Further Praise for *These Fevered Days*

"A lucid narrative grounded in solid research colored by appreciative warmth. . . . *These Fevered Days* makes Dickinson's exploration of that wild terrain [of the mind] and that continent of language palpable, exciting, and accessible." —Wendy Smith, *Boston Globe*

"The Emily Dickinson who emerges in this vivid, affectionate chronicle is a complex and warm-blooded individual—as curious, defiant of convention, and passionate in life as in her poems."
—*The New Yorker*

"Highly readable. . . . By the end, you'll be a believer, in part because of Ackmann's grasp on her subject—both the mountains of scholarship on Dickinson as well as the poet's historical and cultural milieu—and Ackmann's own formidable gifts as a storyteller."
—Ann Levin, *Associated Press*

"Ackmann, a lifelong Dickinson scholar, has a deep empathy for Dickinson's struggles, an expert's knowledge of her poetry and an elegant writing style that will engage even those familiar with Dickinson's story." —Mary Ann Gwinn, *Seattle Times*

"Many thousands of pages have been written about Emily Dickinson, but few capture the elusive Belle of Amherst as succinctly and vividly as Martha Ackmann's *These Fevered Days*."
—Tom Beer, *Kirkus Reviews*

"Evocative yet grounded-in-detail. . . . [I] found myself immersed in Dickinson's world—far more than in the recent films about the

T0018438

poet. . . . [Ackmann's] eccentric way of trying to draw nearer to this most enigmatic of poets is admirable and, ultimately, rewarding."

—Helen Epstein, *Arts Fuse*

"Martha Ackmann is a rare scholar. She is steeped in her subject's work, but also fills her book with the light and sounds of Dickinson's home. Dickinson is at once the most mysterious and yet most accessible of American poets, and she led what has been called the most remarkable unremarkable life in American letters. Ackmann does justice to this creative paradox in her warm and stirring book."

—Cullen Murphy, Editor-at-Large for the *Atlantic*

"Using an ingenious device to capture the whole of Emily Dickinson's life by presenting it in ten distinct tableaux, Martha Ackmann illuminates the poet from her first word as a toddler, 'music,' to her final written ones, 'called back.' In *These Fevered Days*, the author describes a gift from Dickinson to a friend as 'exquisite, tender, and intimate,' words that aptly describe Ackmann's latest triumph."

—Madeleine Blais, Pulitzer Prize–winning journalist

"This utterly enchanting book invites us into the world Emily Dickinson inhabited and made. With exquisite sensitivity to poet and place, Martha Ackmann illuminates a life simple and complex. Treasures abound on every page."

—Ellen Fitzpatrick, author of *The Highest Glass Ceiling*

"*These Fevered Days* is a contemplative, sometimes lyrical endeavor to unlock several of the most important moments of Emily Dickinson's mysterious life. The book brings readers deeply into Emily's world: the sights she sees from the window of her room, the people with whom she corresponds, the sounds of daily life on the streets of nineteenth-century Amherst. Weaving together numerous sources, Ackmann's narrative provides thoughtful insights into both the poet and her craft."   —Julie Dobrow, author of *After Emily*

THESE
FEVERED
DAYS

Curveball: The Remarkable Story of Toni Stone

*The Mercury 13: The True Story of Thirteen Women and the
Dream of Space Flight*

THESE FEVERED DAYS

Ten Pivotal Moments
in the Making of Emily Dickinson

MARTHA ACKMANN

W. W. NORTON & COMPANY

Independent Publishers Since 1923

For information about permission to reproduce selections from this book, write to
Permissions, W. W. Norton & Company, Inc., 500 Fifth Avenue, New York, NY 10110

For information about special discounts for bulk purchases, please contact
W. W. Norton Special Sales at specialsales@wwnorton.com or 800-233-4830

Manufacturing by LSC Communications, Harrisonburg
Book design by Chris Welch
Production manager: Lauren Abbate

Library of Congress Cataloging-in-Publication Data

Names: Ackmann, Martha, author.
Title: These fevered days : ten pivotal moments in the making of
Emily Dickinson / Martha Ackmann.
Description: First edition. | New York, NY : W. W. Norton & Company, [2020] |
Includes bibliographical references and index.
Identifiers: LCCN 2019044493 | ISBN 9780393609301 (hardcover) | ISBN 9780393609318 (epub)
Subjects: LCSH: Dickinson, Emily, 1830–1886. | Poets, American–19th century–Biography.
Classification: LCC PS1541.Z5 A56 2020 | DDC 811/.4 [B] —dc23
LC record available at https://lccn.loc.gov/2019044493

ISBN 978-0-393-86753-4 pbk.

W. W. Norton & Company, Inc., 500 Fifth Avenue, New York, N.Y. 10110
www.wwnorton.com

W. W. Norton & Company Ltd., 15 Carlisle Street, London W1D 3BS

1 2 3 4 5 6 7 8 9 0

FOR
JOANNE DOBSON
AND THE MEMORY OF KAREN DANDURAND
(1946—2011)

✓

WITH LOVE AND GRATITUDE FOR WHERE THIS
CONVERSATION BEGAN

These Fevered Days – to take them to the Forest
Where Waters cool around the mosses crawl –
And shade is all that devastates the stillness
Seems it sometimes this would be all –

F1467

CONTENTS

AUTHOR'S NOTE

On the surface, Emily Dickinson lived an ordinary life: she resided in one town, went to school, never held a job, lived in her parents' home, remained single, and died at age fifty-five. To many who knew her, Dickinson's only acclaim was winning second prize for her rye and Indian bread at the annual cattle show. When she died, her death certificate listed her occupation as "at home." Dickinson's internal world, however, was extraordinary. She loved passionately, wrote scores of letters, anguished over abandonment, fought with God, found ecstasy in nature, embraced seclusion, was ambivalent toward publication, and created 1,789 poems that she tucked into a dresser drawer. Only after her death, when her sister opened the drawer, did the world begin to realize that the life of Emily Dickinson was far from commonplace. "My Business is Circumference," she once declared, and the work she produced over a lifetime is dazzling.[1]

These Fevered Days takes its cue from Dickinson's own words:

This was a Poet –
It is That
Distills amazing sense
From Ordinary Meanings –
And Attar so immense[2]

This book intentionally concentrates, extracts, and distills Dickinson's evolution as a poet. It does not claim to be a comprehensive,
cradle-to-grave biography. Rather it seeks to shed light on ten pivotal moments that changed her. Too often, readers see Emily Dickinson as an artifact in amber: an eccentric spinster who locked
herself away from the world. That perspective, while incorrect, is
partially understandable. Dickinson did indeed keep herself at a
distance—in her own lifetime and ours. "Biography first convinces
us of the fleeing of the Biographied – ," she wrote—as terse a warning to future biographers as there ever was.[3] Yet while part of Dickinson will always be unknowable, much can be discerned. There are
the poems to help us, of course. Fragments, too. Volumes of letters
also are essential. And thousands of archival documents related to
her life in Amherst, Massachusetts; her education; her travels to
Washington, DC, Philadelphia, and Cambridge, Massachusetts;
her reaction to the Civil War; and memories about her from family
and friends. The tangible world surrounding Dickinson is another
resource: her home, the paths she walked, the flowers she loved,
the light in her bedroom. For America's most enigmatic and mysterious poet, Emily Dickinson left a trail of clues.

Readers unfamiliar with Dickinson may benefit from a brief
biographical overview that situates these ten moments. Emily
Dickinson was born in Amherst, Massachusetts, on December 10,
1830, to Edward and Emily Norcross Dickinson. She had an older
brother, Austin, and younger sister, Lavinia. Her father was a law-

yer, and later a politician. Her mother kept the family home. Emily received superior schooling at Amherst Academy, and Mount Holyoke Female Seminary in nearby South Hadley, Massachusetts. She had many friends, and—early on—teachers commented on her facility with words. When she returned home after one year at Mount Holyoke, she settled in, helping with housework and making social calls. The tedium wore on her. Her first publication appeared in an Amherst College student magazine when she was twenty-one. The prose work—not poetry—was printed anonymously. A few years later, *The* (Springfield, Massachusetts) *Republican* published her first poem, also anonymously. Emily Dickinson remained single, and gradually became reclusive. The family's financial status made it possible for Emily to stay home and not teach, sew for a living, or have other outside employment. By her late twenties, she was seriously writing poetry and gathering her verse into hand-sewn packets later called fascicles. She shared her love of words with her beloved sister-in-law, Susan, who read her verse and offered advice.

When Emily was thirty-one, she took the uncharacteristic step of sending several of her poems to Thomas Wentworth Higginson, a well-known essayist who had published an *Atlantic Monthly* article offering advice to aspiring writers. Higginson would become Dickinson's literary mentor and one of the most important people in her life. He read her poems with interest, tried unsuccessfully to "correct them," and—while continuing to write her—eventually gave up offering critiques. After the Civil War broke out, Emily composed poetry with the greatest intensity of her life—sometimes a poem a day. These were compressed verses with striking imagery that focused on her great literary themes of nature, faith, pain, love, and immortality. Toward the end of the war, Dickinson faced a medical crisis. She worried she was losing her eyesight. Emily traveled to Boston on two occasions to be treated by a physician, and lived in a Cambridge boardinghouse. When her personal trouble was finally behind her, she met Higginson face-to-face. That 1870 meeting was remarkable, and Higginson's vivid memory of it offers the best account ever recorded of what it was like to sit across from Emily Dickinson and hear her talk—nonstop. As her reclusiveness intensified, so did the mysteries around her. One riddle concerned Charles Wadsworth, a minister Emily had met on a trip to Philadelphia. The two had written each other and Wadsworth had visited the Homestead. There were also three Master Letters—drafts or possibly copies of mailed letters—later found among her papers. No one knew who the unidentified Master was, or even if he actually existed.

As she grew older, one person Emily knew as a child came back into her life: Helen Hunt Jackson. Jackson had become a renowned poet, essayist, and novelist. She also was a friend of Thomas Wentworth Higginson, and he reacquainted the two women with each other, and their literary work. In 1876, Helen visited Dickinson and implored Emily to submit her verse for publication. The poet refused. In her final years, Emily Dickinson endured one loss after another. First her father, then friends, then others close to her. She kept writing, but admitted, "the Dyings have been too deep for me."[4] Ill health overtook her slowly and she died on May 15, 1886. She was buried next to her parents in West Cemetery in Amherst. Emily Dickinson had published only a handful of poems during her lifetime, and all anonymously. It was not until after her death, when her sister discovered sheet upon sheet of poems, that the staggering sweep of her literary achievement became known. The first edition of her poems was published posthumously in 1890.

Which ten moments are the subjects of this book? Chapter One introduces Emily's family and her budding artistic sensibilities. The chapter focuses on an important announcement she made to a friend: a statement declaring, "All things are ready." Chapter Two presents an evening at Mount Holyoke Female Seminary, where the school's legendary founder, Mary Lyon, asked Emily if she felt prepared to profess her faith. Chapter Three traces the chain of events that led to the publication of Dickinson's first poem. Chapter Four zeroes in on a wintry morning when Dickinson announced she wanted to be distinguished. Chapter Five details the composition of Dickinson's masterful poem "Safe in their Alabaster Chambers." Chapter Six chronicles the day Dickinson took the most startling step of her life and sent four poems to Thomas Wentworth Higginson, asking for advice. Chapter Seven depicts Dickinson during the Civil War under the care of a Boston physician and in the throes of a medical crisis. Chapter Eight portrays the momentous day when the poet met Higginson for the first time. Chapter Nine describes Dickinson's childhood friend Helen Hunt Jackson paying a call and chastising the poet for not publishing. Chapter Ten recounts the day Emily Dickinson died, the subsequent discovery of her poems, and the enduring legacy of her work.

The conceit for this book—its focus on ten pivotal moments— originated in my teaching. For nearly two decades, I taught a Tuesday afternoon class on Emily Dickinson in the Dickinson Homestead in Amherst, Massachusetts. My Mount Holyoke College students discussed Dickinson in the very rooms where the poet created her work. Sitting around that seminar table, the students demonstrated that they understood Dickinson's life and work more deeply when our conversation centered on an important moment in the poet's life. When we considered the poet's stance on religion and poems that confronted God, for example, we found it useful to look at a February night in 1848 when Emily Dickinson went head-to-head with the formidable founder of Mount Holyoke Female Seminary. What did Emily say about that event in letters? Did that moment affect the rest of her life? Do her poems reflect the choice she made then? There were other days that were similar—when the poet was altered, pivoted, and not the same as she was before. Something had transpired in those moments that had moved Emily Dickinson toward the poet she would become. The change might have been prompted by a letter she was writing or had received, an emotion she articulated, a passing thought, a visit, a trauma, a conversation, an event that was supposed to happen but didn't. The moments we studied in class and others that I have added here span almost the whole of Dickinson's life from the time she was fourteen years old until the day she died. The ten moments are chronological, but not consecutive. Each chapter revolves around a specific day and a particular change: a day when the poet was different, say, at ten o'clock at night from how she was at ten o'clock that morning. Other Dickinson scholars could surely offer a different set of moments for reasons that are entirely different from my own. Over the years, selecting ten turning points in Emily Dickinson's life has been a kind of parlor game I have played with colleagues who have long studied Dickinson. My list of ten is not definitive. No list would be. But after forty years of teaching and studying the poet, this set of ten makes the most sense to me.

Emily Dickinson did not keep a diary. Sometimes months went by without a word. Large gaps frequently appear in her correspondence: there is not a single letter for 1857. We also must be reminded that the poems and letters that we have today are the ones that have been recovered. Who knows how many manuscripts have been lost? Compounding these challenges is the fact that Dickinson rarely dated her poems. Establishing an accounting of how she spent her time, while not impossible, can be a hard row to hoe. In addition, Emily Dickinson's life was not filled with action, at least not in the conventional sense of the word. The poet moved through her days in ways some people would see as inactive: she tended to her house and family, read, and wrote. But Suzanne Juhasz in her landmark essay, "The Landscape of the Spirit,' " argues that Dickinson did indeed have an active life, a life that was lived in her mind. Juhasz believes the poet did not retreat and run away from the world. Rather she "was capitalizing upon a technique that women have always known and used, for survival, using the imagination as a space in which to create some life other than their external situation. What Dickinson did," Juhasz states, "was to make art from it."[5] If we read Dickinson's letters looking for action in the usual sense—where she traveled, what chores she did, whom she encountered—we find some details for reconstructing her days, but not many. But if we read the letters for what the poet *thought*, her interior world opens. Reading Dickinson's letters in this alternate way was a revolutionary shift for me. This book attempts to crack open that interior world, re-creating a landscape of Dickinson's consciousness. While each chapter circles around a specific day, it also spools back through time to past thoughts and events informing that moment. For example—in Chapter Nine, Dickinson and Helen Hunt Jackson had difficulty finding a time to visit each other: the poet was grieving her father's death and Jackson had recently married. Certainly those two life events had bearing on the day they eventually met, what they said, and how they acted. "Forever – is composed of Nows – " Dickinson wrote.

Let Months dissolve in further Months –
And Years – exhale in Years – .[6]

Each of these ten chapters, then, is a snapshot of Dickinson's present moment with the past in dissolve like a multiple exposure.

Several themes emerge when considering all ten chapters as

a whole. First, Dickinson was ambitious. From an early age, she keenly felt the passage of time and wanted to make the most of her days. As a girl she dedicated herself to a year of improvement, as a young woman, she announced she wanted to be distinguished, and after her first serious poem was published, she thought about fame. While publication was never something Dickinson actively sought, she frequently imagined a future when poetry would bring her renown. Another theme is Dickinson's long view toward her work. Poems never seemed to fade from her mind, and she constantly revised. When she recognized a good phrase, she reused it, altered images for different purposes, and returned to lines sometimes decades later to make the slightest of shifts. I share Karen Dandurand's view that Dickinson did not publish because poetry to her was never finished. She looked upon her verse as constantly in play and the work of a lifetime. Her attitude is reminiscent of Paul Valéry's assessment: "A poem is never finished, only abandoned." She was—as her nineteenth-century contemporaries would have said—"long-headed."[7] Looking at the span of Dickinson's life, I am also struck by how much the poet knew her own mind, both in terms of her need for solitude and what she hoped to achieve in her work. Dickinson recognized that she required the isolation of quiet days. While she was aware that others occasionally viewed her as strange, she never wavered in seeking solitude and never apologized for it. The poet also knew what she wanted to achieve in her verse. When she sent her sister-in-law "Safe in their Alabaster Chambers" for critique, she listened to Susan's advice but went in another direction. She reacted the same way to Higginson's recommendations: open to his criticism, but holding fast to her own point of view. A final theme that runs throughout Dickinson's life is her belief in the sustaining power of art. Early in her life, Emily witnessed how her aunt Lavinia Norcross confronted sorrow by turning to music and art. No doubt the young

Dickinson was already inclined in that direction, but Aunt Lavinia's example was profound. It's hardly surprising that Dickinson wrote with such ferocity during the Civil War. High emotion fueled her. She turned to writing poetry in times of joy and love, and especially in hours of anguish. "I must keep 'gas' burning," she wrote, "to light the danger up."[8] Creative expression was the fundamental force of Emily Dickinson's life, and writing poetry both defined and sustained her.

In researching *These Fevered Days*, I have consulted Dickinson's letters and poems, and also archives at the Jones Library in Amherst, Amherst College, Mount Holyoke College, Harvard University, and many others to consider the importance of the town of Amherst, the role of women's education in the nineteenth century, boardinghouses in Cambridge, Massachusetts, and myriad other details. But because this is a work of narrative nonfiction that seeks to animate Dickinson and bring her story to life, I also wanted to convey the shape and texture of her world. Since I have lived near Amherst for many years, I am familiar with the play of seasons here, the sheltering mountains that ring our valley, and the sound of the train that ran by her house and now runs by mine. But as familiar as I am with Amherst and Dickinson's home, there were still details I needed to ferret out, and for that I relied on friends and neighbors. Chapter Eight opens with Emily returning from medical treatment in Boston and climbing to the family attic to read Shakespeare out loud. She detailed the moment in a letter to her cousin. To gain a better sense of the sound, smell, and feel of that long-ago reading, I asked Dickinson Museum executive director Jane Wald if I could go into the Homestead attic and have a look. Jane has always been gracious to accommodate my capers and obliged again this time. The attic hasn't changed much since Emily read *Henry VI* up there. I spent an hour examining the dappled light that filtered across wood-hewn beams and read some Shakespeare to test how sound vibrated across the rafters. I sought other experiences as well to bring sensory verisimilitude to this book. I paced off the distance in a snowstorm between the Dickinson house and her brother's home next door for the opening in Chapter Four. I turned the pages of fragile, yellowed newspapers to examine what Dickinson read every day. When I wanted to know what the night sky looked like on the day Dickinson died, Alfred Venne at Amherst College projected it for me on the curve of the Bassett Planetarium ceiling. Weather is not far from people's minds when they reflect on a particular moment. "The day was cloudy," they will remember or "freezing cold" or "hot as blazes." For climate specifics, I consulted the pioneering work of Ebenezer Snell, Emily's neighbor, a nineteenth-century Amherst original, and a man utterly obsessed with weather. For over thirty years, Snell kept a meteorological journal recording Amherst's temperature, precipitation, cloud formations, and atmospheric phenomena. I used his large leather-bound journal and the record his daughter continued to keep after his death to begin each chapter. Most memorably, I spent hours writing this book in Dickinson's bedroom, listening to the sound of footsteps on the stairs, looking out her windows, and feeling the warmth of afternoon sun. I hope these details lend a palpable way to imagine the ten moments, and offer an intimacy and immediacy not found elsewhere.

૮

I FIRST DISCOVERED Emily Dickinson when I was a sixteen-year-old student in high school. I remember sitting in my fifth-period English class at McCluer High School in St. Louis and opening our textbook to Dickinson's monumental poem "After great pain, a formal feeling comes—." I couldn't untangle a single line. I was lucky: at sixteen, I had not known great pain. But after reading that verse (second row, fourth seat back) something changed in me. It's taken me years of study and the rest of my life to understand what that was. Looking back I can now say that after reading the poem, I woke up. A clarity flashed in me that made ideas and writing suddenly visible. It was as though I caught a glimpse of what poet Richard Wilbur calls "a wild shining of the pure unknown."[9] If I were writing the "ten moments" of my own life, that day in high school would certainly be among them. But what happened in my high school classroom said more about Dickinson than it did about me. Even though I did not have the life experience to explain her great poem, I still—on some level—understood it. Part of Dickinson's genius, it seems to me, is her ability to trigger a reader's understanding. We do not need to explicate every line to sense the import of her words. The weight of Dickinson's language—what she would call its "heft"—is felt in a place beyond our intellect and sparks a visceral response. Emily Dickinson tells us as much. In that famous 1870 visit with Thomas Wentworth Higginson detailed in Chapter Eight, the poet declared: "If I read a book [and] it makes my whole body so cold no fire ever can warm me, I know *that* is poetry. If I feel physically as if the top of my head were taken off, I know *that* is poetry. These are the only ways I know it. Is there any other way."[10]

Emily Dickinson has been called everything from "the outlaw of Amherst," "the best friend of reclusive English majors," and "an intellectual terrorist." She even called herself "the only Kangaroo among the Beauty."[11] I hope *These Fevered Days* offers a rich and vivid sense of her unparalleled life. There is no doubt she is a towering poetic voice. But there's something else about her too. Emily Dickinson reminds us what it's like to be alive. And when she does—she takes our breath away.

March 19, 2019
Leverett, Massachusetts

THESE
FEVERED
DAYS

One

ALL THINGS ARE READY

Sunday, August 3, 1845

Ebenezer Snell woke early. Looking east to the Pelham Hills, he saw dawn saturate the Connecticut River Valley. He dressed, careful not to disturb his wife and five daughters, and walked outside to check his scientific apparatus. Snell was forty-four years old, the first graduate of Amherst College, and now a professor of mathematics and natural philosophy at his beloved college on the hill. Not a large or robust man—he had such a modest manner, some of his first students called him "Miss Snell."* They loved him for his kindness, and delighted—like everyone else in town—in his obsession with weather. For the last ten years, Professor Snell had risen every morning to record measurements and scientific observations in a large leather-bound journal. Now he opened the book, skimming past the title page: *The Meteorological Journal Kept at Amherst*

---

* Ebenezer Snell has the distinction of being the first student in the first class (1822) to graduate Amherst College. He also was the first college graduate to teach at Amherst Academy and the first alumnus to return to the college as a professor. His young Amherst Academy students initially gave him the nickname "Miss Snell." [Frederick Tuckerman, *Amherst Academy: A New England School of the Past, 1841–1861* (Amherst: Printed for the Trustees, 1929), 208–9.]

College. Long. W 72 degrees 34' 30." Lat. N 42 degrees 22' 21." Station 267 feet above the Ocean Commencing 1835. Turning to the new day, he wrote, "Sabbath, August 3, 1845." Every year Snell added new columns and categories to his tabulations—wet bulb measurements, dry bulb measurements, mean temperature. "Pure Air" was a frequent exclamation. For today, though, he concentrated on his six original calculations—*barometer, attached temperature, external temperature, clouds, winds and fall of water.* "Sunrise," he wrote, and then recorded: *barometer 30.000; attached thermometer 69 degrees; external thermometer 57 degrees; cloudiness 8 SW cir; winds SW ½; fall of water 0.** In the margin, he jotted down additional remarks: "vegetation suffers from long drought," "plants withering," "smoky in morning." Later that day, Professor Snell would return to his journal and record three additional sets of numbers for 8 a.m., 3 p.m., and 6 p.m. He also included one more observation. When he was outdoors at noon and looked up, Snell saw a parhelion, a bright circle ringing the sun.[1] He picked up his pen and added the note.

Less than a mile down the road, fourteen-year-old Emily Dickinson knew what she wanted to do that summer day. Emily loved Sundays. She enjoyed the visits of friends and family who stopped in the afternoon for lemonade or the family's homemade currant wine. In the evening, she joined other Amherst residents in Mr. Woodman's Singing School—everything about music enthralled her. She especially loved long Sunday conversations with her older brother, Austin, when he was home from boarding school. The two sat by the stove and said whatever entered their minds. That is, until their father opened the kitchen door and the siblings swallowed their words with barely concealed smiles. What Emily did *not* like about Sundays was going to church. The service was long

---

* Snell's cloudiness scale ran from 1 to 10, with 10 being a cloud-covered day.

and the hymns were accompanied by a bass viol, and—according to one parishioner—appalling. Emily was lucky. Her parents did not demand that she attend services, and she occasionally slipped out before communion and walked home. Other times she would endure morning worship in order to earn the "privilege"—as she put it—of avoiding another service later in the day.[2] More often than not, though, she simply chose not to attend at all, and her parents did not protest. It was *not* going to church that Emily loved best about Sundays; with the house empty, she felt unleashed. Not that she did not love her family: living under the same roof with her mother and father, brother Austin, and younger sister Vinnie always felt right to her even as she grew older. But being alone set loose in her a potent force. With no one around, she would proclaim, "I am left alone in all my glory."[3] Today Emily wanted to stay home and write a letter to her friend Abiah Root. Recently Emily's consciousness had shifted. Sitting down at her desk felt more solemn, more purposeful, and she wanted to make an announcement. Her words would be nothing so bold as a manifesto or even a declaration; they would be quieter, but no less convincing. Emily wanted to tell her friend that she could see her future and was ready for the days before her. She was putting Abiah on notice—perhaps the world, as well—that she was serious about writing. Nothing gave her a greater sense of pride or made her feel more alive. Years later, those who marveled at her dazzling words wondered what she could hear that others could not? She answered once. "All have gone to church – the wagons have done passing, and I have come out in the new grass to listen to the anthems."[4]

But before she wrote Abiah, Emily had to settle in: her mind switching as it frequently did from her family to her friends, from school to home, and even Sunday meeting. As much as she tried to avoid church, Emily had to admit that sermons at the First Church of Amherst had been better since Rev. Aaron Colton had become the minister. Congregationalists in town were hard on their clergy: opinionated, demanding, and tight with money. When one of Colton's predecessors was sent packing, the deposed minister's wife spared few words about the good people of Amherst. "New Zelanders would have behaved better," she snarled.*[5] Emily liked that Reverend Colton did not fall into the habit of spouting religious platitudes. If she had to sit in church, she preferred it would be Reverend Colton's—at least his language had color and vitality. Emily always paid attention to words, more so than to the spiritual injunctions. When someone's language was stale and predictable, she lost interest and her mind wandered. But when words made ideas come alive, she was transported. Her father could be caught up in language too—even the language of sermons—although most people would have been surprised that Edward Dickinson could be carried away by anything other than a legal brief. After hearing one sermon at Boston's Park Street Church, Edward had written home, "If I could hear such preaching, every Sabbath, I would walk ten miles, in mud, knee deep . . . I do really wish Providence would so order it, that we could, now & then, have something worth the trouble of hearing. I could never sleep under such preaching—& never tire."[6] There were no reports of Edward sleeping in church that drowsy August morning, although it was growing warmer by the hour. Hot weather bothered Emily and she knew First Church would be stifling with too many people sitting too closely together. In Friday's newspaper, Professor Snell had reported that Amherst had shattered several records for heat. If Emily needed any addi-

---

* Original spellings, misspellings, and errors in grammar—Dickinson's and those of others as well—have been maintained throughout this text, and will not be called out as such.

---

tional excuse for missing church that morning, she had one in Reverend Colton's absence. Colton was away from the pulpit and, in his place, two Amherst College professors assumed the preaching duties: Professor Fowler in the morning and Professor Warner in the afternoon. Spiritual guidance by way of professors of rhetoric on a steamy summer day, squeezed into rigid pews next to townsfolk mopping their faces did not sound inviting to Emily—certainly not as appealing as being alone at her desk.

Emily said the summer of her fourteenth year had been the best in her life and she wanted to share everything in the letter to her friend Abiah.[7] The two girls had attended Amherst Academy together the year before, along with Emily Fowler and Mary Warner, the rhetoric professors' daughters.[*] Now that Abiah had moved and was living hours away, Emily was eager to pour her thoughts onto the page. She had much to tell. There was a new piano in the house— the family's first—and she was learning lively marches and popular songs. The academy's summer term was nearly over and public examinations were around the corner. The *dreaded* examination, she thought. All Emily could think of were "those tall, stern, trustees" staring when teachers called upon her to recite an aspect of biblical law. "I am already gasping," she wrote.[8] But her preoccupations in the letter were not solely about school. She told Abiah about cutting bookmarks, new births in town, gardening, and drying forget-me-nots. All the girls were making herbariums. "I have got an idea that you are knitting edging," she said.[9] Emily also loved sharing gossip, especially accounts of romantic couplings. Who,

---

[*] Before Amherst Academy accepted females, most young girls attended Hannah White's Amherst Female Seminary. A fire destroyed the seminary in 1838 and the institution closed. No doubt the closing of Amherst Female Seminary prompted academy trustees to open the door to girls as well as boys.

she wanted to know, was this Mr. Eastcott, the one who gave Abiah concert tickets. "I think for my part it looks rather suspicious."[10] She noted Abby was taking interest in William. Don't you think he will make a devoted husband, she wrote. Sabra was going back to Baltimore in a few weeks after honoring us poor country folks with her presence, she added, and poor Hatty doesn't seem to have time for anything now that she was teaching school. "I have some patience with these – School Marms," Emily all but sighed. "They have so many trials."[11]

As she wrote, Emily examined the pen stand on her desk. She knew the letter was going to be a long one, and could take a while to compose. So many words and ideas crowded her mind—they seemed to rush ahead of her hand. "I can hardly have patience to write," she once told Abiah. "I have worlds of things to tell you, and my pen is not swift enough to answer my purpose at all."[12] Lately Emily had made a ritual of writing a letter: clearing space and time, and even her small desk in order to gather her thoughts. She studied the surface before her as if moving the inkwell would help her concentrate or anticipate the words ahead. She now took a slow, deliberate, formal, even ceremonial approach that prepared her for writing, and she expected Abiah to be ready as well: she imagined her friend leaving behind every chore and sitting down with her letter. Placing words on the page and envisioning Abiah savoring her sentences carried weight for her. Emily said a voice inside her head commanded her to write. She called it her "faithful monitor" and she could not keep it quiet for long.[13] Nor did she want to. If anyone that Sunday suggested that there was an element of the sacred to her ritual, she likely would have disagreed. There was no open Bible. No sanctified cloth. No preacher or even professors substituting for a divinely inspired voice. Not even a candlestick before her. This ceremony was liturgy of a dif-

ferent order. If her desk were indeed an altar, it was a shrine not
to God, but to words.

That summer the Dickinson family was enjoying hard-won
stability. Gone were the days when Edward and Emily Norcross
Dickinson and their three children had to share half a house with
Edward's parents. As cramped as the living arrangement was, it was
worse when Samuel and Lucretia Dickinson were forced to move
to Ohio for financial reasons. Dickinson's grandfather had been a
pillar in the community: a lawyer, politician, and one of Amherst
College's first trustees. A diligent man with lofty dreams and good
intentions, he often rose before dawn and walked seven miles to
court in Northampton because he was too impatient to wait for the
daily coach.[14] Samuel's impulsiveness extended to financial matters as well. He had been reckless with his own money—and other
people's too—and gave far more to get Amherst College up and running than his personal finances could afford. When he withdrew
to Ohio for a job as head of manual labor at Lane Theological Seminary, his spirits were broken and few thought he could recover. He
did not regain his health, and died of lung fever in 1838 at age sixty-
two. "Ever since I can remember," Edward's sister observed, our
father's "life has been one of anxiety & care & disappointment."[15]

Samuel's death affected the young Dickinson family in a number of ways. For Edward, it meant a lifetime of working to reclaim
the family's prominence and reestablish his father's good name.
For Emily and the rest of the Dickinsons, it meant living with the
specter of Samuel's failure and sharing the house again—this time
with a family unrelated to them. Gen. David Mack and his wife,
Mary, took up residence in the western half of the old Homestead
while the Dickinsons moved all their furnishings to the east. General Mack, the owner of the hat factory in town, was an imposing
figure to Emily and her siblings. As a boy, Austin remembered

the first time he saw the general. "I thought I had seen God," he said. "tall, erect, of powerful build . . . a believer in law and penalty." Austin called him "a Puritan of the Puritans."[16] Living alongside General Mack and his family in tight quarters lasted six years. Then the Dickinsons knew it was time to strike out on their own. By 1840, Edward had earned enough money in his law practice to buy a house on West Street around the corner from the Homestead. The two-story frame home had a grape arbor, lattices, and—with two acres—enough ground for flowers, a vegetable garden, a horse, and chickens.

The chickens were Austin's pride. He once boasted in a letter to the local newspaper asking if anyone's hens laid larger eggs than his. The flock had a habit of wandering off the property and good-natured neighbors frequently could be seen carrying the Dickinsons' feisty prize rooster back to the coop. When sixteen-year-old Austin was twenty-five miles away studying at Williston Academy, Emily kept him up to date with chatty letters of neighbors' foibles and barnyard drama. "The other day," she began, "Francis brought your Rooster home and the other 2 went to fighting him while I was gone to School – mother happened to look out of the window and she saw him laying on the ground – he was most dead – but she and Aunt Elisabeth went right out and took him up and put him in a Coop and he is nearly well now – while he is shut up the other Roosters – will come around and insult him in Every possible way by Crowing right in his Ears – and then they will jump up on the Coop and Crow there as if they – wanted to show that he was Completely in their power and they could treat him as they chose – Aunt Elisabeth said she wished their throats would split."*[17] Letters to Austin were not the

* Elizabeth Dickinson Currier (1823–1886) was the youngest sister of Edward Dickinson and a few years older than Emily. The poet often misspelled her aunt's

same, of course, as having him sit with her by the stove, but they did provide a way for Emily to stay close to her brother. "There was always such a Hurrah wherever you was," she wrote.[18]

The new house suited Emily's mother. Home meant everything to Emily Norcross Dickinson, and she delighted in finally having a place of her own to raise a family. The house was still near enough the town center that she could stroll to First Church to help with the summer Ladies' Fair or drop into Cutler's General Store for oranges, imported French chocolate, or all those coconuts the family loved. Proximity also made it easy to be involved with town events. When the local Temperance Society met at the Amherst Hotel, for example, Mrs. Dickinson joined the crowd in congratulating the proprietors on banishing rum. Yet no one around Amherst would ever call Mrs. Dickinson genial or a natural when it came to socializing. She had a reserved quality that kept others at a distance and her innermost thoughts to herself. Since Amherst was a lively and learned town, it was difficult for her to duck away from conversation after lectures at the college or during political events when officials frequently tapped her husband for a public role. One professor's wife, Deborah Fiske, put her finger on two qualities that made Amherst unique. Amherst, Massachusetts, she said, was filled with "a very spending evening sort of folks" and its best women were "free from the silly birdish airs."[19] Emily Norcross Dickinson, while a serious woman, did not easily fit the expectation when it came to spending evenings. Some residents mistook her diffidence for gloom and went so far as to call her doleful. One acquaintance complained

---

name with an *s*. Known for her strong personality, Elizabeth once earned Dickinson's assessment as "the only male relative on the female side." [L473.] Aunt Elizabeth also wrote poetry and contributed a verse history of the family for its 1883 reunion, praising Dickinson ancestors for being full of muscle and mind.

that a call on Mrs. Dickinson was full of her usual "plaintive talk."[20] There were other criticisms, too, even from family. Everyone grumbled that she did not write enough letters. Her mother-in-law became so exasperated she once declared sarcastically to Edward, "Tell Emily, I wish she would write her *name* in your next letter so as not [to] forget to write. I would write her sometimes, if she would answer my letters."[21] Harsh as such appraisals were, the rebuke did not cause Mrs. Dickinson to change her ways. Even though Sunday was a day when many people caught up on letter writing, she did what she enjoyed most: baked cakes, tended to her exotic figs, darned socks that Austin had sent home for mending, and—according to her elder daughter—surveyed her domain. Writing to her brother, Emily once joked, "Mother taking a tour of the second story as she is wont Sabbath evening."[22]

Although some Amherst residents would quibble that a house abutting the town cemetery—charming residence though it was—was not an ideal location, the Dickinsons felt they had space and privacy at last. But hours alone were not easy to come by for young Emily. The Dickinsons always seemed to have people around. In the early years of their marriage, Emily's parents had taken in boarders to earn additional money and provide protection—as Edward argued—for his wife when he was in Boston on business. Edward's forthright sister-in-law, Lavinia Norcross, did not see the situation that way. All those boarders made for more women's work, she said, and her sister did not need to be kept so incessantly busy with cooking, cleaning, and maintaining a household. With more money in the bank now, the boarders were long gone, but the house still was full. Either Aunt Elizabeth was staying for a few weeks—demanding that young Emily look under the bed for who-knows-what every time she went to sleep—or family friends sent their children to live with the Dickinsons while the youngsters attended the academy. Vinnie or Emily had to double up on those occasions and share their beds when guests were with them for extended stays. As long as Emily was allowed a retreat from time to time, she did not mind the company.*

Strain for Emily, however, came from the demands associated with her father's many obligations. Now that he served as Amherst College treasurer, students trooped in and out of the house with tuition payments, professors stopped by with advice on how he might eke out more money from the State House, and trustees sat in the parlor urging Edward to use his growing political clout to the college's advantage. Edward's responsibilities were not limited to his law practice and college duties either. He was president of the Henry Clay Club, the local lyceum, and the Franklin and Hampden Agricultural Society. As an elected official, he served in the state senate, and became a representative to the General Court and Governor's Council. Edward liked the tumble of politics and was good at it, but being away from Amherst and his family for long stretches grew wearisome. He vowed to stay put and never run for political office again, but then he waffled and won another election that took him back to Boston for months at a time. Nothing curbed his continued civic involvement, not even a furious constituent writing in the local newspaper. "Was there ever standing on two legs," the critic wrote, "such a lump of hypocrisy, deceit, trickery, craftiness, corruption, fraud and cheating, as is filled up in this six foot [sprig] of whigism?"[23] A few years earlier, when enterprising young New Englanders looked west and began purchasing land, Edward had uncharacteristically jumped in. He'd bought acreage

---

* Emily's behavior as a young girl demonstrated this attitude. She would dutifully entertain guests, but then spend hours in her room after company had departed. Her frequent absence from church also underscored her desire for privacy.

in Michigan on the Lake Huron side. For a moment, it looked like the allure of someplace else might take the Dickinsons away from their deep roots in Massachusetts. But recently he'd made up his mind and this time he did not waver; he sold off the Michigan property. Father's life is a boisterous one, Emily observed, and—like her mother—she accepted family duties and the commotion at home.[24] Sometimes, though, she wished she could be as lighthearted as her sister, Lavinia. Vinnie genuinely enjoyed company and could carry on conversations and laugh with ease. Emily would make appearances when she had to, but wearing a public face at her father's events drained her of energy she preferred to expend elsewhere.

To say Emily and her eleven-year-old younger sister shared little in common would be a mistake. Although Vinnie usually dove into female chores with an enthusiasm Emily could not understand—"I dont see much of Vinnie," she once remarked, "she's mostly dusting stairs!"—the sisters shared much, including a similar sense of humor.[25] Young as they were, they both had a cultivated sense of the absurd, and loved scanning the newspaper—Vinnie sewing and Emily reading aloud—searching for articles they found comical. Their favorites were stories of improbable calamities and shocking deaths, articles that Emily described as "funny accidents, where railroads meet each other unexpectedly, and gentlemen in factories get their heads cut off quite informally."[26] What made the stories so funny, she said, was that reporters told them in a sprightly way. Take the article two days ago in Friday's newspaper: "A fine cow, belonging to Mr. William Feeter of Manheim, died a few days since from some intestinal ailing, having taken her food and drink with difficulty for several months past. Resolved, if possible to ascertain the nature of the disease, Mr. Fetter had a post mortem examination of the animal where a *live milk snake nearly three feet long* was found in her stomach."[27] The italics alone would have amused Vinnie, never mind the snake. Like all Dickinsons, Vinnie also was protective, fierce, and loyal to a fault. Although she may not have known why Emily needed privacy and so much time alone, she gave her sister both. Not being overly concerned about reasons and consequences may have been exactly the attributes Emily found indispensable in her sister. After they had grown, Emily looked back on their girlhood and called her attachment to Vinnie "early, earnest, indissoluble."[28]

"Give my love to Biah," Vinnie said when she knew Emily was writing a letter to their friend.[29] Emily was happy to relay the good wishes, since she knew her sister—like their mother—did not correspond much. In delivering the greetings, she tried to capture Vinnie's voice, even noting the way her sister dropped the initial "A" of Abiah's name. Emily's ear was keen and she understood that accurately replicating sound was part of good writing. Episcopalians always say A*amen*, she heard people remark. Abiah calls the piano a "piny," and "Is n't [Ellena] a beautiful name?" she once gushed.[30] While both Emily and Vinnie missed Abiah, they were hardly lacking in friends at the academy. There was Emily Fowler and Mary Warner, their cousin Sophia Holland, who lived around the corner, Mary Louisa Snell, and Jane Hitchcock, Vinnie's best friend.* In particular, Emily held dear the group she called her Circle of Five: smart and lively girls who dove into their studies of mental philosophy, geology, Latin, and botany. "How large they sound, don't they?" Emily boasted.[31] Jane, Sophia, and Emily also took French lessons from Charles Temple, an Amherst College senior, who regularly walked over to the academy to instruct a select group. Occasionally Emily was able to work in German classes too. In addition,

---

* Sophia Holland was Dickinson's second cousin on her father's side. Perez Dickinson was Sophia's maternal grandfather and Samuel Fowler Dickinson's brother.

the girls were fortunate to hear lectures offered at the college. Amherst College president Edward Hitchcock, Jane's father, took an interest in welcoming academy boys and girls to college talks. He loved dissecting a mannequin for science lectures, holding up each anatomical part and explaining the wonders of its function. "I don't think a practicing doctor could have done it as well," one student remembered.[32] Hitchcock, a man with a capacious mind and generous spirit, was an expert in many fields, especially the geologic history of the region. He expounded on dinosaurs and glaciers, and his lectures on volcanoes struck Emily with a force she would long remember. For girls, whose intellect was often ignored by the world around them, the education offered at the academy was substantial. Not every Amherst parent saw it that way, of course. Mary Jones said she wished her daughter would concentrate more on dancing lessons, flower drawing, and attainments that would give her a "polish of manner." Amherst is such a peculiar town, she complained, a "land of *factories equality* and *independence*."[33] When British scholar Harriet Martineau came through Amherst on her American tour of female education, she noted forty to fifty academy girls listening attentively to President Hitchcock's lectures. "No evil had been found to result from it," she reported.[34]

Charles Temple had other talents besides teaching French at the Academy. The young man from faraway Smyrna was accomplished at cutting silhouettes and had asked Emily if she would like one.* She said yes. While Charles snipped the contours of her face, she sat patiently, stealing a glance from time to time as slivers of black paper cascaded to the floor. In only a few minutes, he was finished and handed Emily the silhouette. She studied the image in her hands and saw a girl with a slight frame, bobbed hair, small

---

* Smyrna is present-day Turkey.

nose, and chin tucked in. Alert, some might say, or cautious. Emily knew a silhouette was merely an outline—more suggestion than assertion—but the likeness stared back at her with the insistence of a clue. It was odd that she did not mention the silhouette to Abiah. Lately Emily had been interested in her own looks and the ways her friends were maturing. Over the last few months when former classmates who had been away stopped by to visit, she had looked at them for signs of change and did not see any. But when she looked at herself in the mirror, something was different. Emily joked with Abiah. "I am growing handsome very fast indeed," she crowed, and "expect I shall be the belle of Amherst when I reach my 17th year."[35] Abiah may have laughed when calculating that fourteen-year-old Emily had given herself a few more years before turning heads. But Emily had altered—that was certain—growing taller, wearing long dresses, and sometimes covering her hair in a net cap. Her hair, she said, studying the color closely, was golden.[36]

"I have had no leisure for anything," Emily wrote her friend.[37] The new piano took a lot of her attention, but she did not mind. Emily had been waiting for a piano for many months. From the time she was toddler, she was taken with music, tapping out notes on her aunt Lavinia's piano and calling them "moosic"—the first spoken word anyone could remember her saying.[38] A year ago, Edward had asked his brother in Worcester to search the city for a good piano at a fair price that both Emily and Vinnie could use. "I prefer *Rosewood*," he instructed. "3 pedals—& a stool."[39] Within a year, a piano matching Edward's directives arrived in Amherst: a square Renaissance revival pianoforte with carved legs made of rich Brazilian rosewood. Emily jumped into lessons and made good progress, becoming competent in waltzes and syncopation. She was willing to devote hours to practice, while Vinnie was not. Emily's sister became distracted easily and was unable to sit for long periods of time mastering fingerings and scales. Emily was eager to move ahead, leaping over the initial drills to try her hand at new creations until her teacher reined her in. "She shant let me have many tunes now," Emily had explained, "for she wants I should get over in the book a good ways first."[40] As dedicated as she was to her lessons, Emily understood there was more to music than notes on a page. Music taught her what rhythm, style, and going against the rules could accomplish. A variation in phrasing, tempo, or touch could create a difference that hours of tedious drills never could convey. Her practice book's description underscored the point: "Style is something that cannot be transferred, and for which no rules are given . . . Style is the spirit of the performance."[41] Emily stayed up late at night creating her own compositions and playing what others called odd tunes with weird and beautiful melodies. Once, half apologizing for keeping a guest up at night, Emily had admitted that she knew her music might bother others. The notes, she said, "madden me, with their grief and fun."[42]

Schoolwork kept Emily occupied, too, especially her assignments for Wednesday afternoons. Each Wednesday, Amherst Academy teachers selected a handful of students to read their essays in front of the others. "Autobiography of a Goosequill" was one theme. "Genius seldom satisfied with its own production" was another.[43] "I have written one composition this term, and I need not assure you it was exceedingly edifying to myself as well as everybody else," Emily bragged to Abiah. "Don't you want to see it? I really wish you could have a chance."[44] The school assembly always filled Emily with a tangle of emotions: pride when she was selected and dread when teachers asked her to stand and read to others. Although she was confident in her written work, she did not like to perform. Reading in public made her chest tighten and at times she sensed the envy of other students. Emily knew she was among the best writers at the academy and could be far from charitable when listening to what others wrote. One young man came under her withering scrutiny with his theme "Think twice before you speak." He began with an ill-conceived example: if a young gentleman boarded in a tavern and offered a young lady his arm and had a dog with no tail—think twice before you speak. When the second example was more disastrous than the first, Emily had enough. Afterward, she walked up to the young man with a response she could not contain. Think twice before you speak, she had told him.[45]

Emily knew Abiah would appreciate news of Composition Day. The day was special to them because the two girls had met the previous spring on a Wednesday afternoon. Emily could recall the moment clearly and enjoyed recounting the story even as she grew older. Their first meeting unfolded in her mind like a scene in a play. She was shy, she remembered, and sought the corners of a room. Vinnie, Emily Fowler, Jane, and other students climbed stairs to the third floor as teachers searched for readers. Tall windows flooded the room with light: to the west, the Connecticut River; to the east, the Pelham Hills; to the south, the Holyoke Range; and to the north, Mount Toby's oval plateau. The encircling mountains always pleased Emily, and offered a sense of reassurance and proportion. Perhaps they calmed her jitters too. She looked around the recitation room at the boys and girls: everyone appeared so expectant, high-minded, and serious. Such an august assembly, she had said to herself, with a tinge of amusement.[46] That's when she noticed a girl she did not recognize. The new girl in town, someone said, staying for the school term with cousins.

Maybe it was Abiah's confidence coming up the stairs that first caught Emily's attention or her composure entering that venerable room or perhaps her singular absence of nerves that Emily found difficult to imagine. One thing was certain: Emily could not take her eyes off Abiah's hair. Before coming to school, Abiah had stopped to pick dandelions and then wove them into her dark curls. Emily liked her instantly. Abiah appeared independent and unbridled by convention. But there was something else: something about the dandelions themselves. Emily understood, of course, what a literary image was. She had studied poems in school and read verses that appeared in the newspaper, often clipping them out to save and study later. She understood how a single object could represent something else and trigger emotions, even profound ones. The sight of Abiah's dandelions, however, prompted more than a schoolgirl lesson on imagery. Emily was coming to understand how to make ideas visible. The dandelions utterly transformed the staid Composition Day for her, as if shaking all the stiffness out of the room and flinging it to the fields. In Emily's mind, they were more vivid than the actual children around her. The dandelions made her forget the clambering students and the nonsensical essays and the pulse of anxiety in her throat—and focus instead on the sheer astonishment of yellow weeds. One image could change everything, she thought.[47]

One academy teacher kept a mental note of how exceptional Emily was. Emily Dickinson, he wrote, was an excellent scholar of exemplary deportment, faithful in all school duties. Her compositions were extraordinary, strikingly original in thought and style and far above what a child her age might have produced.[48] He did not comment, however, on her industry or on the ways Emily and her friends sought out additional literary endeavors to satisfy their creativity. Papers flew back and forth among the girls for comment, and occasionally a former female teacher would share one with them as well.* Abiah was writing fiction, too, a romance. "Please send me a copy," Emily implored, "I am in a fever to read it."[49] In their most ambitious project, a group of academy girls—Emily included—had produced a handwritten literary journal of original compositions, *Forest Leaves,* which they circulated among classmates. According to Emily Fowler, Emily Dickinson was known as one of the best writers in the academy and also one of its sharpest wits. Penning the humor column was her responsibility. Their friend Fanny Montague drew the words of the journal's title page, crafting each letter in the shape of a leaf. When the girls distributed *Forest Leaves*, the other students quickly recognized articles by their classmates' handwriting. Emily's script was unmistakable: small, clear, and finished. As much as they were proud of their journal, no one, unfortunately, bothered to keep a copy. The girls gave them all away. We were reckless, Emily Fowler later lamented, adding with disparagement, "Helen Fiske did no special work on the paper for various reasons."†[50]

Helen Fiske had been Emily's friend when they were children. Her father taught Latin and Greek at the college, and her mother

---

* The executive director of the Emily Dickinson Museum, Jane Wald, says it is her understanding that when Dickinson as a girl refers to receiving or sending "papers," she is talking about essays she had written for school or wrote on her own. [Email to author, September 30, 2015.]

† Emily Fowler Ford later remembered that the last copy she ever saw of *Forest Leaves* turned up at the Maplewood Institute in Pittsfield, Massachusetts. According to her, students in Pittsfield started a similar paper. For years, scholars have searched unsuccessfully for *Forest Leaves.* A small archives of the former Maplewood Institute is housed at the Berkshire County Historical Society. A search in those archives did not turn up the publication. [Will Garrison, email to the author, November 2, 2015.]

was the vibrant Deborah Fiske, of the "spending evenings folks." Despite her frequent bouts with fatigue and persistent cough, Deborah was perennially cheerful, townspeople said. She thought nothing of inviting thirteen rowdy children to her house for games of blindman's bluff and checkers, spooning out kind words and treats of raisins and nuts. But after spending her early years in Amherst schools, young Helen left to attend class away from home and only now returned briefly to Amherst on vacations. While Emily and Helen fondly remembered playing together under lilac bushes when they were six years old, Helen had grown into a handful and the two girls did not see much of each other anymore. Her mother with a mixture of pride and exasperation called Helen an "everlasting talker" who begged for the same stories to be told over and over again.[51] "Helen learns very well," she said, but "she is quite inclined to question the authority of everything: the Bible she says she does not *feel* as if it was true."[52] Once when Helen tried to get out of Latin exercises, she wrote her father an elaborate poem, including this self-assessment:

> I'm but a child,
> and rather wild,
> As all the world doth know.
> And this is why,
> It seems so dry,
> For me to study so.[53]

Even though Helen's father was a trustee of Amherst Academy and her mother an active supporter of all Amherst's institutions, her parents determined their clever and imaginative daughter needed a steadier hand and absence from her mother's illness at home. Helen went off to stay with friends in Hadley, then across the state in Charlestown, after that Pittsfield and Falmouth. She tested others' patience as well, trying to be excused from Sunday school and bristling when she had to put down her books to do housework. On one sojourn away, Helen admitted she could be contrary. She could not promise to obey, she told her caretaker, but she would agree to *try*.[54] If Helen Fiske were presented as a cautionary tale to Emily, Sophia, Vinnie, and the other girls at Amherst Academy, it was as a lesson in deportment and the price paid for not following rules. But thinking about Abiah at her new school, Emily did not reject Helen Fiske's example of independence. "I expect you have a great many prim, starched up young ladies there, who, I doubt not, are perfect models of propriety and good behavior," she wrote. "Don't let your free spirit be chained."[55]

There was more Emily could have said about Helen Fiske, but she chose not to—at least not in her letter that Sunday. As much as Emily appeared to tell Abiah everything she thought or did, there were emotions that touched her so deeply she told no one—or waited until the force of the blow had been absorbed to put words to her grief. The previous year had been difficult. Amherst experienced one death after another, with each person closer to Emily than the last. That winter Helen's mother, suffering from consumption, appeared to be doing better. One morning she sat up in bed, dipped toast into her milk, and called for her husband and sister to join her. But before Professor Fiske could reach the bedroom, his wife was gone: one last gasp, neighbors said, and her eyes fixed in death. "The loss cannot be repaired," Amherst College president Heman Humphrey said at her funeral.[56] For Emily, who already wondered how her rambunctious childhood friend could endure being away from home, she now imagined what it would be like to lose a mother. The thought terrified her. In March, Emily Fowler's mother began failing. Everyone knew Harriet Fowler. She was Professor Fowler's wife, the daughter of Noah Webster whose new dictionary Emily treasured, and a woman known for lively conversation and cultivated ways. On the day of Mrs. Fiske's funeral, Harriet Fowler returned home from the service, complaining of exhaustion and chills. Within five weeks, she, too, was dead, and another Amherst girl was motherless. "Death is doing his work thoroughly in this place," Principal Jeremiah Taylor said, and dismissed the academy early so that students could attend Mrs. Fowler's service.[57]

But of all the anguish the year before, Cousin Sophia's illness was especially hard for Emily to bear. Sophia was in nearly every class with Emily, her home was down the street from the academy, and her father sold the Dickinsons dry goods and paint. That awful spring of 1844, Sophia began having chills, a fever, and complained of a headache. Then her fever soared and she became so weak, she could not get out of bed. All the signs pointed to typhus, a disease that hit children with ferocity. An epidemic had been raging in Washington, DC, and was creeping north to New England. When she heard of her cousin's illness, Emily asked to see Sophia, and the physician permitted her a few moments to sit by the young girl's bed. Emily visited often, studying Sophia's face for signs of pain, recognition, submission, or perhaps faith. Then a fearful delirium set in. Sophia tossed, uttering scrambled words that only she could fathom. The scene was frightening for a child to witness and the doctor forbade Emily from entering the room. But when it looked as though Sophia's death was imminent, he gave in, and allowed Emily one last look. She peered through an open door, took off her shoes, and stole into the room. Emily did not know exactly what to expect, but what she found surprised her. Sophia lay peacefully, mild and beautiful. Her pale features lit up, and on her lips an unearthly smile. There was no delirium, no difficult breathing: only motionless peace with eyes half-closed. Emily stared. It was not that look-

ing at Sophia held some ghoulish attraction. Rather, she wanted
to understand—to witness that skip of a moment between life and
death. Friends outside the door worried; they thought she had been
with Sophia long enough, and finally led Emily away. Days later
when mourners laid Sophia in her coffin, Emily was overwhelmed
with grief. Reverend Colton's sermons gave no solace. Mourners'
promise of the afterlife offered little comfort. When she looked out
the north window toward West Cemetery, only one thought entered
Emily's mind—Sophia was not coming back.[58]

Edward and Emily Dickinson were alarmed by their daughter's
melancholy. When she was younger they had seen her through the
gloom of colds and respiratory ailments, and a severe canker rash,
but she had never been as somber as this. They wrote sturdy Aunt
Lavinia in Boston for help. More than any other relative, Lavinia
Norcross seemed to know what to do when someone was down-
spirited. Not only was she forthright, as she had been to Edward
about taking in boarders, she also was practical and believed
meaningful activity was an antidote to sorrow. Within weeks Emily
was in Boston staying with her aunt and uncle and their two-year-
old daughter, Fanny. "We hope you are enjoying yourself," Mrs.
Dickinson wrote, "and that it will be a benefit to you to be away from
home a little while."[59] Aunt Lavinia knew what had sustained her:
family, beauty, and art. She delighted in the city's theatre, concerts,
and horticultural shows, and music at the Bowdoin Street Church—
she told the Dickinsons—simply melted her down. Emily stayed
for more than a month, helping her aunt when even more relatives
descended on her welcoming household. "Aunt Lavinia will really
have quite a family," Emily's mother wrote. "I trust you will lend a
helping hand."[60] While Emily was away, her classmates stopped by
the West Street house and asked Mrs. Dickinson how their friend
was doing. She relayed their greetings. Edward, as usual, fretted.

"Be careful about wetting your feet," he told his elder daughter, "or taking cold—& not get lost."[61] With Austin back at school, young Vinnie appeared to be the only one at home not worried about her sister. She "gets along better without you, than I thought she would," Mrs. Dickinson noted. Vinnie means to brave it out, her father added.[62] After regaining her moorings, Emily returned to Amherst. Aunt Lavinia's disposition had made an impression. She vowed to plunge into a year of improvement, made resolutions, and then berated herself for breaking some.[63] For a young girl, Emily keenly felt the passage of days, and was at turns philosophical and restless. She was determined to be more productive and use her time wisely.

On that warm August day, Emily peered at what she had written in her letter to Abiah and moved into her final sentences. There was barely an inch of space left on the page so she made her script smaller and more compact. "Why cant you pass Commencement here. I do wish you would."[64] The rush of activity that came with the end of summer was about to descend. Days before, nearby Mount Holyoke Female Seminary celebrated its commencement. Amherst Academy would be next. The college would follow soon after. As Emily surveyed the words before her, she was dissatisfied. "I have looked my letter over and find I have written nothing worth reading. . . . Dont look at the writing and dont let any one see the letter."[65] Her standards were high, and it was not by accident that she ended the letter with what was on her mind: her own writing. Emily indeed was changing, even if Charles Temple's silhouette had traced only the edges. She heard anthems in the grass. She wanted weird and beautiful melodies to spring from her pen as well as from her piano. She wanted to break the rules like Helen Fiske. She wanted to understand the particles of moments that others could not see or grasped with a faith she found too easy. There were forces at work spinning Emily into a world her family and friends could not fully understand. I am the same old sixpence, she would tell Abiah—but she was not.[66] Possibility circled her young life like Professor Snell's parhelion—a luminous circumference around a brilliant center. "I have no flowers before me as you had to inspire you," she wrote Abiah.[67] Emily did not need them. Everything she required for inspiration already was taking root in her mind. It was confidence, independence, and self-awareness that were growing in her—qualities that would sustain her for the rest of her life. Emily dipped her pen into the dark well and began a sentence she had never written before. "All things are ready," she wrote, and she knew it.[68]

Two

IT IS HARD FOR ME
TO GIVE UP THE WORLD

Sunday February 6, 1848 6 pm Barometer 29.12. Attached Therm.
64 degrees. Extern Therm. 26 degrees. Cloudiness 10. Winds
NW 1 mph. Clouds Nimb. Snowfall 0 Remarks Some blustering.
Snowing a little in pm.

—Ebenezer Snell, *The Meteorological Journal Kept at Amherst College*

Emily dreamed vivid dreams. She dreamed of planting a rye field with her mother, of the Amherst postmaster seizing her family's property, of bees fighting for pond-lily stems, of a friend meeting Tennyson at a Boston publishing house, of standing before an audience and unveiling a statue. Once a sip of something before bedtime gave her what she called a sherbet dream. She noticed when she dreamed the same dream twice, three times, or night after night, and often told friends and family when they made an apparitional appearance. Sometimes her dreams were so insistent, Emily woke herself up, thinking she had to put on a shawl and hood to meet someone. She dreamed of growing old, her young face staring at her old face with a crown of silver hair— a grandame. "Dreams are couriers," she once said. "Sometimes I wonder if I ever dreamed – then if I'm dreaming now, then if I *always* dreamed, and there is not a world."[1]

For months before beginning classes, Emily dreamed of Mount Holyoke Female Seminary. "It has been in my thought by day, and my dreams by night," she told her friend Abiah. "You cannot imagine how much I am anticipating in entering there."[2] The idea of furthering her education after Amherst Academy excited Emily and the new seminary—then in its eleventh year—already was known for attracting ambitious young women from as far away as Montreal and St. Louis. The four-story building rose out of the center of South Hadley, Massachusetts, like a monolith, dwarfing everything around it, including the church next door. When founder Mary Lyon drew up plans for the school, supporters urged her to name it Mary Lyon's School, but she found the idea boastful. The seminary should be named for something as vital and enduring as education itself, she argued. She studied maps of the surrounding landscape, of the rugged Metacomet Ridge that ran like a spine down the Connecticut River valley. One prominent point, Mount Holyoke, rose 935 feet above farmland. While not the highest peak, its formidable foundation appealed to her. The mountain was carved from seismic shifts that ripped North America from Africa and Eurasia. Its rock—the product of molten lava—was among the most ancient on the planet. Mary Lyon liked the association: a seminary forged by volcanoes.[3]

"I fear I am anticipating too much, and that some freak of fortune may overturn all my airy schemes," Emily told her friend Abiah. Disappointment was in her nature, she said, acknowledging her dreams might be capsized by something unexpected or her own change of heart.[4] As cautious as she told herself to be, Emily was ready for the next step toward adulthood, and looked forward to time away from Amherst—even if "away" meant only eleven miles down the road. When she thought about what she would find at Mount Holyoke, she could tick off predictions with the certainty

of someone who was well prepared. She expected hard work and
an energetic community of young women. She expected teachers
more experienced than the academy's young staff—seasoned edu-
cators devoted to a lifetime of learning and serious scholars themselves. She also expected rules. With hundreds of young women
living under one roof with their teachers, orderliness had to be
maintained. The seminary's list of regulations was long: do not
throw anything out the windows, do not close doors, do not delay in
the hallway, do not leave lamps burning upon retiring, use pumps
properly, devote time to compositions, do not be absent from
church. She would follow the rules—mostly—and knew that the
formidable Miss Lyon was in charge of the whole teeming enterprise.* Emily also understood she would be on her own—away from
home for the longest period of her young life. In February now—six
months since entering the seminary—she had come to two important decisions. She realized she did not want to become a teacher. As
much as she loved learning, instructing others held no interest. At
Amherst Academy when teachers had asked her to rise and read her
compositions, she felt uncomfortable in front of others. She also
recognized she could never be a missionary. Many Mount Holyoke
graduates set out on their own as missionaries to Salonica, Ceylon,
and Ningpo. But Emily did not feel the call, and the idea of travel far
away from Amherst was unthinkable. She was focused on one more
decision, too, a far more serious resolution than those about teaching and missionary work. That decision was not yet clear to Emily
and would not be until later in the day, when she was scheduled to

---

* Emily's infractions included reading and working after the retiring bell, writ-
ing letters during silent study hours, and asking to visit her Amherst home on the
Sabbath—a violation of seminary rules, which Mount Holyoke's assistant principal,
Mary Whitman, sternly pointed out to her.

meet with Miss Lyon herself.[5] She knew why Mary Lyon wanted to see her. She wanted to talk about God. No one would ever confront Emily so emphatically about the state of her soul.

Some Amherst townspeople may have questioned the decision to send Emily to Mount Holyoke Female Seminary. After all, when she'd joined the incoming class that previous September, she was only sixteen—young by seminary standards. Mary Lyon had raised entrance requirements every year and she did not want immature students unable to handle the work. The seminary was bursting, larger than Amherst College by nearly 100 students. Miss Lyon had rejected more pupils than she accepted, and was forced to hire additional teachers. Emily's academic training at Amherst Academy— while enriching—had been sporadic. Like many students, girls in particular, she sat out school terms when her parents worried about her health: a cough that lingered for weeks; complaints of a raw throat, a bout with what her father called *influenzy*. It irritated Emily to be absent from the academy as she had the year before she entered Mount Holyoke. "It cost me many a severe struggle to leave my studies & to be considered an invalid," she complained.[6] For months, she had sulked around the house and helped her mother, learning to bake bread—her sleeves rolled up, mixing flour and milk. She grew to enjoy baking, but housekeeping was a plague to her. Occasionally she sought escape from her imposed "exile"— as she called it—in carriage rides and roaming the fields alone.[7] During the time she was absent from the academy, there had been another restorative trip to Boston to visit her aunt and uncle. Aunt Lavinia had trooped Emily around the city with her usual enthusiasm. They took in Bunker Hill, Mount Auburn Cemetery, a horticultural exhibition, two concerts, and climbed to the top of the Massachusetts State House for a view of the city. Emily especially enjoyed the Chinese Museum, where two scholars—one a professor

of music and another a teacher of writing—practiced their art for
curious onlookers. "There is something peculiarly interesting to
me in their self *denial*," she said.[8]

Not all parents were like the Dickinsons, who believed their
daughters deserved an education. Many families thought educating young women was a waste of time. Why educate girls beyond the
age of fifteen, they argued. Certainly a cultivated mother needed to
provide a proper learning environment for her children, but academy schooling was sufficient. When daughters ended up marrying
and staying at home, it was unnecessary for them to proceed with an
advanced curriculum. Besides, an education was expensive; a year
at Mount Holyoke cost $60—much more than Edward had paid for
Emily at the academy. Even Emily's aunt, Mary Dickinson, thought
women's higher education was foolish. "They have so little business
to do in this town," she once huffed, "they are undertaking to build
a *Female Seminary*."*[9] However, while no one ever would call Edward
Dickinson a champion of women's education, he did want the best
for his daughters, and a commitment to learning ran deep on both
the Dickinson and Norcross sides of the family. Emily's maternal grandfather, Joel Norcross, was one of the founders of Monson
Academy at the same time Samuel Fowler Dickinson was getting
Amherst Academy off the ground. Emily's mother and Aunt Lavinia
had attended Monson, and later Mr. Herrick's School for Girls in
New Haven, Connecticut, where young women regularly attended
lectures at Yale. A woman's life should have a serious purpose, young
Emily Norcross long ago wrote in a Monson Academy composition.
There is satisfaction in contemplation and retirement, she had
written, seclusion based not on what is lost but what is gained.[10]

* Mary Dickinson probably was speaking of Hannah White's Amherst Female
Seminary, which opened in 1832 and closed after a fire in 1838.

Even darker concerns abounded about educating young women: fears about their health, womanhood, and safety. Many detractors, including at least one Harvard professor, thought too much reading and writing drained blood from a young woman's brain particularly during her catamenial period. Women and men were different, he said. Women have a finite amount of energy and should expend it wisely. "With every act of life . . . the uttering of a word, the coining of a thought, the thrill of an emotion, there is a destruction of a certain number of cells."[11] If women spent too much time at their desks, they ran the risk of never being able to have children. Some ministers warned their religious colleagues not to associate with Mary Lyon. The editor of *The Religious Magazine* took the argument one step further, declaring that Miss Lyon's work undercut the very foundation of society, producing masculine women out to supplant men. "In the place of all which is most attractive female manners, we see characters expressly formed by acting a *manly* part upon the theater of life," he wrote.[12] Then there were those who believed Mary Lyon and Mount Holyoke Female Seminary put ideas in girls' heads: ideas about ambition and living lives far different from their mothers. Celia Wright of Blandford, Massachusetts, was one of those girls; Emily knew her through Amherst friends. Celia had graduated Mount Holyoke the year before Emily entered and dreamed of traveling west for missionary work with Choctaw Indians. Her father disapproved. He thought the work was dangerous and did not want his daughter so far away from home. But Celia was defiant and flatly announced she would go. That's what you get, Dr. Wright may have thought, from someone like Mary Lyon who urged young women to "accomplish great things."[13] When Emily's Amherst friend called on the Wright family, she felt tension between father and daughter. Someone had been crying. Later a seminary teacher recorded the whereabouts of recent 1846 graduates. "Celia S. Wright," she wrote in a column of names, "to the Indians."[14]

Edward and Emily Norcross Dickinson did not worry about fifty-year-old Mary Lyon planting preposterous ideas in their daughter's head. Edward did have apprehensions about Emily being away from home, of course, but they were his usual worries about eyestrain from reading too much, and unease about his daughter being in charge of her own money for the first time. "Tell Father, I am obliged to him much, for his offers of 'picauniary' assistance, but do not need any," she instructed Austin.[15] Mrs. Dickinson checked to see if Emily had enough shoe blacking and boxed-up treats to be delivered when the family made an occasional visit. She knew Emily had a sweet tooth and sent gingerbread, a cake, and a pie. Fruit and chestnuts, she probably realized, would remain untouched for days. If they needed any reassurance about Mary Lyon's aims, the Dickinsons had only to look to relatives and friends who supported her. Early on when Miss Lyon put out a call for help with seminary furnishings, Grandfather Norcross had readily supplied the crockery.* Amherst College president Edward Hitchcock and his wife, Orra, had invited Miss Lyon to board with them while she put finishing touches on her dream. Edward Hitchcock said being around Mary Lyon made the wise wiser and the

* Among Mary Lyon's papers from the early years of the seminary is a note from Daniel Safford clearing up an order of crockery from Joel Norcross: "Mr. Norcross understood that you were to write for more *crockery* or *glass* on your return," Safford wrote in 1844, "consequently he had not sent what you ordered." Norcross quickly made good on the request, as Safford informed Lyon: "Crockery with the article from Mr. Whiteman, the tongue in a half barrel, the dryed Beef in a bag, a two gallon jug of *temperance Wine* for Mr. Condit (which you will please inform him of) all go to the depot today." [Daniel Safford to Mary Lyon, July 16, 1844, Mary Lyon Collection, Mount Holyoke College Archives and Special Collections.]

good better.[16] He would do anything for her, including serving as a Mount Holyoke trustee and giving the seminary his old anatomy mannequin that he so loved showing Amherst Academy students. His wife helped too. A skilled artist, Orra had sketched a biblical vignette that the seminary adopted for its seal. The landscape—resembling Mount Zion—suggested Mount Holyoke Female Seminary was a place where women would be raised up.[17]

The seminary seal would have appealed to the Dickinsons. It reassured them that Emily's education would be grounded in the same Christian principles as Amherst College. Emily's mother already had pledged her life to Christ in 1831—the only member of family yet to do so.* Her father had not professed, but regularly attended First Church, where he also served on parish committees and helped search for suitable ministers.† Like her parents and grandparents, Emily knew that Christianity was tightly woven into the everyday life for students at colleges such as Amherst, Yale, Harvard, and Princeton, and female seminaries like Mount Holyoke. Faculty led student prayer groups, roommates encouraged one another to consider conversion, the curriculum was infused with biblical study, and religious revivals were a frequent and serious

---

* "Professors" of faith in the nineteenth-century Congregational Church declared a personal testament of belief and commitment to Jesus Christ. Their profession of faith indicated that they had evidence of a personal experience that changed and deepened their relationship with Christ. Men made a public statement of belief. It is unclear if women, such as Emily's mother, who professed her faith at First Church, made a similar public statement. [Jane Eberwein, email to the author, March 12, 2016.]

† Members who were professed Christians made up the church's inner group. Parish members who had not professed were permitted to make decisions about finances and secular business such as hiring ministers. [Alfred Habegger, *My Wars Are Laid Away in Books: The Life of Emily Dickinson* (New York: Random House, 2001), 80, 81, 125.]

occurrence. President Hitchcock once remarked that religion was at the very core of Amherst College.[18] Area newspapers shared his point of view. In reporting on commencements at Amherst and Mount Holyoke, newspapers listed students who read prizewinning essays as well as the number of seniors who had professed their faith. To be a college or seminary student in New England meant to be a student of faith as well. Edward Dickinson knew firsthand how deeply religion weighed on students' minds. He could remember walking past doorways of student lodging in New Haven and hearing young men's prayers. He kept letters his parents wrote—letters imploring him to take advantage of Yale's revivals and pledge his life to Christ.* Samuel and Lucretia Dickinson counted the number of Amherst College students who had professed, rejoiced when one of their son's friends joined the fold, and used student professions to prompt Edward's own. Even more than studying, listen to the sound of God around you, his mother had urged. It is "the most important of *all calls*."[19]

Emily had not received letters from her parents about professing her faith. As they had when she was home, Edward and Emily Norcross Dickinson left the subject of Christian conversion to their daughter and did not pressure her. But the routines at Mount Holyoke made it nearly impossible for Emily to keep her thoughts

* Congregationalism was the largest denomination in Massachusetts, and the faith embraced by the Dickinson family, Amherst College, and Mount Holyoke Female Seminary. Jane Eberwein states that First Church of Amherst, which the Dickinsons attended, endorsed a Congregational faith with recognizable roots in the New England Puritan tradition, but could no longer be considered Puritan. Theology, she states, made Emily Dickinson's situation more difficult. It posited that a person could choose a commitment to Christ rather than needing to wait for Christ to choose who would be saved. [Jane Eberwein, email to the author, April 12, 2016.]

about religion private. She had to take a stand on faith and she had to do it publicly. During her first month at the seminary, Miss Lyon had asked students to declare their status. Students came forward and identified themselves in one of three ways: those who already had professed, those who were considering a hope in Christ, and those who did not feel a call. Emily was in the latter group—those without hope. She was not the only one. Seventy-nine other young women—nearly a third of the seminary—had joined her. During church services, the large group of "no hopers"—as they were called—sat together every Sunday, a stark physical reminder to themselves and others of their spiritual state. But there were other times during the day when Emily could disappear into her own solitary space and turn over thoughts. As public and communal as the seminary was, Mary Lyon valued solitude and believed it was critical to young women's development. If she'd had her way, Miss Lyon would have built the seminary with private rooms for every Mount Holyoke student. Finances precluded the option, so she settled for "lighted closets"—individual spaces in each room where a young woman could separate from her roommate and have time to pray or think. When Emily wanted to be alone, the lighted closet was a refuge. No one would know if she spoke to God or let her thoughts glide elsewhere to words, images, and poetry.[20]

While Emily took the question of faith seriously, it did not diminish her attention to academics at Mount Holyoke. She was doing well. Before she entered the seminary, she had reviewed arithmetic in order to be to be on the "safe side of things," she had said.[21] During those first weeks back in September, Emily had passed all her examinations—a notable accomplishment for someone so young. Many students were not as prepared: some had been sent home for failing marks or for not completing the three days of exams on time. A few left because they were homesick. Emily's test scores placed her into the first class level. By the middle of the term, she had advanced to the next rung. With three levels of classes at Mount Holyoke, it was possible Emily could complete her studies and graduate in two years rather than the usual three. That is, if she wanted to. The majority of students did not, although her roommate, cousin Emily Norcross, was an exception. Cousin Emily was in her final year at the seminary and looked forward to work as a music teacher somewhere out west. With both of her parents deceased, Cousin Emily knew she would need to support herself, and teaching was her future.* But most parents and many students looked upon a year or two at Mount Holyoke as the final step in a young woman's education—a "finishing stroke," Emily said.[22] Emily's childhood friend Helen Fiske had wanted nothing more than to attend Mount Holyoke and had spent months reviewing her subjects, especially—like Emily—her ciphering. Helen's father worried that his daughter was studying with such intensity that she was neglecting her duties to others. He spoke with Mount Holyoke's assistant principal, Mary Whitman, about his concerns. Either Miss Whitman had persuaded him that Helen should not attend Mount Holyoke—at least not right away—or he had decided himself. Professor Fiske determined Ipswich Female Seminary would be better for his daughter, saying it provided "less stimulus to intellectual effort."[23] Emily knew she was fortunate to be accepted at Mount Holyoke, and realized it was too soon to be talking about successfully completing all her classes and graduating. Besides,

---

* Emily Norcross's parents were Amanda Brown and Hiram Norcross, Emily Norcross Dickinson's eldest brother. Hiram died when his daughter was an infant. Her mother remarried and moved to Springfield, Massachusetts. Emily and her brother were shuttled among relatives, living for a while with their Norcross grandparents, with Aunt Lavinia in Boston, and spent holidays with the Dickinsons in Amherst.

the first year for every student, no matter what level, was proba-
tionary. For now, she enjoyed sharing a room with her cousin,
singing in the seminary chorus, taking piano lessons, and making
the most of her studies in botany, rhetoric, physiology, ecclesiasti-
cal history, astronomy, and algebra. She boasted to Austin after she
had completed each course, and announced to him when she delved
into chemistry, Mary Lyon's principal subject. "Your *welcome* letter found me all engrossed in the history of Sulphuric Acid," she
wrote, adding five exclamation points.[24]

Not only had she done well in her classes, Emily also had
adjusted to the seminary's bustling environment. At times it felt
like she was living in a beehive: swarms of students and teachers buzzed about the building, each with schedules, chores, and
places to go. Few seminaries existed that were as large and complex
an operation as Mount Holyoke. Every action had to be systemati-
cally organized and assessed for effectiveness. As was her custom,
Mary Lyon kept track of it all. She compiled lists of students absent
overnight, notes on sweeping, care of sink pumps, and inventoried
the kitchen contents: one spinning wheel, one blue tub, one meat
barrel, one cheese strayner. She marked who was ill and needed
mayweed tea. Nowhere was Mount Holyoke's organizational bearing more apparent than in domestic work. In order to keep costs
of the school down, avoid hiring outside help, and teach the values
of self-reliance and equality, Miss Lyon created a domestic work
requirement. Each student worked at least an hour every day on
chores that contributed to the "family." Some young women prepared puddings, others ironed tablecloths, several helped out in
the sick room, and a group of copyists sent off a journal letter to
former students who were missionaries abroad. There were 235 jobs
for 235 students. Miss Lyon was adamant that parents not associate
domestic work with academics, and stated her policy in the annual

seminary catalogue: "All members of the school aid to some extent in the domestic work of the family. The portion of time thus occupied, is so small that it does not retard their progress in study, but rather facilitates it by its invigorating influences. But it is no part of the design of this Seminary to teach young ladies domestic work. This branch of Education is exceedingly important, but a literary institution is not the place to gain it. Home is the proper place for the daughters of the country to be taught on this subject; and the mother is the appropriate teacher."[25] After learning she would not be attending Mount Holyoke, Helen Fiske justified her disappointment by disparaging the seminary as a place "to learn to make hasty pudding and clean *gridirons.*"[26] But Emily did not mind the chores. "My domestic work is not difficult," she wrote Abiah, "& consists in carrying the Knives from the 1st tier of tables at morning & noon & at night washing & wiping the same quantity of Knives."[27] Students made light work of their chores, singing as they cooked, needling their classmates for washing dishes "after the manner of the Pharises!," and humorously naming their work circles for lofty church organizations. The dishwashers were known as the American Board.[28] Those scrubbing the baking dishes were the Home Missionary Society. A joke among the domestic groups was Mary Lyon's unending reconfiguration of the dining room. She always looked for a better arrangement to promote efficiency. Around Mount Holyoke, the sound of Miss Lyon moving tables was as constant as the boil of bubbling stew pots.

Nearly every student at one time or another wrote home about Mary Lyon. She was everywhere, they said. Up at five a.m. in her wrapper to check on breakfast, setting buckets of disinfectant in the hallways to ward off illness, shepherding students into coaches for mountain hikes in the fresh air. With everything she had to do—or thought she had to do—she believed focus was key. "Try to be systematic," she lectured the young women. All her life, she told them, she suffered from what she called "regular habits." They had to do better. She warned them about interruptions to their thinking and drains on their time. "I really think it requires more discipline of mind and more grace to meet a lady's duties than a gentleman's," she argued. "He has little minutia to attend to. He can rise in the morning and go to his business without hindrance, but it is not so with a lady."[29] Mary Lyon's command did not escape Emily's notice. Joking with Austin about South Hadley's isolation, she cast Miss Lyon as a military general, leading a charge, and urging her troops to fight back. "Do you know any nation about to besiege South Hadley?" Emily wrote. "If so, do inform me of it, for I would be glad of a chance to escape, if we are to be stormed. I suppose Miss Lyon. would furnish us all with daggers & order us to fight for our lives, in case such perils should befall us."[30] Over and over again students commented on the intensity with which Miss Lyon approached her work. "I wish you could see Miss Lyon," one of Emily's classmates wrote home. "I know you would laugh. She is hard of hearing, has false teeth, wears a cap, and dresses as well as an old washwoman. Yet she is noble for doing business. She runs around here with her nose dripping and does more business than any two men."[31] She is, another student observed, such a "driver and hurrier. There is no standing still where she is."[32] What some saw as rush, Emily might have seen differently. It was not so much *hurry* that defined Mary Lyon, but *urgency*. Emily felt it in herself. A year earlier, during her self-proclaimed year of improvement, Emily told Abiah "life is short and time fleeting" and she wanted to "spend the year. . . . to better advantage."[33] She, too, was driven, and searching for ways to make her dreams take shape.[34] Whether a commitment to God was part of that plan remained uncertain. But she knew that within hours she would need to make up her mind.

Emily was not the only young woman who was imagining her future. Her classmate Sarah Worcester from Park Hill in the Cherokee Nation was already in conversation with tribal officials about opening a school for girls. Margaret Robertson from Sherbrook, Canada, wanted to write a novel. Louisa Plimpton from Sturbridge, Massachusetts, dreamed of going to China.* Fidelia Fiske, Helen's distant cousin, earlier had embarked on her own adventure. During afternoon assembly in Seminary Hall, teachers read aloud from Fidelia's letters, praising her bravery and determination. They told the young women about how Fidelia had started Mount Holyoke in 1839, but contracted typhoid and was forced to leave. How she'd returned several years later and had finished her studies. When a foreign missions board had announced an opportunity to go to Persia, Fidelia jumped at the chance, and set sail from Boston Harbor. Four months later, she arrived in Orumiyeh, where she learned Persian and laid plans for a girls' school modeled on Mount Holyoke. "My dream breathes not yet," Fidelia had written her friends at the seminary. "But I hope that bone is coming to bone."[35] Everywhere around Emily women were taking risks. She knew Miss Lyon insisted that students learn chemistry not from reading books but by conducting laboratory experiments. After a teacher burned her

---

* In 1851 Cherokee chief William P. Ross toured Mount Holyoke and spoke with Worcester and fellow student Ellen Whitmore about working with him. The Cherokee National Female Seminary opened on May 7, 1851, with Whitmore as principal and Worcester as assistant teacher. Robinson became a novelist, most notably of *Christie Redfern's Troubles*. [Carrie MacMillan, Lorraine McMuller, and Elizabeth Waterson, *Silenced Sextet: Six Nineteenth-Century Canadian Women Novelists* (Montreal: McGill-Queens University Press, 1992), 89.] Louisa Plimpton became a missionary in Foochow, China. [Sarah D. (Locke) Stow, *History of Mount Holyoke Seminary, South Hadley, Mass. During Its First Half Century*, 1837–1887 (Springfield, Mass: Mount Holyoke Seminary, 1887), 322.]

hands when a test went awry, the solution was simply to search for a bandage, not abandon the scientific attempt. You learn by trial and error, analysis and contemplation. When something didn't work, Miss Lyon believed, you tried again. Trust your own mind, she always said. Once students had taken to the fields to collect flowers for analysis. They had been so zealous in gathering samples, teachers asked them to temporarily suspend their collecting. Faculty worried there would be no blossoms left. In spring when the snow cleared, Emily would be out in the field again, searching for fossil tracks and evidence of long-ago dinosaurs. Hearing about Fidelia's ambition and being called upon to use her own powers of observation made Emily think about what was ahead for her. Time and again during the year, she introduced herself to new classmates, young women who had never heard of the Dickinsons of Amherst. She thought of these introductions as giving her "dimensions."[36] The introductions forced her to reconsider who she was, what her narrative had been, and what it would become. There was something emancipating about being herself and not solely the daughter of Edward Dickinson. Before long she was signing her letters "Emilie" and wondering if—like Fidelia—she had the independence and courage to set sail.[37]

Of course, for Emily and the other students no woman was a more imposing model of determination than Mary Lyon. In founding the seminary and keeping it afloat, Miss Lyon knew better than anyone the forces against her. She spent hours every day drafting letters to would-be donors and spooling out worries to her friends. This seminary is up against so much, she had written, it has nine chances out of ten of failing. Her words filled pages with lines crossed out, phrases added, words stacked one atop another, and scrawls written up along the sides. In a draft of one difficult sentence about women's education, she had stated, "We must cheerfully

endure opposition," then deleted with a heavy dark line the words
that followed—words about enemies to the cause. It incensed her
that she had to follow expectations for what women should do: she
should not travel alone, she should not directly ask for money, she
should not lead meetings where men were present. "My heart is
sick my soul is pained with this empty gentility, this gentile nothingness," she once fumed to a friend. "I am doing a great work. I
cannot come down." She complained of headaches and had spells
of erysipelas that turned her skin as taut and as hard as an orange
rind.* That November day back in 1837, when Mount Holyoke
Female Seminary opened its doors for the first time, Mary Lyon
wanted everything to be perfect, but it wasn't. The front steps were
not in place, windows were still without blinds, stoves sat uncon-
nected to their stovepipes, furniture had been delayed by storms,
and no one could find the new bedding. The first sight that greeted
many students was Trustee Daniel Safford on hands and knees setting up bedsteads. "We are in glorious confusion," he enthusiastically declared. By nightfall, South Hadley townswomen could be
seen walking through the huckleberry patch with supplies, their
arms filled with donated sheets and blankets.[38]

As much as Mary Lyon inspired young women to be independent, she also made clear that one matter took precedence: Christianity. She believed that the purpose of life was a commitment to
Christ. Yet she also understood the weight of the question Emily
was confronting. While Miss Lyon thought a profession of faith was
necessary to everlasting life, she recognized that making the decision was not a casual one. It was better to wrestle with the question seriously, she said, rather than mindlessly profess to believe.

* Erysipelas is a bacterial infection brought on by an insect bite or a cut. It is now
easily treated with antibiotics.

Besides she had not professed her own faith until she was twenty-five—older than Emily and most other students. Some might have argued that if religion were so important, Mount Holyoke should not have accepted conflicted students like Emily or asked them to leave after a term if they still had not professed. Yale, for example, threatened to expel students who did not believe the Bible was God's word.[39] But expelling students who did not profess to believe missed the point, Miss Lyon would have said. Young women should make up their own minds and come to the Church freely.

Since Christmas in 1847, religious questioning at the seminary had intensified. Like Amherst College, Mount Holyoke decided to spend December 25 in voluntary fasting and prayer. Emily had expected changes in spending her first Christmas away from home, but the seminary's decision to embrace such austerity was nothing she'd ever experienced. Holidays at home were filled with laughter and she enjoyed making a list of her Christmas bounty: a perfume bag, a sheet of music, a china mug with a *Forget me not* upon it, a watch case, an amaranthine stock of pincushions, candy.[40] Nearly every Mount Holyoke student observed the fast. Emily spent the day in church, prayer meetings, and had more time than usual to be alone. After morning services, Miss Lyon invited all who felt a call to Christ to place a sealed note in her note box. Fifty attended. "The house has been very still," one teacher observed. "I hardly heard one 'Merry Christmas' this morning."[41]

Around that time, Hannah Porter, a friend of Emily's maternal grandfather, had been staying at the seminary. Deacon Porter, Hannah's husband, was one of the seminary's most valued trustees. Mrs. Porter was always interested in the spiritual health of students and kept an eye on Emily's development, since she was well acquainted with her family. When she returned home to Monson, she received a letter from Cousin Emily Norcross. "Emily

Dickinson appears no different," the young woman reported. She "says she has no particular objection to becoming a Christian and she says she feels bad when she hears of one and another of her friends who are experiencing a hope but still she feels no more interest."[42] Emily Dickinson had known her roommate was writing and had asked her cousin to relay her best wishes to Mrs. Porter. She also promised to write herself and perhaps explain her views, but failed to do so. With the first term near its end, Emily was short on time, she said.[43]

The Mount Holyoke term concluded in January 1848, and Emily enjoyed a two-week recess at home. On Sunday, February 6, she was back at school, and the seminary whirled into action. That evening before supper, young women again spread fresh white linen cloths over the long tables and Emily set the knives beside each plate. It may have been difficult to keep her mind on the task. The scheduled meeting with Miss Lyon was only an hour away: that is, her *second* meeting. Even though she appeared to have told no one, Emily had first met with Mary Lyon right before the recess. Back in January seventeen students who were considering a profession of faith met with Miss Lyon privately in her rooms—Emily among them. Miss Lyon led the young women through a discussion of Acts, then assigned homework. During the recess, she said, memorize John 6.35: the passage that begins "I am the bread of life." When you return, she told them, we will hear where you stand.[44] After that January meeting, Emily had written Abiah and alluded to what was going through her mind. "This term is the longest in the year," she said. "I love this Seminary & all the teachers are bound strongly to my heart by ties of affection. There are many sweet girls here & dearly do I love some new faces, but I have not yet found the place of a *few* dear ones filled, nor would I wish it to be here." Emily reported on her studies and how much she enjoyed chemistry and physiology. In a long postscript, she inquired of mutual friends and commented on the unseasonably warm weather. Between the two remarks, Emily had inserted an aside—brief and vague—hinting at what had transpired hours before. "There is a great deal of religious interest here and many are flocking to the ark of safety," she wrote. "I have not yet given up to the claims of Christ, but trust I am not entirely thoughtless on so important & serious a subject."[45]

The recess between terms had given Emily time to think. As a girl, she once had joined a prayer group but had stopped attending. Prayer had become—as she put it—"irksome"—and did not sustain her interest.[46] Recently Amherst had experienced a town revival and neighbors flocked to church meetings. Emily remembered the revival well—and uncharitably. She recalled watching those who had "sneered loudest" at religion suddenly professing their faith. "They were melted at once," she said. The comment underscored her wariness: conversions often looked impulsive to her—the product of overexcitement rather than belief.[47] When converts such as Abiah had spoken of their spiritual contentment, Emily was envious, but also skeptical. She thought accepting religious maxims meant abdicating independence and not personally struggling with profound questions. It was like learning chemistry by a book rather than an experiment.

After that first dinner of the new term, Mary Lyon retired to her rooms to prepare for the meeting with Emily and the others. Before the break, she had asked the young women if they felt lost—adrift without a profession of faith. She hoped the time away from the seminary would make their answers clear. Lately Mary Lyon had also been reading about Noah and his search for a rare place where he could hear God. She wanted her students to find their own singular place.[48] Miss Lyon took up the notes that students had dropped into her box and read through them. Of the seventeen who had attended the meeting before vacation, a few said they would not be attending tonight's gathering. She made note of the numbers and checked off who would and who would not be joining her.

As the minutes ticked down, Emily finished her chores in the dining hall. She plunged her hands into hot water and drew a towel across each thin knife blade. Then she went upstairs to the main floor and walked past the mineral cabinet with its shelves of rocks and fossils. Miss Lyon's rooms were behind the double parlors and across from Seminary Hall. Emily could remember the many words Mary Lyon had spoken there. "Don't be a hypocrite," she had told them, "be honest." "Distinguish between what is very difficult and what is impossible. Do what is difficult." "The difference between great and small minds is the power of classification. Little minds dwell on particular things. Great minds take in a great deal." "If you have as much intelligence, energy, and enterprise as you ought to have, you are making much of yourself. Do something. Have a plan. Live for a purpose."[49] Emily looked around her. No one else had a private room on the main floor. Miss Lyon's was there because she wanted to answer if someone knocked at the big seminary door. Last month, when Emily had walked into Mary Lyon's rooms, her keen eye took in everything: a worn copy of *Gorham's Chemistry*, Bunyan's *Pilgrim's Progress*, Miss Lyon's Bible—the pages smooth and bare without a single mark from her hand.[50] On her desk were sheets of writing Lyon had composed deep into the night: lists, letters, drafts, appeals, journals, catalogs, lesson plans, recipes. The shuffled surface of her desk was like a map of her mind: a searching intellect, insatiable, and alive with ideas. Mary Lyon and Emily were alike in so many ways, and in so many ways they were not. While Miss Lyon wanted to wrestle down the unknown and tame it with lists and order and systems, Emily wanted to stare it down and walk straight into the abyss. Emily did not want to live by anyone else's rules, not even the rules of the Church, and the questions for her never stopped. "Does not Eternity appear dreadful to you," she once asked Abiah. "I often get thinking of it and it seems so dark to me that I almost wish there was no Eternity. To think that we must forever live and never cease to be. It seems as if Death which all so dread because it launches us upon an unknown world would be a releif to so endless a state of existence."[51]

That evening Emily did not pause outside Mary Lyon's door, and she did not leave a note. She kept on walking. Darkness flooded her student room. She could barely make out George Smith's Hotel and Livery Stable across the road, and she could not see the town cemetery at all. Cousin Emily was late in returning for the term, and the room felt empty and lonely. It had been a blustery day. Low, dense clouds spread across the sky and snowflakes flew past her window on their way to the ground. A few days before, a storm had dumped eight inches of snow and tree trunks were still lined in white. Miss Lyon had asked Emily Dickinson if she felt lost. She did not. Emily knew where she was. She was as rooted to the soil beneath her feet as was one of her wildflower specimens. In church services the minister asked Christianity's central question: Are you willing to give up the world for everlasting life? Emily knew her answer. No, she thought. Amherst, her family, and the deep mud of March were more sacred to her than any religious doctrine. She would not trade the friends she had, the natural world she loved, or the verses that were beginning to thread through her mind for anything, including the promise of everlasting life. It was here and now that she lived for, not the possibility of eternal salvation—if that even existed. It is hard for me to give up the world, she thought.[52]

For months, Emily had tried to reconcile Mary Lyon's great teachings about independence and ambition with the call to faith. She could not seem to square Miss Lyon's injunction to use one's own

mind with her appeal to join the flock. The two precepts seemed
at odds with each other: incompatible and dissonant. But then she
understood. Emily realized that categories of faith did not fit her:
"professors of religion," "those who have a hope," "no-hopers." They
were too neat. Her mind told her to reject classifications and shun
categories. She made her decision: she had discovered a way to take
religion seriously while also remaining independent. She neither
accepted faith nor rejected it. Emily decided to continue questioning.* "I am standing alone in rebellion," Emily would write a few
years later. Four years before her death, she remained unchanged. I
"both believe, and disbelieve a hundred times an Hour," she said.[53]

Mary Lyon's meeting was still going on downstairs as the young
women on Emily's hallway made preparations for the next day. The
morning bell would rouse everyone especially early. When the
sun came up, Mount Holyoke Female Seminary would begin new
classes for the spring term. Deacon Porter would soon arrive to collect tuition, and later on Professor Snell would travel down from
Amherst College to deliver a lecture on electricity. Already Margaret Robertson from Canada was thinking about a new composi-

* Jane Eberwein argues that Dickinson "withdrew increasingly from communal
religious ritual—not because she ceased questing for God . . . but because she was
probably the only person she knew who felt impelled to continue the quest . . . she
never felt that assurance of salvation for which she yearned even as it evaded her
intensely inquiring ironic mind." [Jane Eberwein, *Dickinson: Strategies of Limitation* (Amherst: University of Massachusetts Press, 1985), 182.] Eberwein also notes
that the phrase "give up the world" did not appear in Amherst's First Church's
1834 *Articles of Faith & Government*. That document asserts on page 7 that professed
Christians should not attend balls, races, theatre, engage in gambling, travel on
a Sunday for business or pleasure, or "make use of ardent spirits, except as medicine." Eberwein suggests that Dickinson would have understood those edicts and
other precepts as abstaining from worldly distractions and pleasures. [Jane Eberwein, email to the author, February 19, 2019.]

tion, trying to imagine life in 1948. In a few days, Mr. Judd, a friend of Miss Lyon's, would appear with his sleigh and take students for a ride. Miss Lyon loved racing along the frozen river and disappearing into a whirling squall.[54] Everyone would soon settle into the old track with recitations, reviews of ancient history, algebra problems, chemistry experiments, and more letters in Seminary Hall from the intrepid Fidelia Fiske. Emily knew she would never set out for Persia or teach Choctaw Indians. She now realized her travel would take her elsewhere. Whether she knew it then or not, she would bore into her own interior, confronting an unknown as wild and uncertain as any new world a missionary had seen. A place as rare as Noah's. Right now, if she squinted and looked far to the northwest, she could almost see that volcanic summit—Mount Holyoke—sitting dreamlike against the night sky.

Downstairs, the prayer meeting had ended. With all the young women in their rooms for silent study hours, Miss Lyon sat alone with her books and her lists and the pulsing exhaustion of her own vision. She drew out a pen to record which students had joined her that night. Five new ones attended, she wrote. One was not there who had been before, she added. She left no note, however.[55]

Three

I'VE BEEN IN THE HABIT *MYSELF* OF WRITING SOME FEW THINGS

Friday, February 20, 1852 2 p.m. Thermometer 18.2 degrees.
Barometer mean 30.38b. Wind NW 2. Humidity 44. Cloudiness 0.
Snow 0. Remarks: Clear and pretty cold. Faint Streamers.

—Ebenezer Snell, *The Meteorological Journal Kept at Amherst College*

The family cat had been missing for a month, and in its absence Emily became the house mouser. She traps one a night, Vinnie boasted.[1] Even when it came to rodents, Vinnie was proud of her sister's accomplishments. Now that Emily had permanently returned from Mount Holyoke, her life revolved around the Dickinsons' home with all its attendant comforts, duties, and grievances. When Emily informed Abiah she would not be returning to the seminary, she said the decision was her father's.[2] The statement was true, partially. As the presumed head of the household, Edward Dickinson rendered most of the judgments for the family, but Emily was coy about what was or was not her choice. Routinely she suggested that others made decisions for her or actions simply happened or evolved by default. Other times she remained mute about personal accomplishments that others would have bragged about. It became increasingly difficult to discern what she chose to do and what she appeared to have no hand in. She was growing intentionally furtive, indiscernible, and tight-lipped about owning up to her decisions. And she appeared to acquiesce easily to her father's determinations—perhaps too easily. In truth, nothing about twenty-one-year-old Emily Dickinson was easy or apparent. Implying the Mount Holyoke decision was her father's alone said as much about Emily's silence as it did Edward Dickinson's dominance. It was not that Emily was capricious or believed she was not entitled to her own point of view. Rather, she did not want to be found out. She preferred being imperceptible. It was as though Emily wanted to set the trap, but be nowhere in sight when it snapped.

The decision not to return to Mount Holyoke was understood. Emily wanted to stay in Amherst, and teaching already had been ruled out. When she looked around, she saw young people her age finding work, leaving town, and establishing their independence. Cousin Emily was teaching in Ohio. Austin had graduated from Amherst College and was teaching in Boston. Her friend Jane Humphrey had accepted a school post in the Midwest. "Why so *far*," Emily asked. "Was'nt there room enough for that young ambition, among New England hills?"[3] Everyone seemed to be moving, Emily said—implying she was not.[4] She was especially sad to see Sue Gilbert leave. She had grown close to Sue and Mattie Gilbert, who lived in Amherst with their sister and brother-in-law, William Cutler. But, worried about being financially dependent on her sister's husband, Sue had moved to Baltimore. As a teacher, she earned $125 a year—not much—she admitted, but enough to make a home for herself and be on her own. Perhaps it was more than financial concern that made Sue distance herself from him. William Cutler believed women who worked exposed themselves to sickness and even death, and labeled Sue's decision to leave "foolish."[5] But Sue had enjoyed herself in Maryland—made new friends, took in operas, sampled food she had never tasted before—and so far she had proved Mr. Cutler wrong.[6] She was, after all, still alive.

Many young men were also no longer around: Amherst College students and former law students who had visited the Dickinsons' home and showed an interest in Emily. One of them, George Gould—a fraternity brother of Austin's—had gone west to seek work as an engineer. Everyone liked George's wit and kindness, and said even shaking hands with him made a person feel better.[7] Long after George left, Emily kept his invitation to a party—a candy pull.* Two law clerks in her father's office also had departed Amherst, but not before giving Emily gifts. The young men shared her love of literature: one had given her a copy of Ralph Waldo Emerson's poems and the other Charlotte Brontë's *Jane Eyre*. While Emily had no serious romantic prospects at the time, she often was amused by those who did. She told Austin about one friend who had two admirers pulling weeds out of her flower bed. "*That's* romantic, is'nt it," she joked.[8] In the winter, the same young woman was with a beau sledding down Boltwood's Hill. "The very last phase of flirtation," she quipped.[9] If teaching were out of the question and marriage not on the horizon—Emily wondered where life would take her. She was ambitious and a clever writer. At least, that's what her friends and teachers thought. But she didn't know if others agreed. She would soon find out. Before the day ended, Emily's first poem would be published. The verse would take a circuitous route passed from friend to acquaintance before finally ending up in the hands of a

---

* Candy pulls were common in the nineteenth century and a way for young men and women to get acquainted. After boiling sugar or molasses, couples would face each other and pull apart a sticky ball of candy. They would lengthen the gooey sweet, double it back up, and stretch it again until the candy became the consistency of taffy. It was a messy exercise, but one New Englanders especially enjoyed.

respected editor. It all started in the most inauspicious way with shenanigans around Valentine's Day and one of Vinnie's suitors.

By any measure, Vinnie's gentleman callers had been plentiful and some ardent. Vinnie had young men come for the afternoon to hear her sing, stop by for pie, and take her riding in a carriage "drawn by six horses"—or so she effused in her diary.[10] One night Emily observed with amusement that a young man took Vinnie to a lecture while she went unescorted and settled for a seat next to Mr. and Mrs. Snell.[11] At one point Vinnie had so many callers, she had to stagger them or dodge one while another was coming through the gate. Many narrow escapes, she admitted.[12] William Howland was the most persistent. An 1846 Amherst graduate, he later tutored at the college and studied in Edward Dickinson's law office. William and Vinnie frequently went walking and rode horseback to a nearby glade. Howland called so often, Vinnie noted he was at the family's home "again & again."[13] His tenacity sometimes annoyed her, or perhaps it was William himself.[14] But when she came back from a visit to Boston, Vinnie had been pleased to see Howland waiting for her. By accepting his invitations, she clearly encouraged him, and one afternoon led to trouble. The two had gone riding far enough away so that no one would see them. Then they exchanged rings. Mr. and Mrs. Dickinson disapproved and—most likely—the incident did not help Howland's prospects at the Dickinson law office. "Did Vinnie tell you that she went with him to Ware, and how it made a hubbub in the domestic circle?" Emily tattled to her brother.[15] A month later, Vinnie noted in her diary: "Received offer of *marriage*"—but no other details followed.[16] Emily couldn't help teasing her father's law clerks; their earnestness made ribbing them irresistible. When Valentine's Day came around, she penned a lively poem to William. She assumed he wouldn't take her words seriously and would enjoy their charm and exaggeration. It was a spoof, after all: merely a way to have fun. Even if her poem was more quick-witted than profound, Emily assured herself that the valentine was for William's eyes only.

Emily loved Valentine's Day. Most everyone did. Local townswomen hosted Valentine's festivals that served up ice cream while residents penned amusing notes that they slid into a mock post office. For weeks, the Adams brothers' bookshop in Amherst had filled its shelves with embossed lace and flower valentines.[17] Esther Howland, an enterprising young woman who had gone to Mount Holyoke, had been mass producing valentines from her father's stationery store in Worcester. Initially she'd hoped her brother could rustle up $200 worth of orders, but was astonished when he came home with sales topping $5,000.[18] When it came to valentines, Emily considered herself old-fashioned. She wanted to compose the words herself and not rely on someone else's sentiments. She used the holiday to scribble poems and long prose declarations bursting with exuberance and made-up words. She also loved the verbal sparring that came with the holiday. When someone shot a humorous volley her way, she welcomed the challenge, and countered with banter as sharp as it was erudite. "A little condescending, & sarcastic, your Valentine to me," she teased a male cousin, "a little like an Eagle, stooping to salute a Wren, & I concluded once, I dared not answer it, for it seemed to me not quite becoming – in a bird so lowly as myself – to claim admittance to an Eyrie, & conversation with it's King."[19] While Emily enjoyed the personal exchange of valentines, one of her fanciful compositions had earlier ended up in a student publication at Amherst College. It happened that a group of young men—some of whom were Austin's friends—had been scrambling to fill pages of their magazine, the *Indicator*. George Gould from the candy pull was on the *Indicator*'s editorial board and had received one of Emily's delightful valentines. When the pages of the magazine had come up short, George offered Emily's witty prose piece to fill the gap. "Magnum bonum, 'harrum scarum', zounds et zounds, et war alarum, man reformam, life perfectum, mundum changum, all things flarum? Sir, I desire an interview," she began. Come, she implored, "meet me at sunrise, or sunset, or the new moon – the place is immaterial. In gold, or in purple, or sackcloth – I look not upon the *raiment*. With sword, or with pen, or with plough – the weapons are less than the *wielder*. . . . Our friendship sir, shall endure till sun and moon shall wane no more. . . . I am Judith the heroine of Apocrypha, and you the orator of Ephesus. That's what they call a metaphor in our country. Don't be afraid of it, sir, it won't bite. If it was my *Carlo* now! The Dog is the noblest work of Art, sir. . . . But the world is sleeping in ignorance and error, sir, and we must be crowing cocks, and singing larks, and a rising sun to awake her; or else we'll pull society up to the roots, and plant it in a different place. We'll build Alms-houses, and transcendental State prisons, and scaffolds – we will blow out the sun, and the moon, and encourage invention. Alpha shall kiss Omega – we will ride up the hill of glory – Hallelujah, all hail!"[20]

Emily had no idea the valentine would be published. Nor did she tell anyone after it had, even though the headnote written by one of the student editors was flattering. "I wish I knew who the author is," the editor declared. "I think she must have some spell, by which she quickens the imagination, and causes the high blood 'run frolic through the veins.' Yes, the author, of such a gew gaw—such a frenzy built edifice—I should like to know and talk with, for I don't believe her mouth has any corners, perhaps 'like a rose leaf torn!' But I'll not keep you in the door way longer, but enter the temple, and decipher the thoughts engraved there."[21] Discovering her prose had been published made Emily realize that others were interested in her writing, even if they were only Austin's friends. She must have been relieved to see her name not attached to the work. It made her invisible. Only the curious letter *C* stood where her name would have been. The initial may have been a reference to Carlo.

For several years now, Emily's big dog, Carlo, had been her protector and what she called her shaggy ally.[22] Edward Dickinson bought the dog—a Newfoundland most people thought—to keep his daughter company. Carlo followed her everywhere and, like most sights and sounds around Emily, he became the object of metaphor—even in a valentine. Emily could hardly get up in the morning without metaphors and images flooding her mind. Often her letters to Austin took on the appearance of a composition exercise, as if she were trying to freeze a moment in words and capture not only the look, but also the feel of an instant. "We have just got home from meeting," she had written her brother one winter, "it is very windy and cold – the hills from our kitchen window are just crusted with snow, which with their blue mantillas makes them seem so beautiful. . . . Father and mother sit in state in the sitting room perusing such papers only, as they are well assured have nothing carnal in them. Vinnie is eating an apple which makes me think of gold, and accompanying it with her favorite [New York] Observer, which if you recollect, deprives us many a time of her sisterly society. Pussy has'nt returned from the afternoon assembly, so you have us all just as we are at present."[23] When she wrote to others mentioning, for example, that she had a cold, she could not merely say she was ill. Instead she drafted entire scenes featuring a wild creature that spread disease by pouncing on her shawl, throwing his arms around her neck and kissing her wildly. She even used dialogue. " 'Marm, will [you] tell me the name of this country," she imagined the beast saying, 'it's Asia Minor, is'nt it?"[24] Emily also spent considerable time writing in her head and marked passages in books about the role of art in expressing the ineffable.[25] When she came across a fine sentence, she shared it with others, and studied how the listeners reacted.[26] She reused phrases she had created, sending them to different correspondents for different effect. Some of the words in George Gould's prose valentine came from an earlier letter to someone else.[27] The natural world also fueled her imagination—birds, rivers, daisies, sunrises, mice. Like one of Mary Lyon's science students, she would study the object before her, registering light, movement, shape, and color, but then slip out of the world of scientific observation and into figurative language. Take snakes, for instance: "*I* love those little green ones," Emily had written Abiah, "that slide around by your shoes in the grass – and make it rustle with their elbows."[28] Unlike Vinnie, who kept a diary, or Sue Gilbert, who wrote in a journal, or her old girlhood friend Helen Fiske, who wanted to start a "character book" for recording observations—Emily said she was not the type to formally organize her thoughts.[29] Perhaps she didn't keep a diary or a journal because she didn't need to. Images never left her. Once she stood in the Amherst rain watching Austin return to Boston. It was not so much the sight of Austin himself that lingered in her mind, but rather the place where he was not. "I watched the stage coach yesterday until it went away," she had written, "and I hoped you would turn around, so to be sure and see me. . . . I thought you saw me once, the way I told was *this*. You know your cap was black, and where it had been black, it all at once grew *white*, and I fancied *that* was *you*."[30]

Lately Emily was pondering an abstract idea some may have found bizarre. She used one of her wildly imaginative letters to sort out what she was thinking. Surely Uncle Joel Norcross would have realized his niece was writing one of her overblown reprimands for not responding quickly enough to her letters; he had received many of them. But in the final paragraphs, Emily's prose took a startling turn, moving from the humorously absurd to the violent with talk of stones and daggers and guns. She was trying to get at a belief that was important to her, but it was difficult to understand what she meant. "Harm is one of those things that I always mean to keep clear of," she had written, "but somehow my intentions and me dont chime as they ought – and people will get hit with stones that I throw at my neighbor's dogs – not only *hit* – *that* is the least of the whole – but they insist upon blaming *me* instead of the *stones* – and tell me their heads ache – why it is the greatest piece of folly on record. It would do to go with a story I read – one man pointed a loaded gun at a man – and it shot him so that he died – and the people threw the owner of the gun into prison – and afterwards hung him for *murder*. Only another victim to the misunderstanding of society . . . Now when I walk into your room and pluck your heart out that you die – I kill you – hang me if you like – but if I stab you while sleeping the dagger's to blame – it's no business of mine."[31] On the surface, she was making a preposterous claim about accountability: the dagger's to blame, the loaded gun is at fault, stones hit the neighbor's dog. But beneath the surface, Emily was trying to understand if writers were responsible for the feelings they prompted in others: if hurling a word had the same effect as throwing a stone. Was imagination—like a loaded gun—the one pulling the trigger?* Emily seemed to say she wanted the freedom to hurl her words without consequences. She did not want to pay a price for daring images or be muzzled into saying only what was acceptable. Invisibility seemed the key for keeping her imagination sovereign. Years later she would remember sitting with her friend Jane in a favorite spot—the big stone step outside the Dick-

---

* The letter prefigures Dickinson's 1863 poem "My Life had stood — a Loaded Gun —." [F764.]

insons' front door. She recalled hearing the faraway sound of an ax being brought down long after a farmer had swung it.[32] What stayed with her was not the action or the farmer. What remained was the lingering sound. Emily wanted to be like that: heard but not seen.

Austin could not always understand what Emily was saying, and it exasperated him. Austin and Emily's friend Sue Gilbert had become close, and in one letter, he complained to Sue about Emily's confounding prose. "I have a sort of land of Canaan letter from Emily yesterday," he had written, "but she was too high up to give me any of the monuments of earth."[33] Vinnie also found her sister abstruse and difficult to comprehend. She "has fed you on air so long," Vinnie told Austin, "that I think a little 'sound common sense' perhaps wouldnt come amiss *Plain english* you *know* such as Father likes."[34] Writing joint family letters to Austin sometimes prompted sharp contrasts. "Vinnie tells me *she* has detailed the *news*," Emily wrote. "She reserved the *deaths* for me, thinking I might fall short of my usual letter somewhere."[35] But when Emily heard that her brother and sister were complaining about her writing, she fired back to Austin with humor and hyperbole. "You say you dont comprehend me, you want a simpler style. *Gratitude* indeed for all my fine philosophy! I strove to be exalted thinking I might reach *you* and while I pant and struggle and climb the nearest cloud, you walk out very leisurely in your slippers from Empyrean, and without the *slightest* notice request me to get down!"[36]

With Valentine's Day over, the Adams brothers cleared their shelves of Esther Howland's red and white cards and made way for new books to occupy the shop racks. Vinnie had been reading a book with a personal connection to the family: a biography of Mary Lyon. Amherst College president Edward Hitchcock spent the last two years writing the book in order to pay tribute to the woman he admired. He hoped his words would inspire readers to emulate Miss

Lyon's ambition.[37] In 1849—the year after Emily left the seminary—
Mary Lyon had become seriously ill. Already ground down by years
of work, she had insisted on caring for a student who was battling
a serious infection. When the infection spread to Miss Lyon, the
erysipelas that had long plagued her returned. A beloved nephew's
suicide may have weakened her physical condition even more. On
March 5, 1849, Lyon died at age fifty-two. In accordance with her
directions, Mount Holyoke resumed activity a few days later, and as
he so often did, Professor Snell came over to help with lectures.[38]
Behind the sprawling seminary building, trustees worked on a
gravestone monument for Mount Holyoke's founder. Teachers and
students had watched as trustees dug postholes for an iron fence
surrounding the grave. When shovels proved inadequate, the men
dug the dirt with their hands. Receiving the news in Persia, Fidelia Fiske vowed to collect memories of Mary Lyon from former students. "I have nothing that I wanted to do here, except to finish
that writing," she said.[39] She recalled the words to a song Miss Lyon
once sang at the spinning wheel. "It's not in the wheel, it's not in the
band,—It's in the girl who takes it in hand." *[40]

Mary Lyon's belief that women's minds deserved to be as active
as their hands taught her students there was more to life than
housework. In place of spinning flax, a young woman might take
up words or metaphor. For Emily, the demands of an active fam-

---

* Fidelia Fiske continued directing her school in Persia (present-day Iran) until
ill health forced her return to Massachusetts. She taught at Mount Holyoke Female
Seminary from 1859 to 1864. When trustees offered her the position of principal
in 1863, she declined. She wanted to return to her school in Persia when her health
improved—but she never did. Fiske died in 1864 at age forty-eight. Her book, *The
Recollections of Mary Lyon with Selections from Her Instruction to the Pupils of Mt. Holyoke
Female Seminary*, was published posthumously in 1866.

ily made housekeeping impossible to escape. Home is a holy thing, she wrote Austin, but her days were far from pleasing.[41] She disliked the drudgery, and begrudged the time it snatched from her writing. There were pies to make and clothing to mend; floors to sweep and seeds to plant; and all those chickens that needed tending. An especially difficult time for Emily had occurred when Vinnie was away at school. Vinnie, like Helen Fiske, attended Ipswich for a short time—the seminary Helen's father thought was less intellectually taxing than Mount Holyoke. Emily complained to a friend that many of the chores had fallen on her shoulders. "Vinnie away," she had written, "and my two hands but *two* – not four, or five as they ought to be – and so *many* wants – and me so *very* handy – and my time of so *little* account – and my writing so *very* needless." Emily said that if she took so much as "an inch on time" to write, she would be castigated – not so much by her family as the world and her own guilt.[42] Housekeeping, to her, was a way to cultivate a woman's submission and steal time, and she wanted nothing of it. "God keep me from what they call *households*," she said.[43]

The labor around the house was coupled with social calls that annoyed Emily all the more. As much as she often felt regimented by the rigorous schedule at Mount Holyoke, at least then her mind had been occupied. But social convention dictated that when she didn't have her hands busy with domestic chores, she should be paying calls on the local citizenry or they on her. One Saturday evening after tea, Emily had fallen prey to a steady stream of callers that nearly killed her, she said. Along with their mother in the kitchen, she was cleaning up when there was a knock at the door. Two gentlemen were standing on the stone step asking for Emily. Surprised by the summons, she hurried across the room as her father shouted to the young men not to keep the door wide open.

Emily joined the gentlemen outside on the step only to have them—
no doubt jolted by Mr. Dickinson's bark—excuse themselves hastily
in the name of pressing business. Then the bell rang again. This
time a cousin and another gentleman walked in. Emily sat in the
sitting room—more dead than alive, she admitted—and struggled to make conversation. "The weather was rather cold today,"
she said, trying to encourage conversation. The gentlemen nod-
ded in obliging unanimity. Frantically, she searched her mind for
another topic, and pulled up a stray thought about a recent sermon.
As soon as she ventured into the subject, the bell rang again and
in trooped another cousin—Thankful Smith "in the furs and robes
of her ancestors," Emily later reported. Trying her best to disappear into what she called a "primeval nothingness," Emily knew
the evening had gotten beyond her control.[44] It wasn't every evening that the Dickinson home saw a parade of callers and strained
conversation. But when it happened—Emily felt depleted. A "constant interchange *wastes tho't* and feeling," she said, "and we are
then obliged to *repair* and *renew*."[45]

The expectation that Emily spend time dusting or calling on
neighbors grated on her, and her irritation began to show. That
winter when the Sewing Society began its meetings, Emily declined
to attend. She knew "the public" would be puzzled by her absence
and make her the object of prayers, and she let loose with a torrent
of sarcasm. "Now all the poor will be helped – the cold warmed –
the warm cooled – the hungry fed – the thirsty attended to – the
ragged clothed – and this suffering – tumbled down world will
be helped to it's feet again," she wrote her friend Jane.[46] It was an
ungenerous and judgmental remark that betrayed her blindness to
the misfortune of others, and underscored her own unhappiness.
Emily said she loved "to be surly – and muggy – and cross."[47] When

she didn't receive replies to her letters fast enough, she became what she called "crusty."[48] She slammed doors, called herself one of the lingering *bad* ones, and disappeared whenever she felt like it. Even Austin said she could be wild. "Savage," Vinnie said.[49] Emily admitted people probably saw her as hardhearted, but she had no idea friends gossiped behind her back. Emily is wholly misinterpreted, they said.[50] She was not the only young woman who felt out of sorts. Her old friend Helen Fiske confessed that her only diversions were reading, writing letters, and practicing piano. With no career and few activities besides housework, she felt adrift. Occasionally Helen went for a walk or varied the routine by "*the breaking of a few lamp shades*," she said.[51] Emily knew even unruffled Abiah could be peeved. "Not in one of your *breaking dish* moods I take it," she joked.[52] Sometimes Emily was so overwhelmed with unhappiness, she cried. There were tears over canceled plans, tending her mother when Mrs. Dickinson was ill, and when friends moved away. As she looked ahead, the future looked grim, lonely, and aimless. She was not exactly angry, she said. She was bitter and sad.[53] "Duty," she said, "is black and brown."[54]

Helen Fiske rarely allowed herself to be downcast, but she had reason to feel unmoored. After her mother's death, her father died on a visit to the Holy Land. His body was not returned to Amherst, and he had been buried on Mount Zion. For several years, Helen shuttled among relatives and boarding schools. She referred to her wanderings with her usual tart tongue. It was like surviving massacres, she said.[55] But recently, things had changed for the better. Helen was in Albany and staying with a guardian who discussed Coleridge and Tennyson with her and encouraged literary interests. He suggested she might translate a French essay, and she had tried—setting herself down to write in her mother's favorite rocking chair.* But soon social invitations pulled Helen away and she lost her urge to write. She castigated herself for being easily distracted and vowed to do something useful. "I *will* not let myself be turned into a young lady 'in society' who sleeps, goes to parties, receives and returns calls!"[56] But she did just that. The French translation was never finished, the character book she pledged to keep lay unopened, and she was off to a Christmas ball at the state capitol. There she met the governor's youngest brother, a recent West Point graduate working for the Army Corps of Engineers. Edward Hunt, she said, "is very tall, very large, very dignified, *rather* cold in his manner at first, but *thaws.*"[57]

After Valentine's Day, a thin layer of February snow covered the ground in Amherst. It had snowed only two inches all month— but since it had been so cold, nothing had melted.[58] When Emily looked at the barren garden, summer's abundance seemed beyond imaging—the whorls of blooms, ripe peaches, the Baldwin apples Vinnie loved.[59] She thought about her father's contentment when the Dickinson lot was flush with green and in order. He loved the sense of dominion he felt when his trees were trimmed, firewood piled high, potatoes planted, and manure evenly spread.[60] That winter Edward Dickinson had reason to feel in command. He was poised to become a delegate to the National Whig Convention and would travel to Baltimore to join others in nominating Dan-

---

* Helen had no idea her mother had literary ambitions. In 1839 Deborah Vinal Fiske wrote five stories for a children's Sunday-school reader: *Youth's Companion*. The stories were published anonymously. [Kate Phillips, *Helen Hunt Jackson: A Literary Life* (Berkeley: University of California Press, 2003), 63.] Like her daughter, Deborah Fiske felt domestic life did not sustain her. "My *life is* slipping away and I am doing nothing but taking care of my family," she wrote. "I know it is my *proper business*, but some do so much good besides." [Phillips, 63.]

iel Webster for president.[61] Then there was the railroad. Edward's long work bringing the train to Amherst finally was paying off. When news came that all the railroad stock had been sold, there was a ten-gun salute in his honor. He had recently joined the church, too, along with Vinnie and Sue Gilbert.* Like his father, Austin also was taking decisive steps. He had already decided to leave his teaching job and return home in a matter of months to prepare for law school. Harvard Law would be next. As much as Emily loved Austin's company, it was dreary to think of spending her days washing her brother's collars, mending his socks, and making sure he had his favorite breakfast: meat and potatoes and that brown bread he asked for.[62] Emily must have found it hard to believe that anything much would be new for her. When she looked at herself, all she saw was a woman with a soiled dress, a worn apron, and unkempt hair.[63]

In spite of Vinnie's occasional ambivalence toward him, William Howland was at it again. He and Vinnie had gone for a ride in the bracing February cold. Emily hoped William had enjoyed her valentine, silly as it was. The poem began with a rush of Latin bombast and some showing off:

"Sic transit gloria mundi,"
"How doth the busy bee,"
"Dum vivimus vivamus,"
I stay mine enemy!

---

* Edward Dickinson and Susan Gilbert joined Amherst's First Church on August 11, 1850. Vinnie joined November 3, 1850. Austin would join the church on January 6, 1856. Emily never joined, the only member of her immediate family not to become a member of Amherst's First Church. [Jay Leyda, *The Years and Hours of Emily Dickinson*, vol. 1 (New Haven: Yale University Press, 1960), 178, 182, 339.]

Oh "veni, vidi, vici!"
Oh caput cap-a-pie!
And oh "memento mori"
When I am *far* from thee!

Hurrah for Peter Parley!
Hurrah for Daniel Boon!
Three cheers, sir, for the gentleman
Who first observed the moon!*

While the poem was typical of valentine nonsense, Emily was proud of it—at least proud enough to send it. She stuffed the seventeen stanzas with images of the Garden of Eden, her father's apples, legislatures, muskets, Bunker Hill, even India rubbers. She included one scientific metaphor, writing about the Earth on its axis turning around the sun "By way of a *gymnastic*." The poem closed with three stanzas of exalted farewell:

Good bye, Sir, I am going;
My country calleth me;
Allow me, Sir, at parting,
To wipe my weeping e'e.

In token of our friendship
Accept this "Bonnie Doon,"
And when the hand that plucked it
Hath passed beyond the moon,

---

* Dickinson's Latin roughly translates to "Thus passes the glory of the world. Remember that we live to die." Peter Parley refers to a series of nineteenth-century elementary readers. ["Lydia Maria Child and the Development of Children's Literature," Boston Public Library, Rare Books and Manuscripts, bostonliteraryhistory.com.]

> The memory of my ashes
> Will consolation be;
> Then, farewell, Tuscarora,
> And farewell, Sir, to thee![64]

How could William not appreciate the poem's absurdity? He knew Emily Dickinson was not headed off to battle.

Emily couldn't help looking at the sky that day. It had been dazzling lately. The day before, an aurora borealis illuminated the heavens. When he went out for his noon weather readings, Professor Snell saw faint streamers traveling through the sun's corona. Emily recalled what she had learned in school about the aurora borealis. Some people said an aurora borealis reminded them of a biblical passage from Acts. "And I will show wonders in heaven above and signs on the earth beneath." *[65] Northern lights were harbingers, they said, of a future people could not see. Earlier, Emily had confessed to her friend Jane that she had been uncharacteristically bold. "I know you would be surprised," she had written. "I have dared to do strange things – bold things, and have asked no advice from any." The winter had been like one long dream, she said. Then she mentioned the gold thread. "What do you weave from all these threads," Emily asked her friend. "Bring it nearer the window, and I will see, it's all wrong unless it has one gold thread in it, a long, big shining fibre which hides the others."[66] Weeks later Emily shared a similar thought with Abiah. This time it was a golden dream that

---

* Edward Dickinson witnessed an aurora borealis in Amherst the previous autumn. So emotionally moved by the display, he rang the church bell, alerting Amherst residents to the phenomenon. "We were all startled by a violent church bell ringing," Emily wrote Austin, "and thinking nothing but fire, rushed out in the street to see. The sky was a beautiful red, bordering on a crimson, and rays of a gold pink color were constantly shooting off from a kind of sun in the centre." [L53.]

wouldn't let her go. "I have been dreaming, dreaming, a *golden dream*," she had written, "with eyes all the while wide open."[67]

By afternoon on February 20, Friday's *Springfield Daily Republican* arrived in Amherst and someone from the Dickinson household retrieved it from the post office.[68] Much to Emily and Vinnie's disappointment, there were no sensational stories in the newspaper—no heads cut off, no yards of snake in a cow's intestine. The four pages were filled with advertisements, transportation schedules, news summaries, and claims of medical miracles. On page one there was a poem entitled "The Wretch" by one Meister Karl. It was about a bickering husband and wife who quarreled over the husband's smoking.

I hope you don't regret, love,
The times when you were free
To puff those vile segars, love,
Which you've resigned for me!

Page two featured a story about the recent celestial wonder. "The exhibition of the Aurora Borealis, last evening, was the most splendid that we have seen for many a night. The King of the North shook out shimmering folds of all his banners, red, argentine, and golden, and from the way in which his threatening scimeters attached the zenith, we judge that it will be found full of holes when seen again. In fact, we saw light shining through in a number of places."[69]

Situated next to the aurora borealis account in a column to the left was another poem. This one entitled "A Valentine." Unlike the segar poem, this one was anonymous. The poem began with playful Latin lines. It was Emily's poem to William Howland: the one for his eyes only. Atop the poem was an editor's note: "The hand that wrote the following amusing medley to a gentleman friend of ours, as 'a valentine,' is capable of very fine things, and there is certainly no presumption in entertaining a private wish that a correspondence, more direct than this, may be established between it and the Republican."[70] William must have shared her poem with the editors. Without her consent. Emily knew Vinnie's beau had lived in Springfield and probably was acquainted with the newspaper's editors Samuel Bowles and Josiah Holland. A poem in the Springfield newspaper was not like having a prose valentine in a college students' magazine, she realized. The *Republican* was more visible, read by people all over New England, and thousands more across the country.* Some readers even clipped poems out of the newspaper and pasted them in personal journals. No one needed to tell Emily she could write; she already sensed that. But with her valentine in the *Republican*, she understood—for the first time—professional editors thought so too.†

Emily did not say a word to Jane or Abiah about the poem. When she wrote to Sue she did not mention it either, saying only that she hoped her letter would travel through hills and dales, across rivers, and "make a poem such as can ne'er be written."[71] A few days after her verse was published, Emily wrote Austin, rattling on about the memorable evening when all the callers arrived, and Thankful Smith in furs brought up the rear. She let her brother know she hadn't finished his laundry. The family would send a bundle of clean clothes by the

---

* The *Republican* claimed that it was read by people in every state except Mississippi and every territory except Utah. [Stephen G. Weisner, *Embattled Editor: The Life of Samuel Bowles*, PhD Dissertation, University of Massachusetts, Amherst, 1986, 52.]
† Eudocia Converse [Flynt], a first cousin of the poet's mother, copied "'Sic transit gloria mundi'" into her 1848–1853 commonplace book, along with the note "Valentine by Miss E Dickinson of Amherst." Within some circles at least, readers knew the poem was Dickinson's. [R. W. Franklin, ed, *The Poems of Emily Dickinson* Variorum Edition (Cambridge: The Belknap Press of Harvard University Press, 1998), 49.]

next person traveling to Boston. There was not much news, she said. Father's rheumatism was acting up. The old cat had not returned, and Vinnie had a new kitten who slept in a basket under the kitchen table.[72] "How much I have said about nothing," she wrote, never mentioning the poem.[73] Emily was eager for Austin to come home, although she would miss his letters. Her brother's writing had entertained everyone, especially their father. It didn't matter to whom Austin's letters were addressed. Mr. Dickinson opened them all, and read them at the post office, again over supper, and once more by the fire in the evening. In fact, Edward Dickinson was so impressed with Austin's prose, he wanted to preserve his letters permanently. "Father says your letters are altogether before Shakespeare, and he will have them published to put in our library," Emily told her brother.[74]

Later that spring, Vinnie and Emily assessed their looks. Vinnie had her picture taken and sent Austin a copy. "I dont like it at all," she said, "& should be sorry to have you or any one else think I look just like it. I dont think my real face is quite so stupid."[75] Emily decided it was time for a change. When the barber came, she asked him to cut her long hair. Vinnie couldn't believe it. Emily cut her hair, she exclaimed to her brother.*[76] With a fashionable new look and a poem in the *Republican*, Emily shot one of her humorous volleys to Austin. "Now Brother Pegasus, I'll tell you what it is — I've been in the habit *myself* of writing some few things. . . . you'd better be somewhat careful, or I'll call the police!" She was teasing, but barely. When it came to having a talent for words, Emily knew *she* was the writer in the family.[77]

---

* Around early 1853, Emily enclosed a lock of her hair in a letter to Emily Fowler [Ford]. "I said when the Barber came, I would save you a little ringlet, and fulfilling my promise, I send you one today." [L99.] Dickinson's ring of hair is now in Amherst College's Archives and Special Collections.

Four

DECIDED TO BE DISTINGUISHED

Tuesday, January 4, 1859 7 am Barometer 29.835. Attached Therm.
35.1. Extern. Therm. 17.9. Cloudiness 10. Winds NW 3 mph.
Humidity 100%. Remarks Stormy all day
—Ebenezer Snell, *The Meteorological Journal Kept at Amherst College*

The snow began before dawn and by the time Emily finished cleaning up breakfast, she could see several inches collecting outside the window. Quite a fairy morning, she thought, but the day wouldn't stay enchanting for long.[1] Already the storm, which had stretched from Virginia to Canada, halted train service, made mail delivery impossible, and caused people down in New York to nearly come to blows. "What right have the stage proprietors to sprinkle salt the whole length of Broadway in order to remove the snow, and thus spoil sleighing for the use of private citizens?" one resident complained.[2] Stage drivers were wise to keep ahead of the storm. By the time the snow ended twenty-four hours later, Boston and Springfield were buried, and towering drifts leaned against houses, barns, and fence posts. The blizzard had Amherst College professors shaking their heads with a mixture of amusement and annoyance. For as long as anyone could remember, the very day students were due back from winter break, a snowstorm roared through New England. Some young men took advantage of the situation and delayed their arrival for one, two, or even three weeks. This snow would give "loiterers"—as they were called—an especially good excuse.[3] By nightfall there would be nearly two feet on the ground. Few citizens of Amherst were out and about, but one was Emily's fearless sister, who had shopping on her mind. In last Friday's newspaper, Vinnie had seen an advertisement for Mr. Cutler's store.* "Wool hoods, hosiery, gloves, furs, cuffs," the notice announced, "For Sale Cheap."[4]

Emily did not join Vinnie on the walk "up-street," as they called it. Sometimes when bad weather moved in, she wanted nothing more than to be left alone. She loved looking out windows, mesmerized by the images before her. Once she saw a pale storm "stalking through the fields" and "bowing" at the window, she said.[5] Other times, she studied how snow turned to rain and then mist. "Soft fogs like vails hang on all the houses," she wrote, and "the days turn Topaz, like a lady's pin."[6] On another snowy day with her dog, Carlo, by her side, she placed both hands on the windowpanes and tried to imagine how birds flew. "I talk of all these things with Carlo, and his eyes grow meaning."[7] It was no secret to members of her family that Emily was always thinking and writing in her head—"poetizing," she said—imagining a phrase from words that churned all around her.[8] Yet it wasn't enough to merely write down what she had imagined, she wanted to share it too. "Do I paint it *natural*," she once asked Sue, "so you think how it looks?"[9] Townspeople braving the storm that snowy morning would have seen her solitary figure at the Dickinson window. Solitary yes, but not detached. As she watched the snow, Emily was thinking about her prospects. She

---

* Mr. Cutler was Susan Gilbert's brother-in-law—the man who believed women who worked ran the risk of becoming ill or dying. He was married to Susan's sister, Harriet.

had just turned twenty-eight, a new year was upon her, and she was at a critical point in her life. Emily wanted to be distinguished.

By 1859 much had changed in the lives of the Dickinson family. Austin had married and Edward had ventured into politics. Vinnie had ended her schooling. Even Emily found herself in new and surprising surroundings. She never thought she would see the White House or travel to Philadelphia. The changes began when the family packed up their belongings and moved. Deacon Mack, who'd bought the old Dickinson family homestead, had died, and Edward jumped at the chance to buy back the house. Although the move was only around the corner from their beloved home on West Street, Emily felt as though she had been thrown in a covered wagon bound for the prairie. "It is a kind of *gone-to-Kansas* feeling," she said.[10] She had been happy in the old home with its trellises, large garden, and the big stone step where she and friends exchanged confidences. But the family decision was her father's and nothing could stop Edward from taking the opportunity to redress his own father's financial failure and reestablish Dickinson prominence on Main Street. When the time came, Emily made the trek by foot. She noted her " 'effects' " were transported in a bandbox and " 'deathless me' " followed.[11] Emily knew her siblings sometimes poked fun at her for being ethereal and she often played the part, calling the move back to Main Street a transit of "heavenly bodies."[12] But displeased with the uprooting as she was, she also laughed at her own melodrama, and offered a more earthbound definition of home: "They say that 'home is where the heart is,' " she said. "I think it is where the *house* is, and the adjacent buildings."[13]

Austin and Sue soon followed with a move of their own. Since Austin's time at Harvard Law School, his relationship with Sue Gilbert had deepened. By 1853 they had become secretly engaged, but it would be another three years before they married. After setting

a date and then changing it several times, Sue and Austin finally
wed on July 1, 1856, in Geneva, New York, with no family present,
not even Emily, who was important to them both. Sue did not go in
for fanfare, at least not then. "I have no *extravagant* ideas of life,"
she had written her brother. "I expect to forego a great many enjoy-
ments that wealth could procure . . . but I can do it very cheerfully
and happily if the man I love well enough to marry, is unable to
give them to me."[14] Sue's brother may have detected some misgiv-
ing in the "well enough" phrase. He might also have known Austin had his own doubts. Seems strange, Austin had written about
Sue, that two tall, proud, stiff people could love so well or hate so
well.[15] But Austin, aware of his reserve, vowed to change. Explaining what held him back, he admitted to Sue, "I have always been
brought up to the idea that it was not a man's part to *show* any one
a tenderness unless in sore distress—but as water finds its level,
so will our hearts find their true expression as the barriers to it
are one by one broken down."[16] Emily—as always—worried about
her brother's well-being. Her credo was: whatever makes Austin
happy. "After that," she said, "I dont care."[17] In starting married
life, Austin's initial impulse had been to get away from Amherst.
Emily knew that when her father and brother were together, the two
men tangled. "Nothing but " 'fisticuff,' " she said.[18] But she also saw
their devotion when they were apart. Austin thought opening a law
practice out West—Chicago, maybe—would be a good idea, a fresh
start. But when Edward purchased the Dickinson Homestead, he
made his son a tempting offer: stay in Amherst, join the Dickinson
law office, and the house on the lot next door is yours. "It has been
something of a sacrifice for Austin's spirit and rather of a struggle
with his pre-conceived ideas," Sue wrote, but "I feel satisfied that
in the end it will be best." She added, Austin goes into partnership
with his father on even terms.[19]

Emily was ecstatic that Sue Gilbert had become her sister-in-law. "My mother and my sister — *thy* mother and thy sister," she wrote.[20] In the weeks before Sue ended her teaching post in Baltimore, Emily had eagerly anticipated her return to Amherst. One day she let her attention in church wander, pondering what to wear for Sue's arrival. Would the fawn-colored dress be better, or the blue one? "Just as I had decided by all means to wear the blue, down came the minister's fist with a terrible rap on the counter," she said. It took a while to regain her composure, she told Sue, and added, "I am glad I reached a conclusion!"[21] As her friends married—Emily Fowler, Abiah Root, Jane Humphrey, Mattie Gilbert—Emily saw her circle shrink. More than any other friend, Sue meant the most to her. "I need you more and more," she confessed, "and the great world grows wider, and dear ones fewer and fewer, every day."[22] Emily had much in common with her. Sue was smart, direct, opinionated, loved books and art, and the two young women could talk for hours. Sue liked being alone too. It had not escaped Emily's attention that Sue took Austin's letters outdoors to read, "to look at the hills and the trees and the blue, blue home."[23] Sue enjoyed being back in New England, where she had room to roam: she'd walk out to the mill or fields fresh with second mowing. Sometimes when she grew weary of housework, she would "saunter"—as she said—until she couldn't take another step.[24] Together, Emily and Sue would tramp for hours by brooks, across meadows, and up to a favorite high, gray rock.[25] On a windy day undaunted by the gusts, Emily and Sue had set out for the train depot to retrieve a package for Vinnie, holding on to each other and their bonnets.[26] Another time in winter at night, they walked to Plainville to hear a sermon. The length of the journey— six miles—was so common it did not receive a single mention in a letter to Austin.[27] A gift Emily had fashioned for Sue's return to Amherst expressed how close the two women had become. While walking alone one day, Emily had found a tiny snail shell, whitened by the snow. It looked like a "cunning artist had carved it from alabaster," she said. She picked it up, nestled it against soft moss, and slipped it inside a leaf. Then she bound the tiny parcel with a blade of summer grass.[28] The gift was exquisite, tender, and intimate. It suggested Emily believed Sue could appreciate—and maybe even understand—all she could create.

On that snowy day when Vinnie ventured out, Emily could discern the outlines of her sister-in-law's home, but remained indoors. When winter bore down, Emily savored "going into the pod," she said.[29] Over the years, Sue and Austin had enlarged the small house Edward presented as a wedding gift, and the Evergreens—as they now called it—had become a fashionable residence with a formal parlor, porches, and a piazza. Only 150 steps separated the two homes, but with snow mounting—Emily knew better than to brave the path between them. As much as she did not like tending to chores, it was warm inside the Homestead, and Emily occupied herself with a basket of sewing. The house was quiet and her mother was resting. Emily recognized that the move to Main Street had been hard on her mother. More often than not, Mrs. Dickinson could be found reclining on a lounger or sitting quietly in a chair. Something was wrong with her, but no one knew exactly what, and the uncertainty of her illness weighed heavily on everyone. For Vinnie and Emily, it also made for more housekeeping—a burden Emily was always quick to point out. But she was sympathetic to her mother. Perhaps Mrs. Dickinson missed the old home with the rooms she knew so well: a domain she proudly governed as her own. Emily stared into the snow and tried to conjure up a phrase from the images. Then she pulled out a sheet of paper. She wanted company—at least, the kind of visit she often preferred—one on paper. "Since it snows this morning, dear Loo, too fast for interruption," she began in a letter, "put your brown curls in a basket, and come sit with me."[30]

Loo was Emily's cousin, the sixteen-year-old daughter of her beloved Aunt Lavinia and Uncle Loring Norcross. Loo and her younger sister Fanny had become Emily's closest relatives now that Cousin Emily Norcross was gone. While teaching in Ohio, Emily's Mount Holyoke roommate had become ill with consumption. A few months after she returned to Massachusetts, she died at age twenty-four. The same independence and ambition that Emily had appreciated in Cousin Emily, she found in Loo. "I am sewing for Vinnie, and Vinnie is flying through the flakes to buy herself a little hood," she continued in her letter. "I often lay down my needle . . . which seriously impedes the sewing project. What if I pause a little longer, and write a note to you! Who will be the wiser?"[31] Emily's aim that day was not simply to write Loo about the snow or Vinnie's shopping expedition. She wanted to return to a previous conversation she could not get out of her mind. "I have known little of you," she continued, "since the October morning when our families went out driving, and you and I in the dining-room decided to be distinguished. It's a great thing to be 'great,' Loo, and you and I might tug for a life, and never accomplish it, but no one can stop our looking on, and you know some cannot sing, but the orchard is full of birds, and we all can listen. What if we learn, ourselves some day!"[32] For months, Emily had thought about their conversation and—as much as she already knew she was a poet—she understood that it would take effort to become a great one. She wanted to learn. She wanted to be brilliant. She wanted fame. The only question was how to achieve it.

One answer already had revealed itself to her. Recently Emily had become acquainted with a literary man—Dr. Josiah Holland, coeditor of the *Springfield Republican*. The newspaper had printed

Emily's comic valentine poem in 1852, praising her verse and inviting her to submit more. Over years of reporting on Amherst for the newspaper, Dr. Holland had become friendly with the entire Dickinson family. Emily and Vinnie had paid a visit to Holland and his wife, Elizabeth, and the sojourn had opened Emily's eyes to a larger world. Emily noted, for example, that when Dr. Holland offered family prayers, he spoke of God as a friend. "*That* was a different God," she said—a warmer, more intimate deity than the one invoked in the Dickinsons' prayers.[33] Holland had no use for orthodoxy and doctrines, and he trusted his own heart above a preacher's decrees. "Christianity, in the form of abstract statement, and in the shape of a creed," he had said, "has not for me any particular meaning. I have to test things through my heart and best feelings."[34] Dr. Holland's approach to religion aligned more with Emily's own. She wanted to think through the question of faith herself, and she held fast to the belief that heaven on Earth would always outweigh heaven above. "My only sketch, profile, of Heaven," she once wrote, "is a large, blue sky, bluer and larger than the *biggest* I have seen in June. . . . no need of other Heaven."[35]

Emily enjoyed writing letters to Josiah and Elizabeth Holland, and they became two of her favorite correspondents. When she wrote to them, the style and tone of her letters shifted slightly, as if she were trying to impress the couple. Emily was aware that her own words occasionally missed the mark: that her meaning could be lost in abstraction and wordiness. With the Hollands, she sometimes had to double back and clarify what she meant. "If it wasn't for broad daylight, and cooking-stoves, and roosters," she wrote Mr. and Mrs. Holland, "I'm afraid you would have occasion to smile at my letters often, but so sure as 'this mortal' essays immortality, a crow from a neighboring farm-yard dissipates the illusion, and I am here again. And what I mean is this – that I thought of you all

last week."[36] As much as she tried to be "sensible"—as she called it—
such practicality in her writing didn't last long. There always was
metaphor and abstraction in her words. "My letter," she told them,
almost apologetically, "as a bee, goes laden."[37]

Emily had reason to respect Dr. Holland: he was a prolific and
successful writer. Besides editing the *Republican*, he wrote fiction,
essays, history, columns, and poems. He also knew publishers in
New York, and word had it that when he had read one of his manuscripts to Charles Scribner, the powerful publisher had halted
him midsentence and said: "Stop there. I'll take the book."[38] That
wintry morning as Emily thought about greatness, she knew the
path to literary fame that Dr. Holland pursued would be difficult
for her to follow: it was too public. In recent years, Emily's solitude
had grown more pronounced. Her family assumed she would rarely
consent to trips away from home and sometimes even visits with
friends in Amherst. They didn't push. Her strategies for avoiding
people were many. She waited to arrive in church until everyone was
seated so she could avoid conversation.[39] She played the piano for
guests, but only if they stayed in another room with a door cracked
open.[40] When delivering a letter to a friend in town, she rang the
bell and ran.[41] Forced to come downstairs to entertain a guest, she
did so with an admittedly "sorry grace"—irritable, reluctant, and
defiant.[42] She even confessed to fleeing to avoid chores. "I do love
to run fast," she said, "and hide away from them all."[43] Her reasons
for seclusion were also numerous: she disdained social chatter;
she was old-fashioned; she disliked some people or found them not
worth her time; socializing left her depleted; people stared; retreat
was invigorating.[44] Emily had a word for her retreats—"flying."[45] On
one of her "flying days" she told Sue about trying to slip into church
unnoticed. The scene she painted was comical in parts, but it also
revealed her distress and panic:

I'm just from meeting, Susie, and as I sorely feared, my "life" was
made a "victim." I walked – I ran – I turned precarious corners
– One moment I was not – then soared aloft like Phoenix, soon
as the foe was by – and then anticipating an enemy again, my
soiled and drooping plumage might have been seen emerging
from just behind a fence, vainly endeavoring to fly once more . . .
I smiled to think of me, and my geometry, during the journey
there – It would have puzzled Euclid . . . How big and broad the
aisle seemed, full huge enough before, as I quaked slowly up –
and reached my usual seat! . . . There I sat, and sighed, and wondered I was scared so, for surely in the whole world was nothing
I need to fear – Yet there the Phantom was, and though I kept
resolving to be as brave as Turks, and bold as Polar Bears, it
did'nt help me any. After the opening prayer I ventured to turn
around. Mr. Carter immediately looked at me – Mr. Sweetser
attempted to do so, but I discovered *nothing*, up in the sky somewhere, and gazed intently at it, for quite half an hour. During the
exercises, I became more calm, and got out of church quite com-
fortably. Several roared around, and, sought to devour me. . . .
until our gate was reached, I need'nt tell you, Susie, just how I
clutched the latch, and whirled the merry key, and fairly danced
for joy, to find myself *at home!*[46]

In Emily's mind, fame was equated with the public sphere. It
was no accident that she found it unlikely to consider a literary
career similar to Dr. Holland's. No doubt Sue, Austin, and Vinnie would have agreed, shaking their heads at the idea of Emily
traveling to New York to speak with an influential publisher.
Emily could hardly transact business in Amherst without feeling drained. In running errands, Emily admitted, "coming to
anchor, is most that I can do."[47] The path to distinction that Dr.

Holland followed—while instructive—suited him, not her. Making connections through business associates, presenting a manuscript for publication, addressing public audiences, receiving reviews, traveling on lecture tours—were activities that Emily would have found presumptive and petrifying. In recent years, she was allowing fewer people into her secluded world, although there always were exceptions. Vinnie was quick to point out that Emily continued to look for the "rewarding person"—someone to spar with and ignite her mind.[48] With so few intimates, it was surprising that Cousin Loo was one of them. Young as she was, Loo was unlikely to help her older cousin puzzle through the large questions Emily was now facing. After all, what would a schoolgirl have known about the balance between privacy and fame? But what others could not see, Emily frequently could. She recognized a quality in her cousin—loyalty, perhaps—that others failed to notice. Emily knew she wanted Loo in her life. "For you remember, dear," she wrote her cousin that morning, "you are one of the ones from whom I do not run away!"[49]

Someone else who could have offered a receptive ear was Emily's childhood friend Helen Fiske. The Dickinsons saw Helen from time to time. One day Austin had caught sight of her on a sidewalk in Boston. She had been with someone, he said, a "large, ambling long-faced, ungraceful, brass-buttoned individual of some forty to fifty years. . . . I took [him] to be her Lieutenant."[50] Austin was wrong about the age of Helen's escort. He had just turned thirty. But he was right about their close relationship. Lt. Edward Bissell Hunt—the military man she had met at the Albany Christmas Ball— had proposed, and Helen had accepted. After they married, the Hunts moved to Washington, DC, where Edward was stationed with the Army Corps of Engineers. In 1853, their son, Murray, was born. After years of loss and transience, Helen's life had finally achieved stability—but there also were frustrations. The boardinghouse was noisy, her husband's work demanded nearly all his time, and the new baby needed constant attention. Once, during a conversation with other boarders, a remark about women writers left Helen fuming. One of Edward's fellow officers had excoriated Harriet Beecher Stowe and *Uncle Tom's Cabin*. He called Mrs. Stowe "a talented *fiend* in human shape!!"[51] Helen spoke up defending abolition and Stowe's right to publish. But any thoughts she had about someday becoming a writer herself soon vanished. The Hunts' infant son died of a brain tumor, and she was emotionally adrift again.

Helen might have welcomed a visit from Emily and literary talk. As surprising as it was, Emily Dickinson had been in Washington, DC. She and Vinnie were with their father who had won election to the US House of Representatives.* The Dickinson sisters stayed at the Willard Hotel a few blocks from the White House and close to Helen's boardinghouse. Vinnie and Emily toured Mount Vernon, sailed down the Potomac in a painted boat, and met dignitaries. Emily found herself swept up in the bustle of Washington and not entirely happy about it. "All is jostle, here – scramble and confusion," she said.[52] The meeting between Helen and Emily never happened. Helen was simply not up to seeing anyone. She spent days reading condolence letters, and declining invitations. "Still my conscience troubles me a little," she admitted, because the Dickinsons "are from dear old Amherst."[53] Before Helen knew it, Emily was gone.

After they departed Washington, Emily and Vinnie proceeded to Philadelphia to visit Amherst neighbors who had taken up residence there. The friends introduced the sisters to Rev. Charles Wadsworth,

---

* Edward Dickinson represented the Tenth District of Massachusetts from 1853 to 1855.

their charismatic minister. The forty-one-year-old Wadsworth was known for his powerful words and poetic sensibility, and had increased his congregation from twelve families to a church bursting with parishioners. He was also rising in national prominence. Mark Twain was among those who recognized the minister's talents, including his humor. "Dr. Wadsworth," he said, "never fails to preach an able sermon; but every now and then, with an admirable assumption of not being aware of it, he will get off a firstrate joke and then frown severely at any one who is surprised into smiling at it." The reverend's words, Mark Twain said, were like "lightning from a clear sky, when least expected there is a flash and a smash."[54] After Emily returned to Amherst from her travels, a friend sent her a pamphlet of Wadsworth's most celebrated sermons. Some said Emily even started writing to the celebrated clergyman, although no one could be certain.

Edward Dickinson had not accompanied his daughters to Philadelphia; he had been closing his office in Washington. After only one term, Edward Dickinson had lost his reelection bid. "Lost" was a generous word for what had happened: he had been trounced. In Amherst, voters turned against him nearly 2 to 1.[55] The defeat had been a disappointment, but not a surprise. Edward Dickinson's Whig Party had become a dying breed.* While he abhorred slavery and spoke out against it as early as his student years at Yale, Edward Dickinson believed the federal government should not interfere with states and argued that a federal law to end slavery was unconstitutional. How Congressman Dickinson could oppose the formation of new slave states while upholding the right of Southern states

---

* Abraham Lincoln was a Whig until 1854, when he became a Republican. His shift represented the change many Whigs made to align themselves more closely with antislavery politics.

to perpetuate slavery struck voters as absurd. They viewed old-line
Whigs as compromised—"fossil politicians" one had called them—
and voted them out.[56] If Emily disagreed with her father's stance on
slavery, she did not say. Initially Edward's election to Congress had
stunned her into silence. She told Sue that when she heard the news
her "mind came to a stand, and has since then been stationary."[57] She
was only half joking. Politics to her was loud, rough, unrestrained,
even bombastic, and visiting Washington had confirmed that. She
often responded to political talk with humor that could be read as
disapproving. Once when dining at the Willard Hotel and presented
with a flaming dessert, she was heard to remark, "Oh, Sir, may one
eat of hell fire with impunity here?"[58] Yet as much as that clamorous
environment ill suited her, Emily could not escape it. She heard her
father and brother discussing "electioneering," read about Edward's
political triumphs and defeats in the newspaper, and when her
father attended a political convention, she quipped to Sue, "Why
cant *I* be a Delegate to the great Whig Convention? – dont I know
all about Daniel Webster, and the Tariff, and the Law?"[59] She certainly felt like an outsider to her father's political world, a bit like the
drawing she scribbled on a piece of his congressional stationery—
a Native American in full headdress strolling past the Capitol dome.
Emily knew she would never be allowed inside—neither did she seek
entry. What she wanted was quiet and solitude. "I often wish I was a
grass, or a toddling daisy, whom all these problems of the dust might
not terrify," she wrote Mrs. Holland. "And should my own machinery get slightly out of gear . . . some one stop the wheel."[60] After his
election defeat, Edward Dickinson may have better understood his
daughter's inclination toward seclusion.* The time for his brand of

---

* Coleman Hutchison writes that when Edward Dickinson was ousted from political office and returned to Amherst, his "self-imposed exile, of stubborn adher-

conservative politics had passed as the fissure between the North and the South widened. Perhaps Mr. Dickinson recognized that the national stage was not for him. He was frequently absent from Congress and his pronouncements from the House floor were to little effect. He left Washington and withdrew to Amherst, where—with his family—he ensconced himself behind a tall hemlock hedge.

Emily claimed the second-floor bedchamber of the new house. She spent hours at her desk at a window that overlooked the town, the college, and Austin and Sue's home. She was writing more, and her writing had changed. For one thing, the valentines were gone. The last one anyone could remember Emily sending was years before, and on commercially produced valentine paper from Mr. Adams's store.[61] With the shift away from composing her own valentines, she also shed her youthful need to exaggerate, flaunt her wit, and trot out erudition. She still sent poems to mark an event or nudge someone to write, but her poems became less about what happened and more about what she was thinking. Poems sent in letters to Sue, Loo, and the Hollands rose above daily concerns to larger contemplations on nature, faith, and loss. Images of boats, sailors, and the view from shore appeared frequently. "Adrift! A little boat adrift!" began one verse—three stanzas that ended with the image of a small boat buffeted by gales that managed to shoot "exultant on!"[62] Another had someone staring out to sea in search of a boat's "mystic mooring."[63] In a letter to the Hollands,

---

ence to principle, of active withdrawal from publicity may seem all too familiar. . . . Edward Dickinson removed himself from politics at nearly exactly the same moment Emily Dickinson began writing poems with the rhetoric of privatism, withdrawal, and remove." Hutchison argues that Dickinson sympathized with her father's outsider status and the "rhetoric of defeat recurs with startling frequency" in her verse. [Coleman Hutchison " 'Eastern Exiles': Dickinson, Whiggery, and War," *Emily Dickinson Journal* 13, no. 2, 5, 6, and 13.]

Emily offered a different turn on the subject that was cryptic and confounding. "Goodnight! My ships are in!," she had written. "My window overlooks the wharf! One yacht, and a man-o-war; two brigs and a schooner! 'Down with the topmast! Lay her a' hold, a' hold!' "[64] Absent from the passage was any attempt to clarify exactly she meant. The "what I mean is" explanation that Emily had included in earlier letters had vanished. It appeared Emily had decided that if her writing were difficult to understand, then her readers would have to make an effort to reach her rather than the other way around. She already had given up on Austin, vowing never again to send him anything lofty, only trifles and "crickets upon the hearth," she said.[65]

By the time Emily told Loo she wanted to be distinguished, she already had written nearly fifty poems.* They were full of edits, alterations, changes in order, and changes of mind. She waffled over opening lines, sent different versions of the same poem to different correspondents, wrote one poem and then recomposed it as prose. There were verses with lines so fiercely crossed out they were nearly impossible to read.

One Sister have I in the house –
And one a hedge away.

---

* The number 50 is the number of poems Dickinson scholars propose she wrote by 1859. Few of Emily Dickinson's poems are dated. Scholars estimate the dates of her verse by using handwriting analysis, examination of paper, and other means. I use Ralph Franklin's *The Poems of Emily Dickinson*, Variorum Edition, as my source for dating poems, and note individual poems by their Franklin (F) number. Cristanne Miller's 2016 *Emily Dickinson's Poems: As She Preserved Them* is another valuable resource. Miller presents approximately 1,100 poems that Dickinson copied in her own hand and retained among her papers.

Emily wrote. Then, as if frustrated, she drew thick loops over every word and started over.[66] Sometimes Emily would carefully write a poem and fold the sheet as if for mailing, but never send it. She dated practically nothing and almost never included titles. One poem was as short as two lines and others extended to five or six stanzas. There were countless images from nature—robins, gentians, owls, snowflakes—and verses that echoed the religious cadences of her youth:

> In the name of the Bee –
> And of the Butterfly –
> And of the Breeze – Amen![67]

Several poems described an aching void that she refused to identify. The mass of poems surrounding her must have looked like a disorganized workshop or the scattered production of an amateur. But nothing was further from the truth. Emily was making a plan, carving out her own route to distinction even if she would not say so directly. Emily was even more indirect about describing the kind of poetry she wanted to write. A clue appeared in a letter to Emily Fowler Ford with congratulations on her wedding. "You stood before us all and made those promises, and when we kissed you," she had written, "it seemed to me translation, not any earthly thing, and if a little after you'd ridden on the wind, it would not have surprised me."[68] Emily could have been talking about her verse. She wanted her poems to translate all she saw and heard and felt, and not be any earthly thing. What she aimed for was evanescence like the brilliance of lightning, the flash of truth, or a transport so swift it felt like flight.

Among the jumble of papers on Emily's desk was also a curious letter—a missive so private and inscrutable it seemed almost an

invasion to read. She was writing to a man, but she did not identify him. He could have been a fancy of her imagination, and it
was unclear if the letter had been sent or remained as a draft.
In spite of all that was not said, it was clear Emily felt urgency.
She feared her correspondent had been ill or perhaps had died.
Although time and distance had passed between them, Emily
wanted to please him. "Dear Master I am ill," she wrote, "but
grieving more that you are ill, I make my stronger hand work long
eno' to tell you. I thought perhaps you were in Heaven, and when
you spoke again, it seemed quite sweet, and wonderful, and surprised me so . . . I wish that I were great, like Mr. Michael Angelo,
and could paint for you. . . . Listen again, Master. I did not tell you
that today had been the Sabbath Day. Each Sabbath on the Sea,
makes me count the Sabbaths, till we meet on shore – and (will
the) whether the hills will look as blue as the sailors say.* I cannot
talk any more (stay any longer) tonight (now), for this pain denies
me. How strong when weak to recollect, and easy, quite, to love.
Will you tell me, please to tell me, soon as you are well."[69] The letter was extraordinary in its vulnerability. And as difficult as it
often was to understand Emily—this letter was even more enigmatic than the rest. She would not—at least for now—make her
reasons for writing clear.

Many times during her Mount Holyoke Female Seminary days
Emily heard Mary Lyon's advice: try to be systematic; develop
effective habits; don't waste time. Mount Holyoke's founder had
urged her charges to avoid succumbing to disorganization and
squandered effort. When Emily surveyed the sea of papers around
her, she knew she needed a better system for preserving her poems.

---

* Words in parenthesis indicate words that Dickinson inserted in the text as
alternates.

She needed to contain the disorder, maintain a record of what she had accomplished, separate good poems from false starts, polish poems in draft form, produce final copies without edits or alternate words, and prepare a compendium in case she wanted to do something with them—something other than sending them to her private public.* There was another reason too. She wanted to place her words on the page exactly as she envisioned them, complete with unconventional capital letters, dashes instead or commas or periods, and her own unique line divisions and stanza breaks. Her published works in the Amherst College *Indicator* and *Springfield Republican* followed the conventions of print, but those choices had been an editor's not hers. What would her poems look like if she created a book of her own? Emily decided that if she wanted to be distinguished, she would have to do so on her own terms. The route Dr. Holland pursued was appropriate for a man, but—like Helen Hunt—she knew a woman faced different obstacles. Emily reached for a piece of cream-colored stationery—fine paper with a formal finish appropriate for something important and lasting. The page already had been folded in half by the manufacturer so she could write on all four sides. She paged through her pile of poems and selected one. "The Gentian weaves her fringes." Emily placed the worksheet draft in front of her and copied the poem onto the elegant writing paper. She made sure the *G* of "Gentian" was capitalized and the *M* in "Maple" in the next line as well. Dashes, commas, placement on the page were all exactly as she wanted. She looked

---

* "Private public" is Dickinson biographer Richard Sewall's apt phrase, describing the poet's reading audience of friends and family. She had a "public" who read her poems, but they were a private readership selected and controlled by her. [Richard B. Sewall, *The Life of Emily Dickinson* (New York: Farrar, Straus and Giroux, 1974), 603.]

through the stack, selected another poem, turned the page, and
began copying again.

> Frequently the woods are pink –
> Frequently, are brown.
> Frequently the hills undress
> Behind my native town –

At the end of the twelve-line poem, she drew a short horizontal line
indicating the poem was finished and then filled out the page with a
third verse. She turned the page and selected another gentian one,
beginning

> Distrustful of the Gentian –
> And just to turn away,
> The fluttering of her fringes
> Chid my perfidy – [70]

When Emily finished with the piece of stationery, she took another
sheet and filled its pages with four more poems, then another sheet
with five more, and another with seven. The boat poems went in;
the valentines did not. When she finished copying each poem, she
destroyed the worksheet.

With four folded sheets in front of her, Emily looked over the
pages. Twenty-two poems in all. It was enough, she thought. Enough
for now. But she wasn't finished. She needed to make the collection
permanent. She wanted to bind the sheets so that she could hold
them in her hand like one of Mr. Emerson's books. Emily picked up
the four sheets, stacked one on top of the other and looked around
for something to attach them. She found a piece of string, cream-
colored like the stationery. It was too thick to be threaded through a

needle, but if she poked holes through the side of the stacked pages, she would be able to push the string through and hold everything together. She reached into her sewing basket and found a needle. It looked large enough to make an opening. She held the stack of pages in her hand, punched a hole on the side and moved the needle back and forth to make a hole big enough for the string. She poked another hole farther down and wobbled the needle. Then she joined the string in front with a knot. It worked. Years earlier, when she was a schoolgirl at Amherst Academy, she'd made a herbarium and filled it with species of leaves and plants and flowers. She had been proud of the collection: her first book, one might say. But like valentines, the herbarium was the project of an ambitious young woman. She was older now—almost thirty. Emily looked up-street to see if Vinnie was returning from Mr. Cutler's store. I "build a castle in the air," she wrote Loo.[71] Her cousin would know what she meant. Emily was writing. She always was—poetizing, reciting lines in her head or sitting at her desk behind the hedge with worksheet in hand. Before long, whatever verse she had composed would join the stack of papers nearby. If she thought it was distinguished, she would pull out another sheet of cream stationery and search for needle and string. "Fascicles" someone would later call her hand-sewn booklets. Emily gave no name for what she had produced. All she knew was that when she opened the volume, the words were her own—and the pinhole in the page before her looked like wings.

Five

TALLER FEET

Saturday, March 1, 1862 9 p.m. Thermometer 23.2 Clouds stra. NW 2.
Wind NW 3 Thermometer Attached to Barometer 39.0. Barometer
29,925. Dry Bulb 23.0. Wet Bulb 21.0. Force of Vapor .089. Humidity
72. Remarks: Near 3 ft of snow on the ground. Pleasant Drifts.

—Ebenezer Snell, *The Meteorological Journal kept at Amherst College*

The Civil War had been going on for nearly a year and had everyone in Amherst on edge. Mr. Merrick worried his tailor shop
couldn't keep up with the demand for new military coats. He
needed more local girls to help with the sewing. Amherst College
president William Augustus Stearns was distressed that his son,
an adjutant lieutenant, might never return to his science studies.
Frazar Stearns had enlisted with other classmates and now was
headed south with the Burnside Expedition and Captain Clark,
their commander and former chemistry professor.* The new minister in town, Rev. Henry Hubbell, had doubts about remaining
at First Church. Parish ministry seemed the sanctuary of the

---

* The Burnside Expedition, led by Union brigadier general Ambrose Burnside,
took place from February to June 1862. The expedition involved troops from New
England, including Amherst, and sought to blockade ports along the North Carolina coast.

timid, he thought. Shouldn't he join other men and enlist? Judge Ithamar Conkey feared the Union couldn't win. After troops lost the Battle of Bull Run, he mounted a box in the center of town and shouted, "You see it is all over. . . . We cannot whip the South!"[1] Widow Adams cared nothing for soapboxes or military bombast. She lay awake at night and wondered if she could get out of bed in the morning. Weeks before, she had received word that her son Sylvester had died of wounds at Annapolis. Earlier another son, Charles, had died of typhoid in camp. The Snells were worried their grieving neighbor would never come out of her darkened bedchamber. "Dead! Both her boys!" Emily had written her cousins Fanny and Loo.[2] For many residents of Amherst, daylight served as an impudent reminder that battles of every kind continued. As dazed as anyone, Emily found herself asking, "When did the war really begin?"[3]

She knew, of course. How could she not? But for Emily, living in fateful times went back further than secession. It began with Aunt Lavinia's death in 1860. "I can't believe it, when your letters come, saying what Aunt Lavinia said 'just before she died,'" she had written Vinnie. Emily's sister had been in Boston staying with their ailing aunt, and tending to Uncle Loring, Fanny, and Loo. "Blessed Aunt Lavinia now," Emily added. "So many broken-hearted people have got to hear the birds sing, and see all the little flowers grow, just the same as if the sun hadn't stopped shining forever!"[4] Emily could not imagine that in less than a year Uncle Loring would be dead, too, leaving her young cousins to fend for themselves. Then came Lincoln's election that November. Amherst had no telegraph, and young men rode to Northampton to await word. When the sounder came alive after midnight and tapped out news of Lincoln's victory, the men mounted their horses and raced back eight miles across farmers' fields to alert the citizens of Amherst. They

jostled awake the sexton at First Church and did the same at the
college chapel. The sound of bells woke up everyone. Months later,
when the dreadful news of Fort Sumter reached Amherst, Reverend
Hubbell said the recruiting office set up in the streets.[5] "Sorrow
seems more general than it did, and not the estate of a few persons,
since the war began," Emily wrote. "If the anguish of others helped
one with one's own, now would be many medicines."[6]

Emily watched men and women doubled up on their daily work
to assist with the war effort. Down in Springfield the armory
speeded up its manufacturing of weapons. At Mount Holyoke,
seminary students prepared boxes for soldiers. One shipment contained seventy-seven pairs of hose, seventeen pairs of mittens,
thirty pairs of hospital slippers, reams of writing paper, and lint
carefully collected for bandages. For the first time in its history,
the *Springfield Republican* printed extra editions to meet reader
demand. As soon as pages slid off the press, newspapermen tacked
them to boards outside, and crowds elbowed their way to search the
latest casualty lists. One Springfield woman—no doubt wondering
what she could contribute—waited as trains loaded with soldiers
pulled out of the station. She reached up and pushed a small object
into a young man's outstretched hands—a jar of preserved gin-
ger.[7] Women were not exempt from the call for help, and government officials asked for their assistance. One day Emily unfolded
the local newspaper to read an appeal aimed directly at her. "The
ladies of Amherst are urgently requested to take into immediate
consideration the recent statement of the Secretary of the Sanitary
Commission at Washington that among the contributions already
forwarded there is a deficiency in the article of substantial woolen
socks. . . . Our long pleasant evenings are before us and we take the
liberty to suggest that every elderly, every middle aged, and every

young lady in our town that they pledge themselves to contribute one or more pairs of socks."* [8]

Emily chose not to knit socks, but she was busy. "I can't *stop* to strut, in a world where bells toll," she told the Hollands.[9] Her pile of fascicles had grown. At least fifteen individual booklets were stacked nearby, all folded and stitched with thread. Emily was writing with the greatest intensity of her life. She had written over three-hundred poems—so many that some were loose and not bound. For several years she had been working on one poem that was unlike anything she had ever written. She couldn't quite get it right and asked Sue for help. The verse consumed her and would embody every literary principle she embraced. Later that March day the poem would be made public. The work was a towering achievement, even if hardly anyone knew it was Emily's.†

As much as Emily and Susan were devoted to each other, the two women had at times a contentious relationship. Emily could be annoyingly insistent, prodding Sue to write when she was away from home or demanding time when Sue's hands were full. Austin and Sue's first child, Ned, was less than a year old, and his care

* The Sanitary Commission was a private relief organization founded in 1861 to support Union soldiers. The commission's president was clergyman Henry Whitney Bellows; landscape architect Frederick Law Olmsted served as general secretary. The work of the commission focused on providing food, clothing, blankets, and medical care to soldiers. In many cities—including Springfield, Massachusetts— the commission ran Sanitary Fairs featuring art exhibitions, parades, and literary publications that raised money for the cause.

† Dickinson's composition of "Safe in their Alabaster Chambers," F124, is the only extant example that demonstrates the back-and-forth editing process between Emily and Susan Gilbert Dickinson. A close examination of its composition reveals much about the women's relationship and Dickinson's artistic principles.

added to Sue's preoccupation.* Emily's professions of love could also be suffocating and sometimes made her sister-in-law distance herself rather than draw closer. Sue had her faults too. She knew she could be cool and imperious, and once likened herself to someone who—while "pronounced"—sweetened under chastisement and discipline.[10] Around town Susan Dickinson earned respect for her intellect. "There is in her," one young man said, "something different from other Amherst girls." But some people noticed insensitivity and what one called no "refinement of feeling."[11] Helen Hunt experienced both sides of Susan Dickinson. The two initially enjoyed conversations and rambles through the woods. But after one huckleberry party, a falling-out occurred. Their quarrel made a sham of friendship, Helen said, and she vowed to have nothing more to do with her.[12] There was no doubt

---

* Edward "Ned" Dickinson was born June 19, 1861. His birth was emotionally difficult for Sue. Her sister Mattie had lost her first child five days earlier, and Ned was born on the exact date that eleven years earlier Sue's other sister Mary had died in childbirth. Ned's crying, teething, and the family's difficulty in hiring help added to Sue's strain. Like their inability to settle on a wedding date, Sue and Austin vacillated and waited half a year to name their son. For months he was called "Jackey" for Union Jack, but eventually the couple named their firstborn after Austin's father. Sue sent a note, in the infant's voice, asking his grandfather for permission to share the name. Edward gave his answer in a tender response. "I have rec'd your letter, asking me if I am willing that you should have a name like mine—And I say, in this reply, which you can *read*, as well as you could *write* the other, that if you will be a good boy, ride in your carriage & not cry, and always mind your father and mother, I will consent to your being called Edward Dickinson; and promise you a Silver Cup to drink from, as soon as you are big enough to hold it in your hands. Your affectionate Grandfather." [Martha Dickinson Bianchi, *Emily Dickinson Face to Face: Unpublished Letters with Notes and Reminiscences* (Boston: Houghton Mifflin Company, 1932), 39; Jay Leyda, *The Years and Hours of Emily Dickinson*, vol. 2 (New Haven: Yale University Press, 1960), 39.]

Sue could be difficult. She seemed trapped, or wrestled with a foe only she could see. Even at the beginning of their relationship, Austin experienced Sue's dark moods. Once during their engagement when he was cradling Sue in his arms, she expressed doubts about their impending marriage. The admission crushed Austin and he responded with an ultimatum: marry me or don't. The next day he apologized and tried to retract his words, but the exchange already had damaged them both.[13]

The first schism between Emily and her sister-in-law came in 1854, the summer after Austin and Sue became engaged. Austin had finished his education at Harvard Law School when Sue took mysteriously ill. She could barely eat, managing only broth and small bites of chicken. Emily worried and suspected nervous fever, remembering other times when Sue's bouts of depression had sent her spiraling. She had contemplated suicide once.[14] If Sue had anxieties about marriage, Emily would have understood. Emily thought marriage could threaten a woman's intellect, imagination, and sense of self. She told Sue so in an earlier letter.

You and I have been strangely silent upon this subject, Susie, we have often touched upon it, and as quickly fled away, as children shut their eyes when the sun is too bright for them. . . . Susie, we must speak of these things. How dull our lives must seem to the bride, and the plighted maiden, whose days are fed with gold, and who gathers pearls every evening; but to the *wife*, Susie, sometimes the *wife forgotten*, our lives perhaps seem dearer than all others in the world; you have seen flowers at morning, *satisfied* with the dew, and those same sweet flowers at noon with their heads bowed in anguish before the mighty sun; think you these thirsty blossoms will *now* need naught but – dew? No, they will cry for sunlight, and pine for the burning noon, tho' it scorches them, scathes them; they have got through with peace – they know that the man of noon is *mightier* than the morning and their life is henceforth to him. Oh, Susie, it is dangerous.[15]

Seeing no improvement in Sue's condition, her sister Mattie whisked her to Albany to recuperate with relatives. With every mile away from the Dickinsons and marriage plans, Sue grew stronger.[16] From New York she continued west to more relatives. Austin visited her in Chicago, but did not stay. During the time Sue was gone, Emily wrote frequent letters and pleaded for a response. Exasperated with not hearing a word, Emily finally put it bluntly. "Sue – you can go or stay – There is but one alternative – We differ often lately, and this must be the last. You need not fear to leave me lest I should be alone, for I often part with things I fancy I have loved. . . . Perhaps this is the point at which our paths diverge – then pass on singing Sue, and up the distant hill I journey on."[17] The letter must have felt to Sue like another high-toned Dickinson ultimatum. But there was a difference. This time Emily included a poem. "I have a Bird in spring," it began, "Which for myself doth sing – ."[18] The metaphor was hardly lost on Sue, and she understood that the last word in the poem—"Return"—carried special weight. A bird still sang and melody connected them, the poem suggested. Whether that melody represented the bond between the two women, the power of poetry, or something else—Sue understood its presence sustained Emily.

The "go or stay" standoff between the women was not mentioned again. Sue returned to Amherst, and she and Austin were married. But around the time of Ned's 1861 birth, tension resurfaced between Sue and Emily. Not wanting to risk another rupture, Sue offered a blanket apology: "If you have suffered this past Sum-

mer," she wrote, "I am sorry. . . . *I* Emily bear a sorrow that I never
uncover—If a nightingale sings with her breast against a thorn,
why not *we*?"[19] Sue knew that Emily often responded to unease by
writing: tumult seemed to propel, not silence her. Emily already
had shared over seventy-five poems with Sue—more than she had
sent to anyone. There were poems about ambition, buried bulbs
sprouting shoots, and unrealized success. There also were poems
of rejection and deprivation. "A *wounded* Deer – leaps highest – ,"
Emily observed in one poem. And in another,

A little bread, a crust – a crumb,
A little trust, a Demijohn –
Can keep the soul alive – [20]

So many poems flew between the Dickinson Homestead and the
Evergreens that Sue dubbed the route the "Pony Express."[21] As occupied as she was, Sue tried to make time for Emily's work. She read
the poems, studied them, and appeared to save every note, scrap, and
word. When they first had become friends, Emily recognized that
Sue understood her in ways that other girls did not. All her life, Emily
searched for what she called "the rare Ear."[22] In Sue, she found one.

But Sue didn't know everything about Emily. She didn't know
that Emily had written another note to the unnamed Master and
then another one after that. She didn't know that Emily had professed her love and now pleaded with the Master to visit Amherst.
The new letters were similar to the first one she had written: passionate, confounding, and unclear if they had been sent or retained
as drafts. But there were differences. The vulnerability of the first
letter had turned to ache. "I am older – tonight," Emily wrote in the
first of the two new letters,

but the love is the same — so are the moon and the crescent. If it had been God's will that I might breathe where you breathed — and find the place — myself — at night — if I (can) never forget that I am not with you — and that sorrow and frost are nearer than I — if I wish with a might I cannot repress — that mine were the Queen's place — the love of the Plantagenet is my only apology . . . Have you the Heart in your breast — Sir — is it set like mine — a little to the left . . . I dont know what you can do for it — thank you — Master — but if I had the Beard on my cheek — like you — and you — had Daisy's petals — and you cared so for me — what would become of you? Could you forget me in fight, or flight — or the foreign land? Could'nt Carlo, and you and I walk in the meadows an hour — and nobody care but the Bobolink . . . I used to think when I died — I could see you — so I died as fast as I could . . . but I can wait more — wait till my hazel hair is dappled — and you carry the cane — then I can look at my watch — and if the Day is too far declined — we can take the chances (of) for Heaven — What would you do with me if I came "in white?" Have you the little chest to put the Alive — in? I want to see you more — Sir — than all I wish for in this world — and the wish — altered a little — will be my only one — for the skies. Could you come to New England — (this summer — could) would you come to Amherst — Would you like to come — Master?[23]

Emily was even more desolate in the letter that followed. Her sentences were torrents of words that stuttered and faltered and then regained their bearing. It seemed that even using the word "I" was too painful for Emily: she cushioned herself with a more distant reference, calling herself "she" and "Daisy" and her Master "it." Most of all, she apologized—for what she did not say—and pleaded for her Master's affection. Edits and second thoughts were more numerous, exposing the poet trapped in doubt, despair, panic, and subjugation.

Oh, did I offend it — (Did'nt it want me to tell it the truth) Daisy — Daisy — offend it — who bends her smaller life to his (it's) meeker (lower) every day . . . she cannot guess to make that master glad — A love so big it scares her, rushing among her small heart — pushing aside the blood and leaving her faint (all) and white in the gust's arm. Daisy — who never flinched thro' that awful parting, but held her life so tight he should not see the wound . . . tell her her (offence) fault — Master — if it is (not so) small eno' to cancel with her life, (Daisy) she is satisfied — but punish — (do not) dont banish her — shut her in prison, Sir — only pledge that you will forgive — sometime — before the grave, and Daisy will not mind — She will awake in (his) your likeness. Wonder stings me more than the Bee . . . I've got a Tomahawk in my side but that dont hurt me much. (If you) Her Master stabs her more — . . . Master — open your life wide, and take me in forever, I will never be tired — I will never be noisy when you want to be still. I will be (glad) (as the) your best little girl — nobody else will see me, but you — but that is enough — I shall not want any more.[24]

As searing as her words were, they may have provided release. Emily always turned to language to soothe or lessen her distress. The letters could have served as a reminder of the pain she had experienced, but survived. Whatever purpose she had in writing remained a secret known only to her. She never shied away from looking anguish in the eye or contemplating its aftermath. To do so was an act of dominion over misery and resistance to inertia. Emily placed the new letters with the old one, tucking all three away and out of sight.

IN THE REMARKABLE new poem Emily was writing, there was no tone of anguish. "Safe in their alabaster chambers," she began, drawing the first letter of the new poem with a bold S. Emily wanted to contrast the stasis of the dead with the vitality of the living. As she read over the poem and examined it, she swapped out commas for dashes, changed lowercase letters to capitals, and experimented with word choice. Something more fundamental also occupied her mind. She was thinking about the nature of literary imagery itself, possibly remembering the first sight of dandelions in Abiah Root's hair and how the weeds had altered everything. She also had been reading Ralph Waldo Emerson's essay "The Poet." Where do images come from? Emerson asked. What should they do? How do they register in a reader's consciousness? Emily recalled the copy of Emerson's poems that one of her father's long-ago law clerks had given her. The essays made clear—as sometimes Mr. Emerson's poems did not—the qualities necessary for great poetry. Don't be too clever with language, he warned. Avoid verse that is a "music-box of delicate tunes and rhythms." Inspiration, he said, should come from the "picture-language" of nature—sunlight, air, and the living world around us. Emerson believed that beauty is more profound, when it is *felt* rather than *explained*. Emily thought about the poems in her fascicles with all their unidentified subjects. She had tried to capture the essence of an object by the way it made her feel, not necessarily by the way it looked. "As, in the sun, objects paint their images on the retina of the eye," Emerson wrote, "so they, sharing the aspiration of the whole universe, tend to paint a far more delicate copy of their essence in his mind."[25] The idea of where images registered was important to Emily. It was not enough to paint a scene with detailed accuracy: the way an eye apprehended it. Adjectives could be piled deep, for example, in describing the multiple shades of a green leaf. But Emerson's essay, with its talk

Fig. 1: Emily Dickinson at about age seventeen. "Small, like the Wren, and my Hair is bold, like the Chestnut Bur — and my eyes, like the Sherry in the Glass, that the Guest leaves."

Fig. 2: Emily Norcross Dickinson. Portrait by Otis Allen Bullard. "Mines in the same Ground meet by tunneling and when she became our Child, the Affection came."

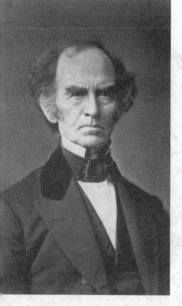

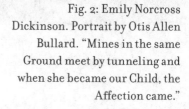

Fig. 3: Edward Dickinson. "His Heart was pure and terrible and I think no other like it exists."

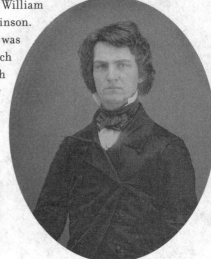

Fig. 4: William Austin Dickinson. "There was always such a Hurrah wherever you was."

Fig. 5: Lavinia Dickinson. Emily's bond with Vinnie was "early, earnest, indissoluble."

Fig. 6: Susan Gilbert Dickinson. "Where my Hands are cut, Her fingers will be found inside."

Fig. 7: Abiah Root. "Don't let your free spirit be chained."

Fig. 9: Mary Lyon, principal of Mount Holyoke Female Seminary. "Do something. Have a plan. Live for a purpose," she told her students.

Fig. 8: Amherst Academy. "I am always in love with my teachers."

Fig. 10: "My domestic work is not difficult & consists in carrying the Knives from the 1st tier of tables at morning & noon & at night." Mount Holyoke Female Seminary domestic work "pie circle."

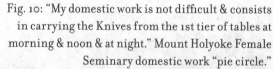

Fig. 11: Ebenezer Snell, Amherst College professor and meteorological record keeper.

Fig. 12: Ebenezer Snell's *Meteorological Journal* for August 3, 1845: "Parhelion at noon."

Fig. 13: The Dickinsons' home from 1840–1855.

Fig. 14: Amherst College student George Gould, responsible for publishing Emily's prose valentine, her first publication.

Fig. 15: Josiah Holland who, along with Samuel Bowles, published Dickinson's first poem. "The hand that wrote the following amusing medley is capable of very fine things."

Fig. 16: Elizabeth Chapin Holland relayed Dickinson's letters to Rev. Charles Wadsworth.

Fig. 17: Samuel Bowles, editor of the *Springfield Republican*. "The most triumphant Face out of Paradise."

Fig. 18: Author and friend Helen Hunt told Dickinson, "You are a great poet – and it is a wrong to the day you live in, that you will not sing aloud."

Fig. 19: Rev. Charles Wadsworth. "My closest earthly friend."

Fig. 20: Dickinson's Amherst was a town of books, learning, and ideas. Its best women, one resident said, were free from "silly birdish airs."

Fig. 21: When writing at her desk, Dickinson looked out the window to the Evergreens, home of her brother, Austin, and sister-in-law, Sue.

Fig. 22: Emily's bedroom in the Dickinson Homestead was a sanctuary where her family did not intrude.

Fig. 23: The Dickinson Homestead on Main Street in Amherst.

Fig. 24: The Evergreens in winter.

Fig. 25: Col. William Clark of the Massachusetts 21st Volunteer Infantry. "War feels to me an oblique place," Dickinson wrote.

of retinas and essence gave her an idea for creating an image that went beyond the retina, beyond what was literally recognizable. She wanted her language to awaken a deeper awareness than what the physical eye could perceive. If she could find the right abstraction and sensation, it might unlock the primeval human consciousness she hoped to touch.* Emily took her pencil and marked a passage in Emerson's essay. "We are far from having exhausted the significance of the few symbols we use. We can come to use them yet with a terrible simplicity."[26]

Emily had another reason for paying attention to Ralph Waldo Emerson—a personal one. Recently, Emerson had dined and spent the night with Austin and Sue. Austin had organized an Amherst lecture series and brought to town an array of impressive visitors: senators, abolitionists, and literary men. Emerson is the "prince of lecturers," the local newspaper proclaimed, days before his arrival. But after Emerson spoke, the room buzzed with disappointment. The problem with the lecture, some said, was it was *too* clear. "It was in the English language instead of the Emersonese in which he usually clothes his thoughts," one had remarked.[27] Sue did not have much of an opinion on the matter. That night she was far too excited about strolling home on Mr. Emerson's "transcendental arm"—as she put it—than to focus on his clarity. During their walk across the town common, Emerson had spoken of Julia Ward Howe and encouraged Sue to read her collection of poetry, *Passion Flowers*. Once inside the Evergreens, he noticed another book he admired—

---

* I am indebted to the teaching and writing of David Porter, who cites Archibald MacLeish in describing what makes Dickinson's imagery unique: " '[Dickinson's images do not] exist upon the retina.... [They can not] be brought into focus by the muscles of the eye.' " [David Porter, *Dickinson: The Modern Idiom*, Cambridge: Harvard University Press, 1981, 26.]

Coventry Patmore's poem "The Angel of the House." He loved Patmore's depiction of wives' devotion to their husbands, a subject on which Sue no doubt had opinions. But Susan did not want to talk about other poets; she wanted to talk about Emerson. His poem "Brahma" had appeared in the *Atlantic Monthly*. It was a meditation on existence and divinity that some readers thought subtle, others absurd, and a few pretentious. What is it about? Sue asked as the two sat near the fire. Is it a kind of Rosetta Stone? Emerson smiled. "Oh there was nothing to understand!" he replied. "How could they make so much fuss over it!" Sue must have been bewildered, perhaps even disheartened by the remark. She thought poetry should have a point, with language that adhered and coalesced toward a center—at least that's what she had been discussing with Emily. Emily was not much help in explaining the mystery of Ralph Waldo Emerson.[28] He seemed, she had said, to have "come from where dreams were born."*

---

* Unfortunately, no historical record exists that indicates if Emily joined Emerson in conversation that evening at the Evergreens. It is likely she stayed home. In her essay depicting the cultural life of her home, "Annals of the Evergreens," Susan Gilbert Dickinson does not say either way. To compound matters, Emerson's visit occurred in 1857—a year for which not a single Dickinson letter has been recovered. All we have concerning the visit are Sue's details in *Annals*, and her memory of Dickinson's remark about Emerson. Scholar David Porter offered a memorable way of thinking about the significance of that evening. He points out that before Emerson's Amherst visit, Walt Whitman had sent him a copy of *Leaves of Grass*. Emerson read the poems, was deeply impressed, and responded to Whitman, declaring, "I greet you at the beginning of a great career." [RWE to WW July 21, 1855, Library of Congress.] Porter argues that the evening Emerson spent next door to Emily Dickinson after writing Whitman marks the genesis of modern American poetry, with all its ambiguity, angles, and disjuncture. At that moment, Porter said, all three—Emerson, Whitman, Dickinson—"were like sides of a triangle that do not meet." [David Porter, conversation with the author.]

Imagery was not the only challenge Emily faced in her new poem. Also on her mind was the large question Sue had raised with Emerson: what is a poem about? Emily questioned how explicit she should be in her poetry. Some of her earlier poems were straightforward, such as one she entitled "Snow flakes": "I counted till they danced so / Their slippers leaped the town."[29] But it was her inclination to come at an idea not directly, but "slant," she would call it.[30] In the verse she was working on, the first stanza started clearly to establish the setting. While she never named exactly what she was talking about, Emily believed the final line left little doubt that she was describing a tomb.

Safe in their alabaster chambers,
Untouched by morning,
And untouched by noon,
Sleep the meek members of the Resurrection,
Rafter of satin, and roof of stone.

Emily was deliberate in beginning the poem with the word "Safe." It sounded reassuring—hopefully too much so. She wondered if the dead were as safe as clergy might suggest. Waiting for resurrection could take a while, the ironic "Safe" seemed to imply. Or resurrection might never come at all. In painting a scene of coffins and tombs, Emily offered no Christian comfort and no reward for a virtuous life. Also absent was the rigorous rectitude that Mary Lyon had preached. The most glaring absence in the first stanza was the omission of heaven itself. The life after death that Emily presented was a world of stasis, passivity and silence: a chamber where the meek members of the resurrection did not move.

When it came to the second stanza, Emily wanted contrast. She wanted to present the natural world flitting above the dead, oblivious to those who slept below: the breeze laughs, the bee babbles, the birds pipe ignorant—even mocking—cadences. In the final line, Emily elected to be clear. She used a compact summation to declare what the poem meant. Yet there was more than summation in the last line—articulated not so much by what was said, but by what was not. The dead have simply perished, the last five words declare. They have not entered the kingdom of heaven. While the meek members may be sleeping—or "lying" as she later changed her mind to assert—they never would awaken. There was no resurrection in Emily's poem—only perpetual internment.[31]

> Light laughs the breeze
> In her castle above them,
> Babbles the bee in a stolid ear,
> Pipe the sweet birds in ignorant cadence:
> Ah! what sagacity perished here!

Emily looked at the poem and deemed it ready—ready to show Sue. She sent the poem to the Evergreens via Pony Express.

Sue was not the only one reading Emily's new poems. *Springfield Republican* editor Samuel Bowles was as well. Sam had been the first dinner guest at the Evergreens after Sue and Austin married, and the three had become devoted friends.* Over the years, Bowles had shared with them his large cultural and political world. They met author Bret Harte, Thoreau's friend Franklin Sanborn, and *Harp-*

---

* Bowles had been coming to Amherst for several years to cover the college commencement season. He had inherited the *Springfield Republican* from his father, and worked his way up from office boy to printing room and from reporter to editor. He hired Josiah Holland in 1849, first as an assistant editor then promoted him to serve alongside him as coeditor.

er's Weekly editor George William Curtis. It was not uncommon for
Bowles to pull a letter out of his pocket from an editor in London or
relay conversations he had had with the president, cabinet members, abolitionists, or prominent literary women. He became a
treasured friend of Emily's, too, bringing her down to earth when
she drifted too high into the ether, and serving as her interpreter of
world events. When she hadn't seen Sam for a while, Emily admitted she needed him to absorb the worst developments of the war. If
Samuel Bowles delivered the news, she said "failure in a Battle –
were easier."[32] An introspective man up to a point, Bowles was aware
of his shortcomings. He could be diffuse, unable to focus, and incapable or unwilling to plumb depths. He was—a friend said—simply
a pragmatic newspaperman through and through.[33] One evening
Sue and Austin had hosted for Henry Ward Beecher and others displayed the core of Sam's character. After Beecher had commented
on the beauty of a vase of flowers, he became pensive, and spoke of
his childhood. I used to sit on the doorstep, he told the gathering,
and listen to the wind in the branches. "I could hear the faint hum
of the spinning wheel in the garret, and a tender sadness seemed
to gather about me and melt my nature 'till I cried like a child."
What was it? he asked. What made me cry? Sue and the other guests
were touched by his emotion and grew quiet. A visiting Episcopal
bishop offered a tentative response: "It was doubtless, Beecher, a
sense of the infinite pressing down upon your young soul." Bowles
was uneasy with the vulnerability he felt and shrugged. "You had
probably been eating green apples, Beecher!!" he joked. The guests
laughed and the poignancy of the moment evaporated.[34] Bowles's
remark underscored that he was often uncomfortable with bor-
ing too deeply and sought to keep situations light. No one could be
harder on Bowles than himself. He called himself "a suggestion,
rather than a realization, & elusive & spasmodic & fragmentary: but

no more to others than to myself."[35] He was right about his scattered ways, but Bowles was wrong about what he meant to others. For the past two years, Emily had been confiding in him and sending him poems.[*]

Given their interests and affection for one another, Sue, Sam, and Emily formed a literary alliance. All three exchanged notes on poets and the latest news from the *Atlantic Monthly*.[36] Sue let Sam know when the *Republican* published a poem she liked, and she clipped and saved verses from his newspaper.[37] Bowles was not hesitant to publish women writers. After a young woman sent her work, he had responded with encouragement. "Though my 'weakness' is not poetry," he had confessed, "I am . . . charmed with your little compact, thoughtful, mysterious & suggestive poems."[38] He also looked for more experienced literary women whose work had a grand sweep. When Julia Ward Howe wrote new lyrics to the battle hymn "John Brown's Body," Bowles lifted them from the *Atlantic Monthly* and reprinted them immediately in the *Republican*.[†] "Mine eyes have seen the glory of the coming of the Lord," the powerful verse began. While Bowles was open to publishing women, he

---

* The dating of Dickinson poems is difficult because she did not assign dates to her verse. Dating also is complicated because while scholars can postulate the date Dickinson included a poem in a fascicle, they cannot know when Dickinson initially composed it. Given these caveats, Ralph Franklin believes that before 1862, Dickinson sent Bowles eight poems: Two swimmers wrestled on the spar (F227); "Faith" is a fine invention (F202); Would you like Summer? Taste our's (F272); Jesus! thy Crucifix (F197); Should you but fail – at Sea (F275); Title divine – is mine! (F194); Through the strait pass of suffering (F187); and *Speech – is a prank of Parliament* (F193).

† It was not uncommon for newspapers to reprint poems from other papers or journals like the *Atlantic*. A poem that appeared in a newspaper in Springfield, Massachusetts, easily could have been picked up by another newspaper in Denver or Brooklyn without editors, readers, or the poem's author knowing it.

also made clear that the *Republican* was not fond of what it labeled gloomy female writing. A *Republican* column spelled it out.[39] "There is another kind of writing only too common, appealing to the sympathies of the reader without recommending itself to his subject. It may be called the literature of misery," he wrote. "The writers are chiefly women, gifted women may be, full of thought and feeling and fancy, but poor, lonely and unhappy. . . . The sketch or poem is usually the writer's photograph in miniature. It reveals a countenance we would gladly brighten, but not by exposing it to the gaze of a worthless world."[40]

But Bowles had been exposing Emily's verse to the world, and without her direct consent. Besides Emily's valentine a decade earlier, the *Republican* had recently published two more of Emily's poems. "Nobody knows this little rose," had appeared in 1858, along with a headnote stating the newspaper had "surreptitiously" received it.[41] In 1861, the *Republican* had printed "I taste a liquor never brewed." Perhaps Sam was growing bolder or more confident in making Emily's poems public, although all the verses appeared anonymously. Years later, Sue all but confessed to being the one who slipped Emily's poems to Bowles. "Love turned to larceny," she said.[42]

Now when Sue looked at a draft of "Safe in their Alabaster Chambers—" she was tempted again. If she had concerns about what some might see as blasphemy in the poem's view of the afterlife, she never said so. The poem impressed her, as did the lingering chill it produced. But before she made any decision about sending it to Sam, she wanted to talk with Emily. Sue didn't entirely *like* the poem, though not because of its provocative view of death as eternal entombment. What gave her pause was the second stanza—the one about the bees and breeze. To Sue, it didn't work. Emily went to work on the poem again. She sifted through the fascicles and all the loose sheets of poems. She knew she had several versions of the verse. All the alternate versions began with the same first stanza. But in version two, Emily experimented with a radically different ending. She hoped Sue would like the new second stanza. Emily placed the fascicle next to her on the small writing table, took up her pencil, copied the poem over, and sent it to the Evergreens. "Perhaps this verse would please you better – Sue," she wrote.[43] Compared to version one, version two was large, sweeping, more abstract, more like Beecher's reverie on the infinite. Emily tried to put into practice what she was learning about imagery, and hoped the final image of the poem would register with Sue. But after Sue read the second version, she liked it less than the first. It was that second stanza again, or "verse" as Sue called it. While she thought Emily's experiment with imagery was exceptional, she argued that its brilliance detracted from the poem as a whole. Stanzas should conform and blend together, she told Emily. Better to cut the second stanza altogether and that final wild image. She put her thoughts down in a note:

I am not suited dear Emily with the second verse – It is remarkable as the chain lightening that blinds us hot nights in the Southern sky but it does not go with the ghostly shimmer of the first verse as well as the other one – It just occurs to me that the first verse is complete in itself it needs no other, and can't be coupled – Strange things always go alone – as there is only one Gabriel and one Sun – You never made a peer for that verse, and I *guess* you[r] kingdom does'nt hold one – I always go to the fire and get warm after thinking of it, but I never *can* again.[44]

Sue wanted it cold. Emily put the second version aside, looked through her manuscripts again, and took Sue's quip about no "peer for that verse" as a challenge. Her kingdom did *indeed* hold others, she thought to herself. Emily located a third version with a new second stanza, and off it went via Pony Express. "Is *this frostier?*" she asked.[45]

> Springs – shake the Sills –
> But – the Echoes – stiffen –
> Hoar – is the Window – and numb – the Door –
> Tribes of Eclipse – in Tents of Marble –
> Staples of Ages – have buckled – there –

Emily also added a personal note. She thanked Sue for her advice and said how much it meant to her. Yet her words of gratitude were oddly crafted—issued in a lurching cadence and as slant as her metaphors. It was unclear why Emily was so indirect in expressing appreciation. Her note seemed to reassure herself that Sue's suggestions were worth taking. The only phrase in the entire note that didn't stammer came at the end. In the years since admitting she wanted to be distinguished, Emily's dream had only grown stronger.

> *Dear Sue –*
> *Your praise is good – to me – because I know it knows – and suppose – it means –*
> *Could I make you and Austin – proud – sometime – a great way off – 'twould give me taller feet –* [46]

No additional versions of "Safe in their Alabaster Chambers" passed between the houses. Emily was at work on other poems, and—as usual—tinkering and adding edits to ones she had already written. The harsh winter lingered. Professor Snell had measured waist-high drifts in the woods around Amherst.[47] Avalanches of ice had demolished chimneys at the college and damaged Mr. Kellogg's store. One frozen slide near the center of town almost knocked passersby to their knees.[48] Then there was the fire that rattled everyone. All Rodolphus Hubbard had wanted to do was support the troops. He'd climbed up to his attic, hoisted the American flag, and set off burning powder to cheer the Union victory at Fort Donelson. But before he knew it, the powder ignited the ceiling and then the floor and soon the entire attic was engulfed. Emily could smell smoke from her window. Lucky for Hubbard, help arrived and his house was saved—but not before there was considerable destruction. Furniture and floors were charred, and Hubbard's pride took a beating. He was so embarrassed he took out an advertisement in the Amherst newspaper and apologized for all the commotion. "We had run up the stars and stripes from the roof of the house, and by burning powder, were doing what we could to testify our joy in view of the triumph of the arms of the Nation," he wrote. "But it was not part of our programme to burn the house."[49]

Given the march of the Burnside Expedition, cascading ice, and fire in Mr. Hubbard's attic, people in Amherst had reason to feel anxious. But that Saturday, March 1, something else startled Emily. Sam Bowles had published "Safe in their alabaster chambers" in his newspaper.* It was the version that Sue least disliked—the one with the second stanza about the breeze and the bees. Before Emily could say a word, Sue dashed off a preemptory note promising they would talk as soon as she could. "*Emily—All's well*," she wrote. Susan had her hands full again. The maid was out and she could not leave

---

* The *Republican* version of the poem changed some of Dickinson's capital letters to lowercase, converted dashes to commas, and indented several lines.

little Ned alone.* "There are two or three little things I wanted to talk with you about without witnesses," she continued. *"Has girl read Republican?* It takes as long to start our Fleet as the Burnside."[50]

Our Fleet? What did Sue mean? Sue suggested she had a hand in the poem—if not in writing and editing, then in securing publication. Did Sue mean to imply that Emily wanted "Safe in their alabaster chambers" printed in the *Republican*? And why did she complain about it taking so long for the poem to appear—comparing its launch to General Burnside's expedition? There was no doubt that Sue was delighted Emily's poem had been published, nettlesome second stanza and all. But did Emily feel that way?

She did not say. As usual—when it came to publication, Emily said nothing. With all the versions of her alabaster poem before her, Emily knew which one she preferred. She disagreed with Sue. Emily liked version two—the one with the experimental imagery. The second stanza read as if the poet were standing at the edge of the universe and looking back at Earth. From that perspective, all of humankind, all of history, all of the world's eminence and strife looked insignificant. The planet was nothing more than a molecule and the dead merely atoms. It was the final image that encompassed everything Dickinson was coming to understand. It was an image evoking Emerson's "terrible simplicity"—abstract and astonishing—and as cold as ice.[51]

---

* One of many Irish immigrants to settle in Amherst in midcentury, Margaret O'Brien came to work for the Dickinsons in 1856. She stayed for nine years, until Margaret Maher began employment with the family. In her astute study, *Maid as Muse: How Servants Changed Emily Dickinson's Life and Language*, Aife Murray argues that Dickinson's great literary productivity in the 1860s was due in part to having more time to work on her poems. With domestic help from O'Brien and Maher, the poet's housekeeping responsibilities lessened.

Safe in their Alabaster Chambers,
Untouched by morning –
And untouched by noon –
Lie the meek members of the Resurrection –
Rafter of satin – and Roof of stone –

Grand go the Years – in the Crescent – above them –
Worlds scoop their Arcs –
And Firmaments – row –
Diadems – drop – and Doges – surrender –
Soundless as dots – on a Disc of snow –

Union general Ambrose Burnside's troops were closing in on
North Carolina. Weeks earlier, Amherst College boys saw their
first battle in a cypress swamp near Roanoke, Virginia.[52] Bullets
fell in a murderous volley, one soldier had said, and there was no
time to count the dead.[53] Amherst residents had to wait for days
before Samuel Bowles's pressmen finally tacked bulletins outside
the *Springfield Republican* listing the casualties. They scanned the
names of the killed and wounded: "Adjutant Stearns in the head and
neck, not badly."[54] Ten days later, a letter from Frazar arrived and
news of the Amherst College president's son swept through town
like a squall. One wound to the neck and one to the forehead, Frazar
wrote. He was fine, and marching with Captain Clark toward Newbern.*[55] Even as she worked, Emily wondered if she could sustain
the concentration her poems required. She thought about writers
who kept working in the face of sorrow. Robert Browning wrote

* Newspapers in Dickinson's time referred to Newbern as one word. Today the city
is identified as New Bern, North Carolina.

poetry after the death of his wife, she remembered. The thought consoled her. "I, myself, in my smaller way, sang off charnel steps," Emily wrote her cousins Fanny and Loo. "Every day life feels mightier, and what we have the power to be, more stupendous."[56] The days before her would be monumental. Within a month, she would share her majestic alabaster poem with someone else. Little did she know, that step would change her life.

Six

ARE YOU TOO DEEPLY OCCUPIED TO SAY IF MY VERSE IS ALIVE?

Tuesday, April 15, 1862 2 pm Thermometer 60.0. No Rain. Stat clouds SW2. Winds SE 2. Therm attached to barometer 55.0. Barometer 30. 279. Dry Bulb 59.64. Wet Bulb 51.14. Humidity 51.1. Remarks No frost in ground. Many clouds.

—Ebenezer Snell, *The Meteorological Journal Kept at Amherst College*

After Jefferson Davis became president of the Confederate States, a group of high-spirited Amherst College boys decided he should be laid to rest in a mock burial. Through means not entirely clear, they obtained an old hearse, dumped an effigy inside, wrangled a white horse from the livery stable, secured oxen and cart for a dirge-playing band, and rounded up classmates to join them in mournful procession. Somehow, they even persuaded one young man to dress as Mrs. Davis, robed in widow's weeds with an infant in her arms—or so it seemed. The whole assemblage paraded in feigned solemnity with stand-ins for Confederate generals Beauregard, Johnston, and Lee leading the way. They marched past the Dickinson law office, past gawking visitors at the Amherst Hotel, past diners at the local oyster house, and around the scraggly town common. Then they headed toward a grove on the south end of the college near Professor Snell's house. When oxen, carriages, band, and mourners finally arrived in a thicket of trees, one student jumped on top of the hearse and delivered a full-throated oration for the late departed. A choir sang, the band played, a military salute rang out, and Mrs. Davis—"the bereaved partner of his buzzum," the boys noted—wailed at just the right time.[1]

Emily was used to displays of youthful exuberance in her college town, but things were different now. In the last month, the war had taken a terrible turn and no mature person in Amherst was pretending about anything, including the demise of the Confederate president. The Civil War was a crucible through which every American would pass, including Emily. She realized, of course, that life was short and offered no promises. But the present moment with its maelstrom of battles and soldiers' deaths galvanized her as never before. She already knew she wanted to be distinguished and make her family proud. She also understood that if she wanted something she'd never had before, she would have to do something she'd never done. The time to share her poems with the world was now. The unprecedented step she would take that day triggered a chain of events that would bear fruit later on. The events would impact her own work, and the course of American literature as well. The developments began on a battlefield with a cannon and smoke and a clash of armies. It would not be long before their reverberations reached Emily's desk.

After their first skirmish on Roanoke Island, where Frazar Stearns, son of the Amherst College president, had sustained a minor wound, the company had advanced to Newbern, North Carolina. They arrived on a miserable day of drizzle and fog, marching twelve miles from the coast in wet uniforms. Awaiting them were Confederate soldiers staked out in a makeshift fort at the brickyard. As thick smoke engulfed them, Major Clark and the Massachusetts 21st led the assault. Aware his men could not adequately see him, Clark jumped atop a cannon and yelled to draw bayonets. He flagged for reinforcements and as he did, he heard the distinctive wail of an approaching Minié ball. He pivoted just as the bullet hit Adjutant Stearns. Frazar slumped. "My God," he murmured, and fell. Charles Thompson, a former custodian at the college, ran with bandages, lint, and wine, and helped carry the young man to a shed. But neither the black custodian, who had known Frazar since birth, nor the surgeon could save him. I wanted you to know, Thompson later wrote President Stearns, I closed his eyes.[*2]

After Union forces seized the brickyard, Frederick Sanderson, Frazar's classmate, searched the battlefield for discarded boards. He gathered up scraps of wood sunk in muddy pools. Then he measured and cut the wood, hammering the boards into a makeshift coffin. Sanderson rowed six miles down the Neuse River to Union gunboats sitting offshore, and for the next eight days, stayed with Frazar's body for the journey back to New England. When Sanderson arrived in Amherst on March 19, he found President Stearns keening with grief. For the Massachusetts 21st, the battles were only beginning. In the months ahead, they would fight in the second battle at Bull Run, then Antietam, and finally Fredericksburg. One soldier wrote that the company of Amherst Boys—once so eager to join the battle—were now "broken, bruised and sheared."[3]

Frazar's death hit everyone hard. The twenty-one-year-old was considered the crown prince of Amherst, beloved, amiable,

* Charles Thompson lived with the Stearns family from the time he was fifteen until his marriage. He worked as a "choreboy" for the family and later as custodian at Amherst College, becoming inextricably connected to both the institution and the lives of students. When Thompson was courting his future wife, Frazar Stearns helped write his love letters. [Abigail Eloise Stearns Lee, "Prof. Charlie": A Sketch of Charles Thompson, Boston: D. C. Heath and Company, 1898.]

and as passionate about music as he was science. People in town especially remembered his enthusiasm for his future. "Sometimes I almost feel as though I could pray to God to *let* me become a chemist," he had said.[4] With his death, many residents of Amherst felt that everything the town stood for—intelligence, learning, dreams of the young—had been snuffed out. Few were more devastated than Austin Dickinson. Edward had first heard the awful news about Frazar and broke it to his son. That's when Austin spun into anguish beyond the reach of his father, his wife, and his sister. He kept repeating his father's words as if in saying them, fate would be altered. His mental state alarmed Emily and she recognized that—for perhaps the first time in her life—she was powerless to reach him. "The World is not the *shape* it was," she wrote.[5] Like Austin, Emily felt untethered and with little she could do, she sat down and wrote a poem, echoing her father's words to Austin.

It dont sound so terrible – quite – as it did –
I run it over – "Dead", Brain – "Dead".
Put it in Latin – left of my school –
Seems it dont shriek so – under rule.

Turn it, a little – full in the face
A Trouble looks bitterest –
Shift it – just –
Say "When Tomorrow comes this way –
I shall have waded down one Day".

I suppose it will interrupt me some
Till I get accustomed – but then the Tomb
Like other new Things – shows largest – then –
And smaller, by Habit –

It's shrewder then
Put the Thought in advance – a Year –
How like "a fit" – then –
Murder – wear![6]

Emily knew her heartache stemmed from more than the Battle of Newbern. She was painfully aware—as was her brother—of the price Amherst College men were paying in the war. Austin was thirty-two years old and married with a child, but Amherst graduates in similar circumstances and even decades older had already enlisted for the Union. William Nelson, Class of '29, was well over fifty and serving as a hospital chaplain. Robert Wilson, Class of '32, was hunting rebel guerrillas with a regiment in West Virginia. His former classmates were also on the front lines. All Austin had to do was look out his window to realize the price others were paying. From his law office he could see the college flag flying at half staff. By the end of the war, thirty-one Amherst men would have died for the Union. No one knew exactly how many students from the South had perished.[7] With no military draft yet in place, Austin was not required to enlist, but the inescapable knowledge of what other men had stepped up to do and he had not—carried weight. Emily knew that. "The Heart with the heaviest freight on – ," she wrote Samuel Bowles, "Does'nt – always – move – ."[8]

Emily hoped Bowles might be able to help. Although she knew Sam was often uncomfortable in emotional moments, there was no one who could speak more candidly to her brother. Shortly after hearing the news about Frazar, Austin asked to see Sam, but Bowles could not get away. Seeing his disappointment, Emily intervened. She rarely asked an outsider for help with Dickinson family matters, but she was deeply concerned. "Austin is chilled – by Frazer's murder," she had written Bowles. "He says — his Brain keeps saying over 'Frazer is killed' — 'Frazer is killed,' just as Father told it — to Him. Two or three words of lead — that dropped so deep, they keep weighing — Tell Austin — how to get over them!'"* [9] But Sam Bowles could not help. Frazar's death had shaken him as well. Since the war began, he frequently stayed in his newspaper office unable to move. Consumed with dispatches, he stared at the telegraph, and once he was home, sat alone in front of the fire, eating grapes and drinking brandy.[10] The long hours brought Bowles to the breaking point.[11] Dr. Holland, who had been on the lecture circuit, returned to the *Republican* to temporarily relieve him.[12] But even with respite from work, Bowles did not improve. Some feared his energy and vitality had been lost forever. "I am unhorsed, literally and figuratively," he admitted.[13] The day he read the words "Stearns, Frazar. Killed," Bowles took the newspaper and threw it away. "The news from Newbern took away all the remaining life," he told Austin and Sue. "I did not care for victories—for anything." Later Bowles apologized to Austin for not being able to rally when needed. "Some of the reasons for my incapacity, & consequent disappointment to you, you know because I have told you.—I have many cares & small power."[14] Samuel Bowles was in emotional tumult and he knew it. "I am going through a 'crisis,' " he said. "I don't know whether it is religious, mental, or physical, but I shall be better or worse when I get through. Whatever it is, it is awful night-mareish."[15]

Emily never used the word "nightmare," but she was in crisis too. She had been seized with anxiety since the previous autumn. Few people in Amherst would forget September 20, 1861, the day the Amherst Boys—students, graduates, and townsmen—shipped off to camp. One hundred men marched past Emily's window fol-

* Dickinson consistently misspelled Frazar Stearns's first name.

lowed by a long line of neighbors cheering and waving flags—the largest crowd ever assembled in town, one person said—a "sea of human beings." As the official ceremony commenced at the train depot down the hill from the Dickinsons' home, Emily watched. A locomotive sat heaving and sputtering, poised to take the company on the first leg of its journey. Edward Dickinson, as always, presented remarks on behalf of the town. He urged the young men to seek valor, and warned them of camp vices. A local clergyman was less scolding, offering prayers and comfort. Then the train whistle blew and loved ones embraced. A ladies' chorus sang "The Star Spangled Banner," with townspeople joining in the final verse. The last words the Amherst Boys heard as they pulled out of the station were "land of the free and the home of the brave." For nearly everyone, patriotic fervor was an attempt to keep dread at bay. They hardly wanted to admit fear to themselves let alone one another. Yet they knew what was coming. First came the death of a town blacksmith, next one of Mrs. Adams's boys, then another Adams son, and now Frazar at Newbern.[16] "I had a terror – since September – ," Emily wrote. "I could tell to none – and so I sing, as the Boy does by the Burying Ground – because I am afraid."[17]

Emily was indeed singing—as she often called writing poetry— at times composing nearly a verse a day. As feverish as her productivity was, the poems were marked not by haste or carelessness but control. They were taut, intentional verses made more so by constant revision. Like townspeople at the depot, Emily confronted fear with hymns, even if writing at times felt brutal.

It is easy to work when the soul is at play –
But when the soul is in pain –
The hearing him put his playthings up
Makes work difficult – then –

It is simple, to ache in the Bone, or the Rind –
But Gimblets – among the nerve –
Mangle daintier – terribler –
Like a Panther in the Glove – [18]

In many poems, a more forceful first-person voice emerged, as if she were squaring her shoulders and announcing who she was and what she believed. Often she presented herself as an outsider, especially when writing about religion, and in many poems she wore nonconformity as a badge of honor and insignificance a point of praise. She delighted in standing apart, and sneered at puffed-up somebodies who forever croaked about themselves. "I'm Nobody! Who are you?" she wrote in one verse. "Are you - Nobody - too?"[19]

Yet it was unclear—as it always would be—if Emily were speaking for herself in her poems or inventing a persona with vastly different opinions. Amherst residents would have been surprised if they had discovered the shy, reclusive daughter of Edward Dickinson was capable of writing such bold lines as

I'm "wife" – I've finished that –
That other state –
I'm Czar – I'm "Woman" now – .[20]

She rarely showed such audacity in person. Perhaps the voice on-the-page was so different because Emily was writing for someone else—a yet-unknown reader—beyond her circle of correspondents and beyond her own time as well. "*My* business is to *sing*," she stated unequivocally.[21] Writing poetry had become to her the work of a lifetime and as fundamental as breathing.

Emily was aware that her circle of preferred readers was not as available to her as they once had been. Sue was busy with the new baby, Fanny and Loo Norcross were still grieving their parents, and Samuel Bowles struggled with precarious health. Given life's inevitable changes, she had fewer people to turn to. Vinnie was her strong supporter in everything, but her sister was not a serious judge of poetry, nor was Emily's mother. Edward, too, was not one who could talk about her work. "Father," she said, is "too busy with his Briefs — to notice what we do."[22] Helen Hunt might have provided an ear, but she and Emily were destined to be at cross-purposes. After the death of their firstborn, Helen and her husband had a second son, and all were living in Newport, Rhode Island. Helen and Edward had been in town recently and paid a call on the Dickinsons. Emily enjoyed meeting Edward Hunt; he was intelligent and quick with humorous observations. During their time together, a scrap of food had dropped from the table and Carlo gobbled it up. Your dog seems to understand gravity, Major Hunt had noted wryly.[23] Helen was a wit, too, and—although she had joked about becoming a poet—she was an insightful reader. Around the tea table that afternoon, Emily might have excused herself and retrieved her fascicles to show Helen, but she did not.

Rev. Charles Wadsworth was another person who had moved beyond Emily's reach. After Emily visited Philadelphia and became acquainted with the charismatic minister, the two had exchanged letters. No one knew how many. As far as anyone could tell, the mysterious relationship was not open to questions. Emily mentioned Reverend Wadsworth on a few occasions, but did not say much about a surprise call he had made when visiting friends nearby. His mother had recently died and he was dressed in mourning. "My Life is full of dark Secrets," he had told Emily.[24] Whether her connection with Wadsworth revolved around pain, faith, or poetry no one knew. But those who were aware of their relationship recognized that the somber clergyman meant a great deal to her. He had written her once addressing an obscure crisis Emily said she was confronting. "My Dear Miss Dickenson," he had written. "I am distressed beyond measure at your note, received this moment, — I can only imagine the affliction which has befallen, or is now befalling you. Believe me, be what it may, you have all my sympathy, and my constant, earnest prayers. I am very, very anxious to learn more definitely of your trial — and though I have no right to intrude upon your sorrow yet I beg you to write me, though it be but a word. In great haste Sincerely and most Affectionately *Yours*—."[25] Wadsworth had left the letter unsigned and embossed it with his personal crest, "C. W."* But now the minister—like so many others—was further away. He had resigned from his church and had accepted another assignment in San Francisco. With his wife and two children, Wadsworth was moving to minister at Calvary Church. The early months of 1862 had brought many losses and Emily looked at spring as a cruel affront. "I dreaded that first Robin, so," she wrote in one poem, and called herself "The Queen of Calvary."[26]

Around the time of Wadsworth's departure, an article appeared in the *Springfield Republican* that caught Emily's eye. No doubt Dr. Holland wrote it, she thought; he usually reported on literary developments. Under the headline "Books, Authors and Art," was a suggestion for reading. "Atlantic Monthly for April is one of the best numbers ever issued," the column began. "Its leading article, T. W. Higginson's Letter to a Young Contributor, ought to be read by all the would-be authors of the land. . . . It is a test of latent

---

* Scholars have confirmed the handwriting in the letter (L248a) is Charles Wadsworth's. While the letter is undated, Thomas Johnson theorizes it was sent in spring 1862. Other scholars concur that Wadsworth's concern may address Dickinson's "terror since September" and therefore could have been written in the 1861–1862 time frame. [Margaret Dakin, email to the author, Amherst College Archives and Special Collections, April 3, 2017.]

power. Whoever rises from its thorough perusal strengthened and encouraged, may be reasonably certain of unlimited success."[27] Emily had heard of Thomas Wentworth Higginson. He was a literary man whose essays on nature and the importance of exercise had often appeared in the *Atlantic*. Sue was familiar with him, too, and had once asked Sam Bowles to locate a photograph of him. After being dismissed from his pastorate in Newburyport for preaching too forcefully on abolition, Higginson had been living in Worcester, some fifty miles away. Emily's uncle William Dickinson knew him. Within weeks of the *Republican* notice, the family copy of the *Atlantic Monthly* arrived and Emily flipped through the pages to Higginson's essay. "My dear young gentleman or young lady," the article began—a remarkable introduction considering he included women in advice to would-be writers. "No editor can ever afford the rejection of a good thing . . . as Ruskin says of painting that it is in the perfection and precision of the instantaneous line that the claim to immortality is made . . . there may be years of crowded passion in a word, and half a life in a sentence . . . Charge your style with life." In the article, Higginson offered practical tips for novice writers: use good pens, black ink, white paper, don't be hasty or slipshod, be neat, and avoid dashes. "Be neither too lax nor too precise in your use of language: the one fault ends in stiffness, the other in slang." Don't be pedantic, too mannered or stylish. Revise as much as you can and don't be in a hurry. " 'Genius,' " he wrote, quoting the French writer Rivarol, " 'is only great patience.' " He spoke of the need for solitude and warned against fame and other distractions. "If a person once does a good thing, society forms a league to prevent his doing another. His seclusion is gone, and therefore his unconsciousness and his leisure . . . a wise man must have strength to call in his resources before middle-life, prune off divergent activities, and concentrate himself on the main work. . . . Literature is the attar of roses, one distilled drop from a million blossoms." He urged writers to avoid looking to England for inspiration. We need new words, he said, look instead to Emerson. "The American writer finds himself among his phrases like an American sea-captain amid his crew: a medley of all nations, waiting for the strong organizing New England mind to mould them into a unit of force." The article concluded with an appeal to patriotism: This "American literature of ours will be just as classic a thing, if we do our part . . . If, therefore, duty and opportunity call, count it a privilege to obtain your share."[28]

A few weeks later, on the morning of April 14, 1862, the Dickinson household bustled. Emily kept track of the family's schedule and needed no reminder of the day's importance. Once again, Edward was preparing to present official remarks—this time at the college. That afternoon at one thirty a dedication ceremony would take place for a cannon captured in the battle of Newbern. Brig. Gen. Ambrose Burnside himself gave it to Amherst College in memory of Frazar Stearns and other men who fell that day. So many people were expected for the ceremony that the railroad added extra cars to transport passengers from as far away as Boston. By noon Emily could hear the last carriages pulling into Amherst for the event. Someone estimated as many as one thousand people jostling for space on the terraces outside Johnson Chapel.[29] Everyone was straining for a glimpse of the cannon, draped in the Stars and Stripes and looking smaller than expected, less brutal somehow—a single barrel, burnished and smooth as glass. Precisely at 1:30 the ceremony began, and Edward spoke first. This moment is pregnant with suggestion, he declared. We are sorrowful, yet grateful. This dedication occurs on the anniversary of the Fort Sumter, he said,

an attack that "startled the nation like a clap of thunder in a clear
sky."*[30] That alignment between then and now represents the way
individual lives are tied to history, he said. We are all connected
to the sweep of larger events, whether we wish to acknowledge it
or not. What ties us, he said, are "sacred associations"—the bond
between the individual and the everlasting.

To many in the audience, the magnitude of the moment, the rush
to see the cannon, and Edward's remarks about "sacred associations"
were indelible. They were a rallying cry to act. One person affected
was a young chemistry professor hired to replace William Clark after
he left to lead the Massachusetts 21st. The young professor wrote Clark
afterward, telling him the ceremony stirred in him a feeling of greatness. I could almost imagine, he wrote, how it felt to jump atop the
cannon and lead the charge. Later the young professor sat down with
his wife and discussed their future. "You can better afford to have a
country without a husband," he told her, "than a husband without a
country." In a matter of weeks, he left the college and enlisted.†[31]

The next day, on April 15, 1862, Emily's thoughts returned to Mr.
Higginson's article. His essay had all but invited writers to send
samples of their work. She wondered if this literary man—a man
she had never met—would be open to reading her verse. In many
ways, the thought was preposterous. A professional writer and abo-
litionist whom many said was willing to use violence for political means—why would he be interested in a middle-aged woman
writing alone in her father's house? But Emily was at a juncture.
The distance she felt from Sue, Austin, and Samuel Bowles grieved

* Fort Sumter was attacked on April 12, 1861. The Amherst College cannon ceremony occurred on April 14, 1862.
† Newton Spaulding Manross enlisted July 22, 1862, and was killed two months
later at Antietam on September 17, 1862.

and stirred her. Frazar Stearns's death gave life an even more fragile edge. Her father's words about "sacred associations" incited in
her a boldness to act. "To take the lead in bringing forward a new
genius," Mr. Higginson had written, "is . . . a privilege."[32] Emily
never would describe herself as a "genius," but she was confident
in her work, and she made up her mind. She took out her poems—
over thirty fascicles and dozens of unfinished drafts, hundreds of
verses in all—and read opening lines, deciding which to send.

I taste a liquor never brewed –
From Tankards scooped in Pearl – [33]

Wild nights – Wild nights!
Were I with thee
Wild nights should be
Our luxury! [34]

I can wade Grief –
Whole Pools of it – [35]

"Hope" is the thing with feathers –
That perches in the soul – [36]

There's a certain Slant of light,
Winter Afternoons – [37]

After great pain, a formal feeling comes –
The Nerves sit ceremonious, like Tombs – [38]

The Soul selects her own Society –
Then – shuts the Door –

To her divine Majority –
Present no more – [39]

Because I could not stop for Death –
He kindly stopped for me – [40]

Some – keep the Sabbath – going to church –
I – keep it – staying at Home – [41]

These poems would not do, she thought. She selected three others
and set them aside: "We play at Paste – "; "I'll tell you how the Sun
rose – "; and "The nearest Dream recedes – unrealized – ."*[42] She
wanted to include one more and studied the poem she had been
working on so intently—"Safe in their Alabaster Chambers." Emily
knew Sue liked the version published a few weeks before in the
Republican. But Emily preferred another, the one with the apocalyp-
tic second stanza and the image of dots on a disc of snow. The sweep
was larger, she thought, more impressive, and the image one of her
best. Emily copied the four poems and lifted out a sheet of paper
for the accompanying letter. She debated about what to say, how
much to tell, and what tone to assume. Don't be too forward, Higginson had warned in the article. Draw near your editor with "soft
approaches."[43] Emily wondered if she should mention the hundreds
of poems she had already written, the decade she had spent drafting and redrafting, the many verses she had shared with Fanny
and Loo, Sue, the Hollands, and Samuel Bowles. She decided not to
mention the poems that had already been published or the careful

* Ralph Franklin believes "We play at Paste" may have been written in direct
response to Higginson's article. [Ralph Franklin, ed. *The Poems of Emily Dickinson*.
(Cambridge: The Belknap Press of Harvard University Press, 1998), 24.]

reading Susan had given to her alabaster verse. But she wanted to be clear with Mr. Higginson about what she thought poetry should do. Words had to live and breathe and spark a physical response. She remembered Sue's reaction to the alabaster verse. "I always go to the fire and get warm after thinking of it, but I never *can* again."44 Poetry had to affect the body, Emily believed, and trigger a visceral response. She would never be content to reach only a reader's mind and heart, she wanted to touch bone and muscle and nerve.

> *Mr. Higginson,*
>
> *Are you too deeply occupied to say if my Verse is alive?*
>
> *The Mind is so near itself – it cannot see, distinctly – and I have none to ask –*
>
> *Should you think it breathed – and had you the leisure to tell me, I should feel quick gratitude –*
>
> *If I make the mistake – that you dared to tell me – would give me sincere honor – toward you –*
>
> *I enclose my name – asking you, if you please – Sir – to tell me what is true?*
>
> *That you will not betray me – it is needless to ask – since Honor is it's own pawn –* 45

Emily did not sign the letter. She placed the four poems and the letter in an envelope, affixed two three-cent stamps to the top left, and wrote the address: "T. W. Higginson Worcester, Mass." She had never sent poems to a stranger before: her action was unexpected and startling. The next day when Mr. Higginson opened the envelope, he was surprised by what he saw: an almost indecipherable scrawl, sentences strewn with dashes, and—strangest of all—no signature. Something else tumbled out: a smaller envelope inside the larger one. Higginson slipped his finger into the tiny packet and pulled out a card. There he found her name, written in pencil in the same hurried scribble as the letter. The card-in-an-envelope-in-another-envelope seemed a kind of game to him. Cat and mouse. A bold introduction and a hasty retreat. A correspondent who introduced herself and then promptly disappeared.[46] His wife had warned him about lending a hand to too many would-be writers, especially those he deemed "half-cracked poetesses."[47] They took too much of his time, she cautioned, were an unnecessary burden, and downright odd. But Thomas Wentworth Higginson was intrigued. He took the letter home.

Emily Dickinson had no idea if Mr. Higginson would respond. In her room that day, she listened to the world around her: the creak of steps on the kitchen stairs, the muffled clop of horses' hooves pulling carriages to the center of town, the sound of a distant train whistle. The ground that spring had softened and crocuses were starting to bloom. By late afternoon, a chorus of spring peepers would be chirping in nearby swamps. Occasionally, Emily's reverie was punctured by the sound of blanks fired on the town common. College students and local men were mustering and practicing military drills. Last month there had been two musters. By August there would be many more.[48] Emily looked out her window and watched as Sue—busy with Ned—wheeled the little boy in his baby carriage. Big scruffy Carlo and two cats trotted behind as if in a grand parade.[49] Emily liked to observe the perambulations of people along Main Street. They always seemed busy and full of purpose. It was easy for her to feel distant from them—a "Nobody"—sitting as she so often did alone at the window, quiet and removed. But Emily knew something had changed. There was a letter with her poems sitting on Mr. Higginson's desk in Worcester, Massachusetts. Now as she raised her eyes above the hemlock hedge, Emily watched— but this time she also waited.

Seven

BULLETINS ALL DAY
FROM IMMORTALITY

*7 p.m. November 11, 1864: Thermometer 35.6 degrees, clouds 0, Winds
NW 2, Therm Attached to Barometer 51.2. Barometer Observed Height
29.532 Dry Bulb 35.0 Wet Bulb 40,532.0 Humidity 70% Remarks:
Cloudy and Chilly.*

—Ebenezer Snell, *The Meteorological Journal Kept at Amherst College*

Evening was calm and clear, vivid moonlight.

—*Cambridge* (Mass.) *Chronicle*, Nov. 11, 1864

Thomas Wentworth Higginson answered immediately. He
wanted to know more. He wanted to know everything. And he
barraged Emily with questions.* How old are you? How long have

---

* Unfortunately, Higginson's letters to Dickinson have not survived. Some of his
questions to Dickinson can be construed by her responses. Dickinson frequently
reiterates Higginson's question or places his query in quotation marks. The letters upon which this chapter is based had previously been misdated. This letter
most likely was written on November 11, 1864, when the Lincoln Clubs of Cambridge held a torchlight procession. Contemporaneous newspaper accounts attest
to the re-dating. On November 13, the date Johnson and Leyda assign to the letter, a
powerful storm swept through New England. Parades could not have taken place in
such bad weather. [Beverly Gill, email to the author, April 28, 2017, Boston Public

you been writing? What writers do you read? What kind of education have you had? Who are your companions? Tell me about your
family. Have you read Walt Whitman? In her return letter, Emily
apologized for not responding sooner, although it had been only
a matter of days. "You asked how old I was?" she wrote. "I made
no verse – but one or two – until this winter – Sir."[1] Her response
was confusing and in a sense, true. Emily measured everything
by a yardstick of poetry. But her answer also made clear that she
did not want Mr. Higginson to know how long she had been working at her craft or that she had written hundreds of poems. Other
answers were similarly coy, such as one about her companions.
"Hills – Sir," she wrote, "and the Sundown – and a Dog – large as
myself, that my Father bought me – They are better than Beings –
because they know – but do not tell." She said her family consisted
of a brother and sister, a mother who "does not care for thought,"
and a father who bought her books but begged her not to read
them. He "fears they joggle the Mind," she added. She shrugged
off her study at Amherst Academy and Mount Holyoke by saying,
"I went to school – but in your manner of the phrase – had no education." Her literary influence, she reported, included the Reve-
lations, Keats, Ruskin, Mr. and Mrs. Browning, and Sir Thomas
Browne.* When it came to expressing her opinions of the Church,
Emily was unequivocal. Her family was "religious – except me,"

Library Archives; George E. Clark, email to the author, April 28, 2017, Houghton
Library, Harvard University.]

* Dickinson loved the Brownings and mentioned them often in her letters. She wrote
of Keats only twice in her life, and after her letter to Higginson, she never mentioned
Ruskin again. She might have been currying favor with Higginson when it came to
Ruskin and Sir Thomas Browne, writers he cited in his essay "Letter to a Young Con-
tributor." [Thomas H. Johnson, ed., Theodora Ward, associate ed., *The Letters of Emily
Dickinson* (Cambridge: The Belknap Press of Harvard University Press, 1958), 405.]

she said, "and address an Eclipse, every morning – whom they call their 'Father.' " She dispatched his question about Walt Whitman with a wave of the hand. "I never read his Book – but was told that he was disgraceful."*

Emily told Higginson other things, too, and with rare candor. She wrote of tutors—her father's young law clerks—who had taken her early literary ambition seriously. "My dying Tutor told me that he would like to live till I had been a poet," she said. For years, she continued, "my Lexicon – was my only companion."[2] She carefully chose details to paint herself as a solitary writer in search of a teacher. Multiple times she expressed frustration in being ill equipped to evaluate her own work. "While my thought is undressed," she wrote, "I can make the distinction, but when I put them in the Gown – they look alike, and numb."[3] Something happened, she suggested, between the thinking stage and the moment she put pen to paper. "I could not weigh myself – Myself" was the way she put it.[4] Yet as much as Emily emphasized an amateur status, she could not resist telling Higginson that professionals were interested in her work. Two editors had called on her at home. They "asked me for my Mind," she said, adding they "would use it for the World."[5] As usual, Emily was silent about specifics that others might have shared. She could have been more forthcoming about

---

* Higginson may have been thinking about Whitman, whom he had bumped into in Boston. Whitman, perched on a counter at his publisher's office, was reading proofs of the third edition of *Leaves of Grass*. He did not impress Higginson. The "personal impression made on me by the poet was not so much of manliness as of Boweriness," he wrote. Higginson admitted he may have been prejudiced against Whitman's poetry because he had read it while seasick—"a fact which doubtless increased for me the intrinsic unsavoriness of certain passages." [Brenda Wineapple, *White Heat: The Friendship of Emily Dickinson and Thomas Wentworth Higginson* (New York: Alfred A. Knopf, 2008), 113.]

the identity of the editors—Higginson would surely have known them—but she said no more. She also hid the fact that she had already published poems.* The most striking absence concerned Sue. Her astute sister-in-law did not merit a single word, not even as a member of the family.

Shortly after their correspondence began, Emily Dickinson would be overcome by adversity. Her burgeoning literary relationship with Thomas Wentworth Higginson would be threatened as her physical health faltered. "The Physician has taken away my Pen," she would tell him.[6] Emily had begun to notice serious problems with her eyesight a year before contacting Higginson, although the disease may have begun its insidious advance much earlier.† For the woman who keenly observed the world around her, the thought of losing her vision was terrifying. Emily's crisis reached a peak on a cold November night in 1864—not in at her home in Amherst—but in a boardinghouse in Cambridge, Massachusetts. She knew she was at a turning point. She wanted to write more poems, but she didn't know if her eyesight would allow it. The letters she had already exchanged with Higginson made her realize that a larger world beyond Amherst and Springfield was interested in her work. In the perilous situation she was in, Emily recognized she was not who she once had been. But she also knew she wanted to be more.

* One editor had to be Bowles or Holland representing the *Springfield Republican*. Karen Dandurand suggests the second editor was Richard Salters Storrs. An Amherst College graduate, Storrs was a friend of Samuel Bowles and frequent commencement guest of Sue and Austin. [Karen Dandurand, "New Dickinson Civil War Publications," *American Literature* 56, no. 1, March 1984, 17–27.]

† Dickinson scholar James R. Guthrie believes the poet's eye problems may have begun as early as 1851. He cites a Boston visit Dickinson made that year to consult Dr. William Wesselhoft. [James R. Guthrie, *Emily Dickinson's Vision: Illness and Identity in Her Poetry* (Gainesville: University Press of Florida, 1998), 178.]

In the time before her health problems escalated, Emily and Higginson inched toward each other—he posing questions and she responding or dodging them—and they settled into comfortable roles as teacher and student. Her eagerness to be instructed must have been irresistible to Higginson. "I would like to learn," she told him. "Could you tell me how to grow – or is it unconveyed – like Melody – or Witchcraft?"[7] He had done his best in offering advice, noting that when a shift in word choice could have provided a rhyme, she rejected it. She opted instead for surprise and defiance of form. Miss Dickinson didn't appear to be careless or motivated by whim, he thought.[8] Rather she seemed to be reaching for something more evocative—an arresting bump in rhythm, a rhyme more minor-key than major, or an image as startling as those in her alabaster poem: "Dots, On a Disc of Snow." Her refusal to conform, he would learn, had less to do with satisfying the reader's expectations than upending them.

Emily wrote to Thomas Wentworth Higginson nearly every month when they first began corresponding. She relished his queries, later telling him, "You ask great questions accidentally."[9] Members of her own family had given up questioning Emily—about her reclusiveness, her resistance to travel, or mysterious callers such as Reverend Wadsworth. Since Emily and Higginson had never met, their relationship was built on letters only, words she could manipulate or hide behind. Letters were "the Mind alone, without corporeal friend," she had said.[10] Do you have a photograph, Higginson once had asked.* No, she replied—but I "am small, like

---

* Emily did have a photograph, a daguerreotype taken around the time she was a student at Mount Holyoke Female Seminary. Perhaps she did not offer it because she was so much younger in the image. She was thirty-one in 1862 when writing her initial letters to Higginson.

the Wren, and my Hair is bold, like the Chestnut Bur – and my eyes, like the Sherry in the Glass, that the Guest leaves."[11] When he had suggested she wait to publish, she scoffed. "I smile when you suggest that I delay 'to publish' – that being foreign to my thought, as Firmament to Fin – If fame belonged to me, I could not escape her . . . My Barefoot-Rank is better."[12] He asked about her seclusion and received a playful, cagey reply. "Of 'shunning Men and Women' – they talk of Hallowed things, aloud – and embarrass my Dog."[13] There was also conversation about the work itself. Higginson had asked about her poem's perplexing pronouns and she told him she was not writing autobiography. "When I state myself, as the Representative of the Verse," she declared, "it does not mean – me – but a supposed person."[14] It was one of the most emphatic comments of her life.

Perhaps most revealing was her description of how it felt to write a poem. Nature, she said, was an inspiration. The impulse to create occurred to her on walks when the sight of a tree or an angle of light would suddenly seize her. At that moment she simply *had* to transform what she saw into words, she said, and the urge affected her physically. "A sudden light on Orchards, or a new fashion in the wind troubled my attention," she explained, "a palsy, here – the Verses just relieve." At those moments something took hold of her—violently. "My little Force explodes," she told Higginson, "and leaves me bare and charred."[15] Yet as forthcoming as she could be, Emily continued to be elusive. Higginson quickly realized he was not dealing with an amateur poet—the kind who taxed his generosity and peeved his wife. He worried Emily might be too brilliant for him, beyond his ability to help. When he told her so, she tossed aside the concern. She was used to men not understanding her. They always asked her to repeat what she said or explain herself in plain language. "All men say 'What' to me," she admitted, with a touch of weariness.[16] But Thomas Wentworth Higginson seemed different to her; he was willing, steady, open, someone who would not interrupt or ask what in the world she was talking about. When his letters to her stopped suddenly, she was alarmed. Perhaps she had told him too much.

"Did I displease you, Mr Higginson," she urgently wrote him in October 1862.[17] She had not. As much as Emily had shared with her correspondent, she knew little about him. Months after their correspondence began, Higginson had joined the Union Army. He was thirty-eight. Dickinson had no idea Captain Higginson had been drilling troops at Camp John Wool in Worcester fifty miles away from Amherst. Higginson's entire life had been a battle between two poles: a life of the mind and one committed to action. The decision to put aside his literary career for a political cause was a familiar one. Three years earlier, he'd been one of the Secret Six who'd financially supported John Brown's raid at Harpers Ferry, and, before that, he'd brought axes to Boston's Faneuil Hall to help abolitionists free a captured slave. The summer of 1862, when President Lincoln had called for 300,000 more troops, Higginson found he could not live with himself. It was unprincipled, he believed, to spend his days writing nature essays for the *Atlantic* when other men risked their lives.* "I never could hold up my head again, in

---

* When Lincoln initiated the military draft in 1864, thirty-five-year-old Austin Dickinson, like other men of financial means, bought a substitute to serve in his place. Paying a substitute between $300 and $500 was legal and not entirely uncommon. The amount of money was based on an unskilled laborer's yearly income. Many men looked upon paying a substitute as shirking one's duty and labeled the Civil War a "rich man's war and a poor man's fight." [Wayne E. Phaneuf and Joseph Carvalho III, *A Not So Civil War: Western Massachusetts at Home and in Battle*, vol. 1 (Springfield, MA: The Republican, 2015), 131; Jay Leyda, *The Years and Hours of Emily Dickinson*, vol. 2 (New Haven: Yale University Press, 1960), 88 and 89.]

Worcester or even elsewhere, if I did not vindicate my past words by actions though tardy," he said.[18] Within weeks Union officers put him in charge of preparing young and untested Worcester boys. Later that fall he was promoted and reassigned; Captain Higginson would become a colonel and assume leadership of the first Negro regiment of Union soldiers.* Emily read about it in the *Republican*. "I should have liked to see you, before you became improbable," she wrote, her letter somehow catching up with him in camp off the coast of Charleston, South Carolina.[19] She had hoped to meet him in person, but a visit would have to wait. "Best Gains – must have the Losses' Test," she said. She had no idea how prophetic she was.[20]

At first things went well for Colonel Higginson. He was impressed with his troops, did well in recruiting others from nearby rice plantations, and understood he had to earn the respect of Negro soldiers who had reason to doubt the goodwill of any white man. He gained his soldiers' trust by listening to stories about their families and lobbying for pay parity with white Union troops.† Yet as much as he found purpose in training soldiers, Higginson yearned for real battles instead of meaningless

---

* It is often believed Robert Gould Shaw commanded the first regiment of freed slaves in the Civil War. Shaw commanded the Massachusetts 54th, but he was not the first to lead a black regiment. Shaw's regiment mustered in 1863 and Higginson's in 1862.

† Higginson wrote many letters to newspapers, criticizing the federal government on pay inequity for black soldiers. His letters appeared in the *New York Evening Post*, *New-York Daily Tribune*, and the *New York Times*. Black soldiers received $10 a month with a deduction of $3 for clothing. [Christopher Looby, ed., *The Complete Civil War Journals and Selected Letters of Thomas Wentworth* Higginson (Chicago: University of Chicago Press, 2000), 55, 61; Wayne E. Phaneuf and Joseph Carvalho III, *A Not So Civil War: Western Massachusetts at Home and in Battle,* vol. 1 (Springfield, MA: The Republican, 2015), 130.]

skirmishes. He soon received his wish. While commanding 250 troops in a transport boat headed up the South Edisto River, Higginson's boat snagged and became a target. Confederates fired from bluffs and he was hit on the side. He didn't know with what. A bullet? A piece of wood? A spent shell? Higginson survived and was hospitalized, but did not improve. "I am in rather a state of collapse," he finally confessed to his mother.[21] His old friend Louisa May Alcott volunteered to come south and help him regain strength.*

When the letters from Higginson stopped as he convalesced, Emily sent another frantic note.[22] She had reason to feel on edge. Problems with her eyesight had been worsening and she was anxious. There were good days and bad, she said, and that intermittency only exacerbated the misery. She never knew when pain and blurriness would hit, and she didn't know if the problem had gone away for good or would come back with greater intensity. Lately the trouble had become so serious her family thought she needed medical help from a specialist in Boston. Her symptoms were many: sensitivity to light, headache, pain around the eyes, eyestrain, tearing, diminished clarity, fatigue from any task that demanded concentration from her eyes—certainly writing. Sometimes her eyes felt gritty, as if she were standing in a dusty field on a windy day. Daytime itself had become an enemy. Bright lights, reflections off snow, even a glint of light off white paper caused problems. The sun was even worse. It felt dangerous, and

---

* Alcott seemed to want to get away from Concord as much as anything. "Don't you want a cook, [or] nurse," she wrote Higginson. "I am willing to enlist in any capacity . . . to be busied in some more loyal labor than sitting quietly at home spinning fictions when such fine facts are waiting for all of us to profit by & celebrate." She did not make the journey to South Carolina. [Looby, 318]

triggered every affliction—ache, fuzziness, and disorientation. Staying indoors on bright days and not being able to garden must have felt like incarceration to her. While Emily may not have articulated it, the psychological effects of her diminished sight had to take a toll too. Household tasks were more difficult to accomplish, making her less independent and reliant on others to help. With reduced vision, she had to be more vigilant, keenly aware of what she couldn't do or couldn't see. She may have seen things that weren't there because her eyes could not be depended on for precision. She sought the dark during daylight and inhabited the night—upside down with the natural order of the day. Her life had become liminal, experienced in a twilight where sensory experience could not be fully felt. In place of sharp perception— what she had depended on and used to such a rich extent in her poetry—was now dimness, ambiguity, and haze.[23]

Emily knew something was profoundly wrong, and she would probably need to leave Amherst for diagnosis and treatment. When his children were young, Edward Dickinson always worried about their eyes. He told Austin to ease up on studying, as if he had a premonition that reading would lead to blindness. When Edward caught Emily stealing a few snatches of Melville one morning after her eye problems had become worse, he scolded her.[24] She also seemed to have given up reading newspapers. She did not know Higginson had been wounded, even though the *Republican* had reported it. Neither did she know Major Hunt had been killed—her friend Helen's husband—the man whose humor about Carlo and gravity had delighted her.* Writing to her Norcross cousins, Emily

* Major Hunt died in the Brooklyn Naval Yard while testing a new submarine battery. A shell exploded and gas overwhelmed him. He fell into the submarine's hold and died of a fatal brain concussion. Edward Bissell Hunt was forty-one. [Leyda, vol. 2, 82–83.]

admitted she felt desolate. "Nothing has happened but loneliness, perhaps too daily to relate," she wrote.[25] Carlo stood by her,
as faithful a dog as he always had been, but she was discouraged
and frightened.[26] On top of everything else, the house was cold,
she was forced to wear a bonnet indoors, and when she reported
on the weather she wrote, "No frost at our house yet. Thermometer frost, I mean."[27] In February 1864—with Vinnie by her side—
thirty-three-year-old Emily met with a physician in Boston. Dr.
Henry Williams, New England's preeminent ophthalmologist,
might know what to do. He was known as an excellent surgeon and
prolific scholar. Williams suggested a treatment, and—as Emily
feared—she would have to move near him for care.* Cousins Fanny
and Loo offered a solution for lodging. Emily could move into the
Cambridge boardinghouse where they resided and travel across
the river to Boston for treatments with Dr. Williams. She had only
two months to prepare for the long stay and an uncertain future.
She would be busy.

It was one thing for Emily to gather up her belongings and say
goodbye to her dog and the rest of her family. It was quite another
to step away from her desk and her poetry. Something remarkable happened that spring of 1864 as she made plans to move to
Cambridge. She published more poetry—all anonymously—than
at any other time in her life. Anonymity had always suited her; it
protected her privacy and seclusion. Within months, five poems
appeared in six different publications, and in newspapers and

---

* Patients such as Emily who could afford good medical care were not usually
treated in a hospital. Instead they moved into hotels or boardinghouses near a physician in order to be treated. [Martin Wand and Richard B. Sewall, " 'Eyes Be Blind
Heart Be Still': A New Perspective on Emily Dickinson's Eye Problem," *New England
Quarterly* 52, no. 3, September 1979, 400–406.]

magazines from Brooklyn to Boston. Her sunset verse, "Blazing in gold, and quenching in purple," appeared first on February 29 in the *Drum Beat*, a daily newspaper released during the two-week Brooklyn Fair. Proceeds from the fair supported the US Sanitary Commission aiding injured Union soldiers. Dickinson admitted she could not refuse to "help the sick and wounded soldiers," yet it was unclear—as it always was—just how involved she was in submitting the verse.*[28] After the poem appeared in the *Drum Beat*, it was also published in the *Springfield Daily Republican* and once more in the weekend edition. Three days later a second verse was published in the *Drum Beat*, "Flowers —well, if anybody." The poem made the rounds in the *Republican* too. It also appeared in the *Boston Post*. No doubt a Boston editor who liked the work had simply clipped it out of the *Drum Beat* or the *Republican* and republished it in his paper without comment or authorization. Who knows how many editors in Chicago, Philadelphia, or Cincinnati did the same? Nine days after the flower poem, a third verse appeared, her elegy "These are the days when birds come back." The next day a fourth was published, "Some keep the Sabbath going to church," and circulated in the *Round Table,* a national literary magazine from New York. At the end of April, a fifth poem, "Success is counted sweetest" was published in the *Brooklyn Daily Union*. Readership for the five poems in six publications was impressive. The *Drum Beat*

* Other *Drum Beat* issues included the works of Louisa May Alcott, Oliver Wendell Holmes, and William Cullen Bryant. Dickinson's verse was published anonymously, as was all her work that spring. Even though *Drum Beat* contributors received complimentary copies of the newspaper, Alcott and others would not have known the author of the sunset poem. But Richard Salters Storrs may have. Storrs was Austin and Susan's old friend and an Amherst College trustee. He edited the *Drum Beat* and would have encountered Emily's verse through Samuel Bowles.

published 6,000 copies of the newspaper every day. The ambitious *Round Table* rivaled the *Atlantic,* and boasted of readers from Chicago, Boston, and London. The *Boston Post*'s circulation was 9,500 daily, and the readership for Samuel Bowles's *Daily Republican* stood at 15,000, the weekly at 14,000, and was for sale on newsstands all over New England. Although they did not realize it, thousands of people were reading Emily Dickinson in the spring of 1864, and a circle of New York literary men were doing their best to promote her.*[29] But Emily sought no further exchanges with the editors and did not take advantage of their publishing connections to further her work.[30] The explosion of publications ended when she dropped her bags in Fanny and Loo's rooms in late April 1864.† Certainly Emily wanted to aid the Union cause, but the flurry of published poems suggests she may have had another concern. Worried about her eyes and the possible end of her creative production, Emily may have wanted to make her mark while she still could.[31]

As improbable as it sounded, Colonel Higginson could have seen some of Emily's New York publications while he was in camp, recovering from his wounds. Earlier she had sent him "Success is counted sweetest" and "Some keep the Sabbath going to Church";

---

* One of the editors of the *Round Table* was Henry Sweetser, Emily's first cousin. His coeditor—his cousin Charles—was a Dickinson neighbor who worked for a time at the *Republican*. Even the *Brooklyn Daily Union* had an Amherst connection. Gordon Ford, husband of Emily's girlhood friend Emily Fowler Ford, was one of the newspaper's founders.

† Emily moved to an area of Cambridge one mile east of Harvard College referred to as Cambridgeport. The two names were used interchangeably. The boardinghouse stood near what is now Central Square on Bishop Richard Allen Drive. [Hiroko Uno, *Emily Dickinson Visits Boston* (Kyoto, Japan: Yamaguchi Publishing House, 1990) 58.]

he would have recognized the poems even though they had been published anonymously.[32] He might also have been aware of Dickinson's burst of publication through soldiers' unsanctioned gift exchanges across enemy lines. When Confederate and Union forces were not engaged in combat, pickets often rigged up small boats and floated gifts, including newspapers, to their counterparts across the river.* Massachusetts troops across the Rappahannock River in Virginia sailed copies of the *Springfield Republican* and received issues of the Richmond *Daily Dispatch* in return. During the spring of 1864, it was possible that Emily's two poems in the *Republican* may have sailed aboard clandestine crafts and ended up in Higginson's hands.[33]

After his wounding, Thomas Wentworth's Higginson's health improved, but not by much. Doctors finally diagnosed his weakness as malaria and he rested in camp presiding over courts-martial, and walking once or twice a day to the river. Many days Higginson sat with Charlotte Forten and edited her manuscript on life in the Sea Islands. Editor James T. Fields at the *Atlantic Monthly* might enjoy it, he thought.† Higginson seemed constitutionally unable to turn aside a serious woman who asked for literary help. It was not merely courtesy that propelled him. He believed in women's rights, and his impulse was political as much as literary. Colonel Higginson suspected he would not stay in the military any longer. He loved his men and the soldier's life, but with his health

* On April 28, 1863, the US War Department issued a call for wounded men to serve in the Invalid Corps, later called the Veteran Reserve Corps. The call sought former Union troops who had lost arms or legs or were otherwise injured to reenlist for light duty, including work as pickets.

† Charlotte Forten [Grimke]'s essay "Life on the Sea Island" appeared in the May 1864 issue of the *Atlantic Monthly*, and detailed her work as an African American teacher in what became known as the Port Royal Experiment.

impaired, he no longer felt useful. "I can understand a gradual sliding into slippers & dressing gown," he admitted, perhaps
with a touch of guilt—the old tug between a life of the mind and a
life of action continuing to trouble him.[34] He thought of returning to Cambridge, Massachusetts, his hometown. He had no idea
Emily Dickinson had moved there herself. By the spring of 1864,
Higginson resigned his post. His wife, Mary, had grown tired of
Worcester and proposed moving to a boardinghouse in Newport,
Rhode Island: the rent was affordable and the city was filled with
artists and writers. Higginson wrapped up his military business
and set sail for New England. He did not know what awaited him.
"I have no restless ambition, never have had," he wrote Mary.[35] In
June the *Springfield Republican* reported, "Col. T. W. Higginson is
now at Newport, R.I., in poor health."[36]

Emily was in Cambridge when she heard the news. "Are you
in danger – I did not know that you were hurt," she wrote. "Will
you tell me more?"[37] Months as an invalid had made Emily more
considerate of Higginson. "A nearness to Tremendousness – / An
Agony procures," she had written in a poem.[38] Her previous letters
always had focused on *her* needs, but this time she asked about
him. "I wish to see you more than before I failed," she said.[39] The
news of Higginson's health left Emily distressed, and she worried
his letters might not find her at the boardinghouse. Her handwriting was larger and more disjoint, and she didn't trust her eyes
to legibly write her new address.* She scissored the details from

---

* Dickinson's handwriting from this era is strikingly different compared to
earlier years. Thomas H. Johnson, editor of the first complete edition of Dickinson's poems, observed that the poet's handwriting showed significant "change in
appearance: letters elongated and uneven. . . . Strongly slanted. Tendency toward
separation of letters, a few words of four of five letters being entirely unligated.

another letter: "Miss Dickinson 86, Austin Street, Cambridge, Mass."[40] She described her new surroundings unfavorably. "I work in my Prison," she told him. "Carlo did not come, because he would die, in Jail, and the Mountains, I could not hold now, so I brought but the Gods."[41] Was Higginson to understand "the Gods" were her verses? With Emily's figurative turns, he could not be sure. She reported the barest of details about her health, telling him only that she had moved in April and did not expect to leave anytime soon. Her doctor, she said, "does not let me go." Emily acknowledged she was at a low point in her life and that word of Higginson's recovery "would excel my own." Yet she did not tell him what was exactly wrong with her. "Can you render my Pencil?" was all she said.[42]

Emily's eye problem, it appeared, was iritis. Her primary symptoms—dim vision, pain, and red eyes that ached in light— were consistent with that diagnosis. There would be treatments in Dr. Williams's Boston office and instructions for protecting her eyes during the day: proscriptions that included rest and limiting her exposure to light.* She could need bandages to block the sun.[43]

Some capitals, such as A and C exaggerated in size." [Thomas H. Johnson, ed. *The Poems of Emily Dickinson* (Cambridge: The Belknap Press of Harvard University Press, 1955), liv.] In this early June 1864 letter to Higginson, Dickinson's handwriting is noticeably larger—some lines include two or three words at most. See https://www.digitalcommonwealth.org/search/commonwealth:kho4mv993/.

* There is no definitive diagnosis for Emily Dickinson's eye problems. Theories have included exotropia (or strabismus), lupus erythematosus, iritis/uveitis, and a kind of psychosomatic blindness. I favor the iritis diagnosis, with the possibility of exotropia as well. Iritis is an inflammation of the muscles of the eye. With exotropia, the eyes turn outward. Interviews I conducted with descendants of Dickinson's Norcross relatives indicated exotropia ran in the family and has been present for generations. My descriptions of Dickinson's likely treatment for iritis derive from comments in the poet's letters, Dr. Williams's written protocols for addressing the

Williams used several protocols, medication, eye drops, and a new instrument for the treatments.[44] An ophthalmoscope illuminated the interior of her eye and enabled him to examine muscles controlling her pupil, blood vessels, and the surrounding nerves. If pressure within her eyes did not improve, he might puncture her eyes' anterior chambers. Mercury could be administered. Cocaine, too, for pain. If all treatments failed, a portion of the iris might be removed, although that was considered a step no one wanted to take. To make her more comfortable, a darkened room and dry flannel wrapped around a jug of hot water would help. She could hold the jug against her face. Doctors reported they could detect changes iritis brought to a patient's eyes. The iris lost its brilliance, they said. A once shining, clear appearance became muddy-looking. In severe cases, the iris could take on another shape, sometimes looking like the ace of clubs. Physicians also knew that the emotional effects of the disease were just as pronounced. One medical text stated, "Cases of iritis, especially those occurring in men accustomed to an active independent life, often produce a very irritable condition of mind, followed by great depression, the result of the pain, partial blindness, and resultant dependence on others."[45] No one knew how Emily had contracted the disease. Medical professionals later theorized iritis stemmed from a bacterial infection such as consumption. Cousin Sophia Holland and Aunt Lavinia both had succumbed to consumption. Emily herself had a bad cough for weeks as a young girl. It was possible her early respiratory problems later triggered

---

disease, and medical texts from the nineteenth century. [Polly Longsworth and Norbert Hirschhorn, "'Medicine Posthumous': A New Look at Emily Dickinson's Medical Conditions," *New England Quarterly* 69, no. 2, June 1996, 299–316; Martha Ackmann, "'I'm Glad I Finally Surfaced': A Norcross Descendent Remembers Emily Dickinson, *Emily Dickinson Journal* 5, no. 2, Fall 1996, 120–26.]

iritis. If his treatment did not work, Dr. Williams knew inflammation within Emily's eye could form clots and lead to permanent blindness. Even if his procedures were successful, the condition might reoccur. He wrote to Edward Dickinson, saying—while satisfied with progress—recovery would be gradual. Emily was not so sure. "I suppose I had been discouraged so long," she said."[46]

Not being able to read was the worst complication of her illness. Dr. Williams had forbidden it, or at least told Emily to drastically limit her time with books. She later said not being able to read was the only restriction in her life "that ever made me tremble." It felt to her like "shutting out . . . the strongest friends of the soul." Emily never looked upon books as her "tormentors," but that's exactly what they had become. Dr. Williams "might as well have said, 'Eyes be blind,' 'heart be still,' " she lamented. She mostly conformed to her doctor's dictates. She did read letters from Vinnie and Sue and kept up with news as she could: she noted Nathaniel Hawthorne had died. But what she had first called her prison, she said, now felt to her like "Siberia."[47] Then there was her writing, of course. Dr. Williams "is not willing I should write," she wrote Vinnie.[48] Perhaps Emily saw abandoning books as the more severe blow, because she continued to write. She wrote letters from Cambridge, telling first Vinnie then Sue that she missed them the most.[49] She corresponded with Higginson. She wrote her nephew Ned on his third birthday, trying to amuse him with a description of a bumblebee: "Emily knows a Man who drives a Coach like a Thimble, and turns the Wheel all day with his Heel."[50] And she wrote poems, perhaps as many as one hundred during the time of her distress.* She real-

---

* Alfred Habegger contends Dickinson continued to write while being treated for eye disease in 1864. He believes she brought her penciled rough drafts home to Amherst and in 1865 copied many over in ink. [Alfred Habegger, *My Wars Are Laid*

ized using her eyes to write might subvert Dr. Williams's treatment plan and perhaps prolong or further endanger her eyes, but she was willing to take the risk. Writing must have felt to her like stolen time, a precious transgression that might exact a devastating price.

From Blank to Blank —
A Threadless Way
I pushed Mechanic feet —
To stop — or perish — or advance —
Alike indifferent —

If end I gained
It ends beyond
Indefinite disclosed —
I shut my eyes — and groped as well
'Twas lighter — to be Blind — [51]

While Emily's verse always drew from more than the literal details of her life, impaired vision made her rely on her imagination even more. If she could not see distinctly or at all, she would have to tap into her metaphorical reserve. She may have found that imagination gave her a richer sense of perception than what she could discern with her eyes.[52] She also may have discovered that her other senses—touch, taste, smell, sound—had grown keener or were able to instruct her in ways she had not fully explored.* Emily's eyesight

---

Away in Books: The Life of Emily Dickinson (New York: Random House, 2001), 489.]

* Recent medical studies have confirmed that the loss of sight does enhance other senses as well as bolster memory and language use. A 2017 study by researchers at the Massachusetts Eye and Ear Infirmary discovered that the "brain 'rewires' itself to enhance other senses in blind people . . . [that enhancement] is possible through

reduced what she saw, but not what she could understand. Years later an appreciation for a more penetrating power than her eyes could produce may have been on her mind. She told Sue, "Cherish Power – dear – Remember that stands in the Bible between the Kingdom and the Glory, because it is wilder than either of them."[53] She could still imagine, and she might still stitch more poems into fascicles.

Dont put up my Thread & Needle –
I'll begin to Sow
When the Birds begin to whistle –
Better stitches – so –

These were bent – my sight got crooked –
When my mind – is plain
I'll do seams – a Queen's endeavor
Would not blush to own –

Hems – too fine for Lady's tracing
To the sightless knot –
Tucks – of dainty interspersion –
Like a dotted Dot –

Leave my Needle in the furrow –
Where I put it down –
I can make the zigzag stitches –
Straight – when I am strong –

---

the process of neuroplasticity or ability of brains to naturally adapt to our experiences." [Public Release, Massachusetts Eye and Ear Infirmary, March 22, 2017.] It is reasonable to assume that Dickinson, suffering from diminishment of her eyesight, may have experienced a degree of such enhancements herself.

Till then – dreaming I am sowing
Fetch the seam I missed –
Closer – so I – at my sleeping –
Still surmise I stitch – [54]

Although Emily initially felt her lodgings had been a "prison," she tempered her view as time went on. She later confessed that she had found friends in the "Wilderness."[55] Her rooms were in Mrs. Bangs's Boarding House, a mile from Harvard College, and a block from Cambridge's main thoroughfare with its bustling shops, livery terminal, and banks.* The greatest adjustment in her new residence was lack of privacy. Most lodgers had a private chamber and sitting area but encountered one another over meals. Emily's adaptation to so public an environment must have been a wonder to Austin, Sue, and Vinnie. Yet, within a month of arriving, she yearned to come home. She was impatient with her progress, reported "calls at the Doctor's are painful," and that she wasn't allowed to walk alone.[56] Cambridge simply was not Amherst, Emily said, even though Fanny and Loo took good care of her.[57] She missed the sound of the whippoorwill in the family orchard, wondered if apples were ripe, whether the wild geese had already crossed, and how Austin's tobacco crop had fared.[58] She was worried about her mother's cough and yet another of Vinnie's cats that had gone missing.[59] She wrote lonely letters to Sue, saying she felt at the "Centre of the Sea" as if she were submerged, and later told her "I live in the Sea always and know the Road."[60] She admitted that she "flew" most of the time, hiding from others as much as she could.[61] But she couldn't avoid eating and had to gather with the other boarders for dinner and

---

* Louisa Norcross was twenty-two at the time she lived in Mrs. Bangs's Boarding House, and her sister Frances was sixteen. Emily Dickinson was thirty-three.

polite conversation. Everyone around the dining table seemed in transition—on the verge of something better or something worse. Emily could not determine which prospect awaited her. All seemed to her a "Foreigner," she told Vinnie.[62]

By November 1864 Emily Dickinson prepared to return home. She was relieved to be leaving Cambridge, but felt hopeless about her eyes. Her problems were "sometimes easy, sometimes sad," she said.[63] Emily asked Vinnie to meet her train alone, and cautioned her sister. "Emily may not be able as she was," she told her, "but all she can, she will." She had taken on an odd habit of using the third person in talking about herself, as if the healthy Emily were as distant to her as a stranger. But she wanted to be clear with Vinnie so her sister would not be shocked by her altered appearance. "I have been sick so long I do not know the Sun," she wrote, "now the World is dead."[64]

Thomas Wentworth Higginson was feeling spiritless himself. "This turning of the leaf is a trying epoch," he wrote.[65] What he considered the most important chapter in his life—his days in the military—was over. All that remained to him were words, and he had begun to doubt if they mattered as much as he once thought. He hoped he might be able to transform his war experience into essays. "Grind it into paint," he had said, but the work did not come easy: his mind was clouded, his wife was suffering from rheumatism, and his beloved mother was near death.[66] He was grateful for distractions. A clever new boarder had moved into Mrs. Dame's Newport boardinghouse. She was a young widow with an eight-year-old son—a Mrs. Helen Hunt, originally from Amherst. He continued writing Emily and hoped to meet her someday. While he knew better than to assign autobiographical details to her poems—there was always that "supposed person" speaking in her verse—one poem appeared to address the medical crisis she now endured.[67] She had sent the poem to him earlier.

The verse struck the tension between what she could imagine and what her eyes could no longer see. She suggested that seeing with her eyes—taking in as much as she could and *owning* the visible world—was lethal. Perhaps, the poem implied, she wanted to see too much.

Before I got my eye put out
I liked as well to see –
As other Creatures, that have Eyes
And know no other way –

But were it told to me – today –
That I might have the sky
For mine – I tell you that my Heart
Would split, for size of me –

The meadows – mine –
The Mountains – mine –
All Forests – Stintless Stars –
As much of Noon as I could take
Between my finite eyes –

The Motions of The Dipping Birds –
The Morning's Amber Road –
For mine – to look at when I liked –
The News – would strike me dead –

So safer Guess –
With just my soul opon the Window pane –
Where other Creatures put their eyes –
Incautious – of the Sun – [68]

That November of 1864, voters went to the polls to cast their
ballots for President Abraham Lincoln or Gen. George McClellan.
Near Emily's boardinghouse, crowds gathered at City Hall, where
men carried a wounded Union captain up the steps. The officer
tipped his cap and told the gathering he was casting the first vote
of his life. Onlookers roared and offered three cheers.[69] The next
day, when news of Lincoln's victory reached Cambridge, supporters paraded through the streets, shouting and cheering. Two days
later—on Friday, November 11—marchers were at it again. The evening was so bright with moonlight it almost seemed like noon. As
she listened to the parade, Emily thought about what was ahead
of her. She knew her health was far from certain. Her eyes might
recover or they might become worse. Permanent blindness was
not out of the question. But what she could not see, she could hear.
"The Drums keep on for the still Man," she wrote Vinnie. The beats
for Lincoln were like a meter, counting out her prospects.[70] When
the noisy parade reached Harvard College a mile down the road,
marchers wondered if Robert Todd Lincoln would come out to greet
them. The president's son was a law student at the college, although
he had chafed under his studies and wanted to join Ulysses S. Grant
in action. In the White House, Abraham Lincoln read a telegram
from General Grant extending congratulations on his reelection.
The greeting offered the president respite from lists of the dead—
those awful bulletins as they were known—that crowded his mind.
Lincoln realized there was much to do—unfinished work—he had
called it in his address at the Soldiers' National Cemetery in Gettysburg.* For Emily, the coming days felt like an uncertain pause

* The *Springfield Republican* ran the complete text of Lincoln's Gettysburg Address
in its November 20, 1863, edition. The newspaper praised Lincoln's speech, declaring, "His little speech is a perfect gem; deep in feeling, compact in thought and

between the life she once knew and life she could not yet see. "The only News I know," she wrote Higginson, "Is Bulletins all day / From Immortality."[71]

An old friend would never forget the look of Emily's wounded eyes. Once bright hazel, they had become "melted & fused," he said, like "two dreamy, wondering wells of expression."[72] In two weeks, Emily would return home to Amherst, where her mother would cook the fricassee beans she liked so much, her father would read her news of Sherman's March to the Sea, and Vinnie would treat her older sister like a delicate teacup, fragile and liable to crack. Once again she would be surrounded by all her poems with their images of bandages, stitches, and finite eyes.*[73] "War feels to me an oblique place," Emily said.[74] Few could tell if she were talking about General Sherman or the growing darkness around her.

---

expression, and tasteful and elegant in every word and comma. Then it has the merit of unexpectedness in its verbal perfection and beauty." Surely the praise for Lincoln's address would have resonated with Dickinson. [Walter L. Powell, "'So Clear of Victory': Emily Dickinson's Gettysburg Address." November 9, 2013, Lecture at the Amherst History Museum, sponsored by the Emily Dickinson Museum.]

* Images of eyes, seeing, and sight became one of Dickinson's most frequently used tropes. Their frequency is her poetic lexicon—over three-hundred references—is topped only by pronouns and words such as "day," "know," "away," "more," "sun," "life," and "never." ["Index Words in Order of Frequency," in *A Concordance to the Poems of Emily Dickinson*, ed. S. P. Rosenbaum (Ithaca: Cornell University Press, 1964), 865.]

Eight

YOU WERE NOT AWARE THAT
YOU SAVED MY LIFE

*Tuesday, August 16, 1870 2 p.m. Thermometer 76 degrees, clouds
1 cumulous, Winds W 2, Therm Attached to Barometer 66.5, Dry Bulb
76.0, Wet Bulb 62,557.9. Humidity 43%, Remarks: Smoky.*

—Ebenezer Snell, *The Meteorological Journal Kept at Amherst College*

Although Emily knew she should lessen the strain on her eyes by not reading, she simply could not help herself. After she arrived home from medical treatment in Boston, she grabbed the family's volume of Shakespeare and looked for a place to hide. Her bedroom—private as it was—was too open to intrusion: too many raps on the door, too many calls from the kitchen to help chop chicken or bang spice for cakes. She wanted to be left alone and she wanted to raise her voice. Up on the second floor, she opened a door near the front of the house that hardly anyone ever used and climbed steep stairs to the attic. The attic was cavernous, running nearly the full expanse of the house and crowned with towering, roughhewn beams. On either side, two rounded windows cast faint pools of light. Another set of narrow steps led from the attic to the cupola, but Emily decided to stay put. She knew the views from the top were beautiful, but she needed more space than the small cupola offered. Less light too. She wanted to follow doctor's orders and not endanger her eyes. The attic was perfect for her purpose. She opened her Shakespeare to *2 Henry VI* and ripped through pages until she found the passage. "I thought I should tear the leaves out as I turned them," she said.[1] She hungered for words after months of being forbidden to read or even use a pen. She wanted to experience their full force—out loud and dramatically proclaimed. It was no accident that she sought this austere place for her performance. The words—and nothing else—were all that mattered. Then she let loose. " 'Let me hear from thee,' her voice rang out. 'For whereso'er thou art in this world's Globe / I'll have an Iris that shall find thee out.' "[2] No one found her out, alone in the attic—a would-be Shakespearean actress performing for an audience of spiders and stumbling flies. That was just what she wanted.

Emily's garret performances did not continue. Within weeks of coming home, Emily realized she would need to return to Boston for additional medical attention. Frustrated and impatient, Vinnie simply could not understand why Emily did not get well. In April 1865—only four months after she had returned from her initial treatments—Emily again was back in the boardinghouse, living with her cousins, and under the physician's care. "The Doctor says it must heal while warm Weather lasts, or it will be more troublesome," she wrote home.[3] Emily longed for the kind of solitude she'd sought in the family attic, but she would not find it in the city, and certainly not during that tumultuous spring. At almost the very moment she arrived at the boardinghouse for a second time, word came of the Confederate surrender at Appomattox. The terrible war was over. Years of battle had devastated the country and left no one untouched, not even in bucolic Amherst. Seventy-five Amherst homes mourned loved ones who had been killed, wounded, captured, or were still missing.[4] Celebrations of the war's end were everywhere across Massachusetts. Parades marched up and down

Cambridge streets, the Boston telegraph clattered so incessantly, newspapers could barely keep up, and Emily's boardinghouse buzzed with elated conversation. But a week later, Abraham Lincoln was dead, murdered by a Confederate sympathizer. The shock of Lincoln's assassination was so profound, people did not know what to say or do. For want of something more solemn than a nod, Cambridge men saluted one another. The day of Lincoln's funeral, citizens gathered at City Hall around the corner from Emily's boardinghouse. After somber speeches, people sat frozen in their seats, as if moving would unleash another nightmare. But it was the *sound* of the city that people remembered most. One person said Cambridge felt like "one mighty ocean of sound . . . rolling through space like a deep sob of anguish."[5] Emily must have found the city's grief deafening, and it intensified her own worry. She was concerned about Sue, whose sister, Harriet Gilbert Cutler, had died unexpectedly, leaving a husband and young children. Of Sue's three sisters, now only Mattie remained. "I would have drowned twice to save you sinking, dear," she wrote. "If I could only have covered your Eyes so you would'nt have seen the Water."[6] Grief returned later that fall when Mattie's two-year-old daughter died. Another "ice nest," Emily wrote.[7]

In October 1865, Emily returned to Amherst, hopeful this time that Dr. Williams's treatment had been successful. The next spring, still experiencing minor trouble, she considered going back for another round of care, but Edward Dickinson thought the crisis had passed. Deferring as she usually did to Edward's wishes, she remained at home. Father "is in the habit of me," she said.[8] As far as anyone knew, Emily's eye problems had been cured. Thankfully, blindness had been averted, although the family did purchase a copy of Dr. Williams's new book on ophthalmic science, just in case another emergency occurred.[9] Emily never again complained of complications and returned without comment to her usual activity—housework, cooking, reading, writing poems, and corresponding with Thomas Wentworth Higginson.

When Higginson realized Emily had been in Cambridge, he bombarded her with invitations to meet in Boston. Even though she was nearly forty, she again used her father as an excuse for staying home. "I must omit Boston," she told him. Father "likes me to travel with him but objects that I visit."[10] But Emily did want to see Higginson and extended her own invitation to visit Amherst. The timing for him was not right, though. Higginson was worried about his wife's health. Mary's mobility had become so compromised and her muscles so stiff, she had to turn pages of a book with a wand.[11] Then there were concerns about money. Higginson was doing everything he could to generate income. At times it seemed like he was on and off trains every week, lecturing with Emerson, speaking to women's clubs. The conflict he always felt between literature and activism remained: he should be doing more to ensure his soldiers received equal treatment under the law; he should work for woman's suffrage. He wanted to be in the thick of political action and not like one of those writers disparaged for having their heads in the clouds: men Henry Adams called poorly dressed hypocrites who gazed out windows and proclaimed, "I am raining."[12] Higginson should have taken his own advice. Years before he had written, "The more bent any man is upon action, the more profoundly he needs the calm lessons of Nature to preserve his equilibrium."[13] It was balance he needed, not a choice between action and writing. Literature kept him balanced and Emily Dickinson kept his mind on literature. The day was coming when he would finally meet his mysterious poet—a day they both would remember for the rest of their lives. From the moment he set foot on Emily's doorstep that day, Higginson would write down as much as he could recall about

what she said and how she said it. His memory would provide the
most intimate account anyone ever recorded of what it felt like to
sit across from Emily Dickinson. The two would have to wait until
August 1870 before meeting each other. The wait would be worth it.
In the meantime, they continued to write.

When another of her poems appeared in print in 1866, Emily was
immediately in touch. She was worried Higginson might have seen
the verse and doubted her vow to avoid publication. "A narrow fellow
in the grass" appeared on the front page of the February 14 *Springfield Republican* and again in the weekend edition. Even though the
poem was anonymous, she fretted about what Mr. Higginson might
think and thought it best to explain. "Lest you meet my Snake and
suppose I deceive it was robbed of me," she wrote.[14] Apparently Sue
had shared the verse with Samuel Bowles, who in turn published
it. But this time Emily was angry about its publication, especially
because someone had changed her line breaks. She was "defeated,"
she said, "of the third line by the punctuation" and complained, "the
third and fourth [lines] were one." The question mark at the end
of line three especially disturbed her. Emily did not want so hard
a stop, preferring lines three and four to glide together. The words
should move continuously to the fifth line, she may have thought,
mirroring the motion of the snake sliding from one patch of grass to
the next.* She was not pleased her literary intention had been tam-

---

* The question mark the *Republican* inserted in line 3 stayed on Emily's mind for
years. Ralph Franklin notes that in 1872, Dickinson sent another version of the
poem to Sue and placed a question mark in the middle of line three: "You may have
met him? Did you not/ His notice instant is — " [R. W. Franklin, ed., *The Poems
of Emily Dickinson* Variorum Edition. (Cambridge: The Belknap Press of Harvard
University Press, 1998), 954.] Franklin states that Dickinson probably sent Higginson a copy of the poem in 1865 before it appeared in the newspaper, hence her

pered with and added, "I had told you I did not print." She folded a
clipping of the poem into her letter as evidence of her complaint—or
perhaps to lend proof that she had another poem published.[15]

THE SNAKE.

A narrow fellow in the grass
Occasionally rides;
You may have met him—did you not?
His notice instant is,
The grass divides as with a comb,
A spotted shaft is seen,
And then it closes at your feet,
And opens further on.

He likes a boggy acre,
A floor too cool for corn,
Yet when a boy and barefoot,
I more than once at noon
Have passed, I thought, a whip-lash,
Unbraiding in the sun,
When stooping to secure it,
It wrinkled and was gone.

Several of nature's people
I know, and they know me;

anxiety about him seeing the verse in print. [Variorum Edition, 952.] The poet
continued to rework "A narrow fellow in the grass" over several years—changing
lowercase letters to capitals, inserting alternate words, taking out punctuation and
putting it in again—demonstrating her lifelong commitment to revision.

I feel for them a transport
Of cordiality.
Yet never met this fellow,
Attended or alone,
Without a tighter breathing,
And zero at the bone.

If Samuel Bowles felt the wrath of Emily's grievance over publication or the bungled lines, he did not mention it. His only comment on the poem was surprise that Emily knew the proper agricultural conditions for growing corn. "How did that girl ever know that a boggy field wasn't good for corn?" he asked Sue.[16] For Emily, the criticism over an intrusive editorial hand was her last word on the subject; it was the last time she voiced an objection to any editorial interference ever. Even when additional poems were published, she never articulated another criticism about line breaks, titles, or other changes to her manuscript text. Either she approved, disapproved and kept opinions to herself, or—as with so many other moments in her life—she simply remained silent.

With Emily home again in Amherst and Thomas Wentworth Higginson more confident his ailing wife was being well cared for in their Newport boardinghouse, the two correspondents renewed their conversation about a visit. Higginson went first and again invited Emily to Boston. He frequently made the short trip from Newport to Boston and thought the location would be a good halfway meeting point. But Emily declined, using Edward Dickinson as her old excuse. In place of Higginson's suggestion, she extended her own, but they still could not find a time. A few years later, Higginson mentioned the prospect to a botanist friend who taught at Amherst College. "I have always dreamed of coming to Amherst, to see you," he said, "& my unseen correspondent Emily Dickinson."[17] Yet, Higginson's schedule again wouldn't work, and instead he presented another meet-you-halfway invitation to Emily, this time adding Boston literary and social events as enticements. "You must come down to Boston sometimes?" he wrote. "All ladies do." Would it be possible to lure you to meetings on the third Monday of each month at Mrs. Sargent's, when somebody reads a paper and others discuss? Mr. Emerson will read next Monday, he said, and there is also a meeting of the Woman's Club, where I'll read a paper on the Greek goddesses. When it seemed he still did not have enough attractions to offer, Higginson threw in even more, adding he would be in Cambridge in June for his Harvard reunion, and later for a music festival. If that weren't enough, he gave one more desperate push. "Don't you need sea air in summer," he asked.[18] She did not. Nothing Higginson suggested could convince Emily to leave Amherst, but she wanted to see him. After corresponding for almost a decade with the man she now called her friend, she needed to tell him something important. "Could it please your convenience to come so far as Amherst I should be very glad," she carefully wrote. "Of our greatest acts we are ignorant — You were not aware that you saved my Life."[19]

Higginson decided to go. It was not Emily's startling admission alone that prompted him, but also a tragic turn of events. On August 11, 1870, his older brother Stephen Higginson died of a stroke.[20] Perhaps "Wentworth," as his family called him, could help make arrangements for burial. The very least he could do was to check on them and their home in Deerfield some twenty-five miles away from Amherst.* Sad as his duty was, Higginson realized there would never

---

* Stephen Higginson II was a merchant in business with his older brother George. In 1853, he purchased a home on Main Street in Deerfield, where the family spent most of their time. According to the 1870 census, Stephen Higginson died in Deerfield, but Thomas Wentworth Higginson's diary lists his brother's death as occur-

be a better time to visit Emily. He also wanted to visit his botanist friend, pay a call on Amherst College president William Stearns, and see chunks of meteors and dinosaur tracks in the college's acclaimed museum. He planned to drop in on the sister of a new friend too—the young widow who recently had moved into the same Newport boardinghouse where he and his wife were living. In spite of her bereavement, Mrs. Helen Hunt was outgoing, good-natured, and full of energy. With his wife unable to join him in most outdoor activities, Higginson enjoyed taking his new friend on picnics and sailing. She was kind to his wife, too, decorating the boardinghouse parlor with flowers and organizing piano evenings she thought Mary might enjoy. One night, with Mary unable to make the steps, Higginson and his new friend climbed to the boardinghouse roof to take in a lunar eclipse. "She is in deep mourning," Higginson wrote his sisters, but is also "bright & sociable & may prove an accession."[21]

Helen was mourning not only the loss of her husband in the tragic naval yard accident but the death of their remaining son as well. Young Warren Horsford Hunt—"Rennie" to his family—died of diphtheria in 1865. He was nine years old. Helen once again traveled to West Point, this time to bury Rennie next to her husband and their firstborn child. At that moment, she realized—more than at any other time in her life—she was alone. Higginson suspected Mrs. Hunt's sunny disposition masked deeper sorrows, and he was right. After Rennie died, Helen first thought she would never have the concentration to work. But when her sister urged Helen to take steps forward, she uncharacteristically snapped back. "I do not

ring in Boston. Stephen Higginson II was buried at Mount Auburn Cemetery in Cambridge, Massachusetts. [Margaret Dakin, email to the author, August 7, 2017; Cynthia Harbeson, email to the author, August 8, 2017; Thomas Wentworth Higginson's 1870 diary, Houghton Library, Harvard University.]

see why you urge me so to take myself in hand," she wrote. "As if
I had not done it!"[22] What she meant by "done it" was to immerse
herself in their parents' prescription for any malady: hard work
and cheerfulness. She also was writing. While Helen had always
wanted to write, she had produced nothing. She needed to feel
the full weight of her loss and isolation before she could re-create
herself. "I myself never took an upward step, till I left happiness
behind me," she later said.[23] She began by publishing poems about
grief. The next year she wrote book reviews and essays. She then
turned her attention to travel writing and discovered she was good
at describing places and people. Every year, when her seasonal
allergies fired up, Helen escaped to Bethlehem, New Hampshire,
where she wrote accounts of the charming town and the price it was
paying for an influx of visitors. Once, after returning to her Newport boardinghouse from a research trip, Higginson and fellow
boarders greeted her with a playful note applauding the "GREAT
AMERICAN OVERLAND TRAVELER WOMAN!"[24] Helen also set
out for Europe and wrote more essays from the continent. But it
was her poetry that captured Higginson's highest praise. He shared
her work and called Mrs. Hunt "one of the most gifted poetesses
in America."[25] Even Ralph Waldo Emerson was paying attention.
After meeting her in Newport, he said Mrs. Hunt's work deserved
recognition. He found it original, elegant, beautifully compressed,
and even pasted a newspaper clipping of one of her poems in the
front of his journal.[26] Helen grew to rely on advice from "the Colonel," as she called Higginson. She was grateful for his suggestion to
take herself more seriously, and asked him to wield his blue pencil over awkward phrases. "If you see a rent in any of the lines, you
might perhaps patch it for me, dear Col. as you so often used to," she
wrote.[27] Now that Higginson was reading both Emily's and Helen's
manuscripts, he wanted to make sure the old friends were aware of

each other's endeavors. They had much in common: both fiercely independent, both brilliant writers, both preferring to publish anonymously. Higginson knew Mrs. Hunt was preparing a small volume of poetry for publication—frantically churning out travel pieces to cover the cost of printing. Even her publisher thought she was crazy, working so hard for a book that probably wouldn't earn a cent. But Mrs. Hunt's ambition revealed her growing confidence. Self-possession was something else the two women shared. "There is always one thing to be grateful for," Emily once said, "that one is one's self & not somebody else."[28] Higginson wondered if Emily might reconsider the question of publication. Perhaps his visit to Amherst could convince her to do what Mrs. Hunt—and all literary ladies did.

Mr. Higginson's visit would be no ordinary call for Emily—not that she received many guests. Since her beloved dog, Carlo, had died, Emily seemed different.* Without her silent companion beside her, she stayed indoors and was more reclusive. The great literary productivity of the Civil War years had tapered off. She also stopped collecting her poems into stitched fascicles, and new poems remained unbound in loose sheets. There continued to be revisions to some of the eleven hundred poems she already had written—there would always be revisions—but urgency no longer propelled her. She had practical reasons for writing fewer poems. Losing the family's maid, Margaret O'Brien, to marriage in 1865

---

* Carlo died around January 1866 at approximately age seventeen. Dickinson never had another dog. One is reminded of the words Dickinson wrote about Carlo in her 1850 valentine published in the Amherst College *Indicator*: "His mistress's rights he doth defend – although it bring him to his end." [L34.] Habegger notes Carlo's death marked the "end of something" for Dickinson. [Alfred Hebegger, *My Wars Are Laid Away in Books: The Life of Emily Dickinson* (New York: Random House, 2001), 497.]

placed more household demands on all the Dickinson women. When help could not be retained, Austin noted the strain. "No girl at the other house yet," he had written Sue, who was away visiting relatives. "Consequence—depression."[29] But later, Margaret Maher joined the Dickinson family as a housekeeper and cook. Although she wavered about staying at first, she became an invaluable presence, adding stability to the household and providing more time for Emily to write.[30] But other changes were evident besides the number of poems she was writing. She was more patient, less insistent, and more forgiving of perceived slights. Although others around her were busy with their own lives, she did not feel as forsaken as she once had. When Sue gave birth to a daughter—Martha, born in 1866—Emily did not pester her sister-in-law with notes seeking attention. She showed similar acceptance of Austin's many town involvements. One night in the dark, she accompanied her brother across the street to admire the new First Church building, a construction project that had consumed Austin for years. Even Emily's aging parents were absorbed in new callings that she noted with pleasure rather than rejection. Emily Norcross Dickinson delighted in her two grandchildren and Edward joined Col. William Clark working to start an agricultural college in Amherst.* Emily's sense of self made the difference. She knew who she was. Vinnie once observed that her sister's primary job was to think. "She was the only one of us who had that to do," she said.[31] Emily no longer was *hoping* to make her family proud, as she once told Sue. The hundreds of poems in fascicles and sheets hidden away in her room bore witness to what she already had accomplished. One

---

* Edward Dickinson was one of the founders of Massachusetts Agricultural College, now the University of Massachusetts at Amherst. The college was chartered in 1863 and offered its first classes in 1867.

had only to look at her to see the maturity. Her russet hair, once the object of girlhood impulsiveness—first long, then cut short—had settled into permanence: parted in the middle and pulled back in a knot. Then there was her clothing. The fashionable fabrics she had once asked Austin to bring from Boston—the calicos, the colored cloth—had given way to dimity. She now wore one style—white dresses—all year round. They were loose-fitting, down to the ankles with lace trim, pearl buttons, and a pocket large enough for paper or a pencil. Words had shifted for her, too. When she was young, she said, words were cheap and weak: the exuberant valentines, the effusive letters to Abiah. But nothing had grown mightier to her now. Sometimes she would write a word and trace the outline of its curves with her finger. She said the word before her glowed.[32] Emily had chosen deeper rather than more abundant sustenance, a life where—as she put it—she would eat evanescence slowly.[33] Thomas Wentworth Higginson also noticed a change. In her letters, she no longer signed her name on a card, slipped inside the envelope: a game played as much for effect as reticence. Largely gone, too, were the callow signatures of "Your Gnome" and "Your Scholar." Now she signed her name with a single word: "Dickinson." That is who she had become.

Colonel Higginson was excited and nervous about paying calls. As a boy he was shy around women outside his family. To mitigate awkwardness, he would write down conversation topics. If tongue-tied, he would pull the paper from his pocket and select a matter to discuss.[34] But Higginson had plenty of questions for Emily, chief among them inquiries about her seclusion. In a letter before his visit, he had asked if Carlo's death had made her even more detached from society. It was difficult for him to understand how she could live so isolated. He certainly was awestruck by the extraordinary images that flooded her mind, but wondered if she paid a price for brilliance. It "isolates one anywhere to think beyond a certain point or have such luminous flashes as come to you," he said.[35] At times her talent made him reluctant to answer her letters, aware he never could match her artfulness. He was clumsy with words, he told her, and often missed the fine edge of her thought. But he forced himself to put aside timidity and continued to write, knowing what he could not offer in useful criticism he might be able to offer in dependability, friendship, and generosity. Higginson thought she needed someone—a person who admired her, even if he did not always understand what she was saying. "Sometimes I take out your letters & verses, dear friend," he wrote, "and when I feel their strange power, it is not strange that I find it hard to write & that long month pass. I have the greatest desire to see you, always feeling that perhaps if I could once take you by the hand I might be something to you; but till then you only enshroud yourself in this fiery mist & I cannot reach you, but only rejoice in the rare sparkles of light."[36]

Eight years had passed since Emily had first asked Higginson if her verse were alive. That was a long time to wait before meeting each other face-to-face. The night before he was to arrive in Amherst, Emily dreamed all night—not of Higginson—but of his wife, Mary, a woman the poet had only heard of infrequently. Mary Higginson's spectral appearance puzzled Emily and she was eager to share the dream. But she would have to wait twenty-four hours before telling Mr. Higginson. All day Monday, August 15, 1870, Emily expected him to arrive, but he did not. There had been a mix-up. He thought they had agreed on Tuesday, not Monday. The next day when they both realized the error, Emily sent a kindly note up-street to his Amherst House hotel. "Dear friend," she wrote, "I will be at Home and glad. I think you said the 15th. The incredible never surprises us because it is incredible."[37] With

the day straightened out, Higginson prepared to meet her. To be
honest, he was exhausted. He had spent the past year writing two
books. The *Atlantic Monthly* serialized his first novel, *Malbone; An
Oldport Romance,* and then there was an upcoming book based on
his Civil War diary. Living in Newport had also lost its allure. He
now found society life superficial and draining.[38] Perhaps Emily
knew better after all how to preserve the energy needed for creativity. As tired as he was, Higginson must have wished he could
find a place to exercise in Amherst. If he were home, he would chop
wood or swing on parallel bars at the Newport gymnasium. Exercise always invigorated him, he realized, and warded off feeling
glum.[39] But Higginson found no parallel bars in Amherst and so
he made himself comfortable. The hotel Emily had suggested was
convenient: four stories tall in the center of town with a dining
room and livery stable around the corner. It was not as hot as it had
been that summer, but it was dry. Many town wells had dried up,
and the Connecticut River was low with brown banks stretching
from shore. The town common looked terrible—scraggly and barren. It's "higglety-pigglety," one embarrassed citizen said, "with
patches of grass, gravel pits . . . old frog holes and snakes."[40] Near
the common, a few workers were pouring tar. Amherst was putting
in sidewalks, and one would run directly in front of Austin and
Edward's law office.[41] The sounds Higginson usually heard—the
clatter of Boston omnibuses, ships coming into dock at Newport's
Narragansett Bay—were nowhere to be found. An unspeakably
quiet town, he thought.

Calling card in hard, Higginson set out walking toward the
Homestead in long, loping strides. Outside the hotel, new farm
machinery was on display. Men listened to a salesman touting a
thresher's efficiency: with a boy to turn and a man to feed, it could
produce 100 bushels of oats a day.[42] Across the street, the *Amherst*

Record newspaper office posted its current edition: a "peotry" column featured a verse by Bret Harte and there was a lengthy article on growing corn. The best way to cultivate corn in New England, an expert reported, was to plow in the autumn and spread green manure in the spring. It was all about chemistry.[43] A few steps further on, at Frank Wood's Dining Rooms waiters served stewed oysters, a favorite of the local citizenry. Higginson passed a Chinese laundry, a harness shop, and Mr. Marsh's cabinet- and coffin-making establishment. A dry-goods store was draped in mourning. One of the store's proprietors, William Cutler, had died suddenly the same day as Higginson's brother. He didn't make the connection, of course, that Cutler was Susan Dickinson's brother-in-law—the man who feared she might die if she left Amherst to teach in Baltimore. Higginson followed the road down a gentle slope until it leveled off near a copse of trees and the start of a wooden fence. The fence marked the beginning of the Dickinson property. First the Evergreens, Susan and Austin's stately home, then the Homestead, Edward Dickinson's manse. The walkway rose again as it approached the front steps—a not-so-inconsequential reminder of the family's prominence. Higginson took in the sight so he could tell Mary everything. A large house. Like a country lawyer's. Brick. Flower and vegetable gardens to the east and an apple orchard. Pears too.[44] From where he stood, he could see the train depot and the distant line of the Pelham hills. Mrs. Hunt used to laugh at how timidly Colonel Higginson would knock at her room in the boarding house. He knocks like a baby, she said, and then slides in edgewise.[45] Higginson made no such hesitant entrance at the Dickinsons. He knocked, presented his card, and was ushered into a dark parlor on the left. Then he waited.

First he heard her. From upstairs on the second floor came the sound of quick, light steps—footsteps that sounded like a child's.

Then she entered. A plain woman with two bands of reddish hair, not particularly good-looking, wearing a white pique dress. The white stunned him. It was exquisite. A blue worsted shawl covered her shoulders. She seemed fearful to him, breathless at first, and extended her hand, not to shake—but to offer something. "These are my introduction," she said, handing him two day-lilies. "Forgive me if I am frightened; I never see strangers & hardly know what I say."[46] Then Emily looked at him. A tall man in his mid-forties with joyful face, she thought.[47] Dark-haired, whiskered, graceful, he looked kind. Higginson did not reach into his pocket to fish out a topic for conversation. He did not need to. Once they sat, Emily began talking and she did not stop. "When I lost the use of my Eyes," she told him "it was a comfort to me to think there were so few real *books* that I could easily find some one to read me all of them."[48] She wondered how people got through their days without thinking. "How do most people live without any thoughts," she said. "There are many people in the world (you must have noticed them in the street) How do they live. How do they get strength to put on their clothes in the morning." She was full of aphorisms, sentences that seemed to have been crafted earlier in her mind and that she wanted to share. "Women talk: men are silent: that is why I dread women; Truth is such a *rare* thing it is delightful to tell it; Is it oblivion or absorption when things pass from our minds?" At times Emily seemed self-conscious and asked Higginson to jump in. But every time he tried, she was off again, and words tumbled out, almost uncontrollably. He tried to recall every phrase, every thought, even her tone, humor, and asides. "My father only reads on Sunday – he reads *lonely & rigorous* books," she said. Once, she recalled, her brother brought home a novel that they knew their father would not condone. Austin hid it under the piano cover for Emily to find. When she was young, she said, and read her first real

book, she was in ecstasy. "This then is a book!" she had exclaimed.
"And are there more of them!" She boasted about her cooking and
said she made all the bread for the family. Puddings, too. "People
must have puddings," she said. The way she said "puddings"—so
dreamy and abstracted—sounded to Higginson as though she were
talking about comets. Emily said her life had not been constrained
or dreary in any way. "I find ecstasy in living," she explained. The
"mere sense of living is joy enough." When at last the opportunity
arose, Higginson posed the question he most wanted to ask: Did
you ever want a job, have a desire to travel or see people. The question unleashed a forceful reply. "I never thought of conceiving that
I could ever have the slightest approach to such a want in all future
time." Then she loaded on more. "I feel I have not expressed myself
strongly enough." Emily reserved her most striking statement for
what poetry meant to her, or rather how it made her feel. "If I read
a book [and] it makes my whole body so cold no fire ever can warm
me I know *that* is poetry," she said. "If I feel physically as if the top
of my head were taken off, I know *that* is poetry. These are the only
way I know it. Is there any other way." Emily was remarkable. Brilliant. Candid. Deliberate. Mystifying. After years of waiting, he
was finally sitting across from Emily Dickinson of Amherst, and
all he wanted to do was listen.

Following goodbyes, Higginson walked down the granite steps
and headed toward town. He needed to clear his head and let settle what had just happened. Perhaps he could drop by President
Stearns's office over at the college, he thought, or look up Mrs.
Hunt's sister. Maybe stare at fossils. When he reached the college, the natural history museum was closed, so he made his way to
Mrs. Banfield's home. He found Helen Hunt's sister engaging and
lively; the two women even looked alike. Higginson and Ann Banfield wished that Helen could have joined them, but she was in New

Hampshire working—she was always working. With only months left before her book of poems would go to press, Helen was writing essays nonstop in order to pay for the poetry collection's printing. "I am working away at my *trade*," she had written her sister, "send off $45 worth of Ms. tomorrow. . . . I must earn every cent I spend till Jan."[49] Higginson returned to the college after his social call and met with President Stearns. William Stearns knew Emily, of course, and mentioned how proud Vinnie was of her sister. Everyone knew the Dickinsons were proud people, but Vinnie—Stearns emphasized—was especially loyal to her older sister. Stearns noted he would be on the same train as Higginson the next morning. They could talk more then about the Dickinsons.

Before returning to the hotel for the night, Higginson called once more on Emily. On the parlor table, he caught a glimpse of his nature book, *Out-Door Papers*, as well as his new novel. Emily had read everything he had ever written, even if she was not subtle about acknowledging it. She must have felt more relaxed than earlier in the day, and entered the parlor informally. Her mind was still on her family and she still wanted to talk. "I never had a mother," she said. "I suppose a mother is one to whom you hurry when you are troubled." She spoke of her father, too, and shared a story Higginson could hardly believe, a tale about not knowing how to tell time. "I never knew how to tell time by the clock till I was 15," she said. "My father thought he had taught me but I did not understand & I was afraid to say I did not & afraid to ask any one else lest he should know." They talked of Helen Hunt and Emily recalled the afternoon that Helen and her husband sat at her tea table and Major Hunt fed Carlo scraps from the table. She thought Mr. Hunt was the most interesting man she had ever met. It struck Higginson that the time he spent with Emily that day had been an act of self-definition for her: her torrent of words was like a personal and literary manifesto.

She reminded him of Bronson Alcott, Louisa May's father—although Emily was not pompous or overbearing. Higginson hoped he could remember everything. Before he rose to leave, Emily placed a photograph in his hand. It was an image of Elizabeth Barrett Browning's grave, a memento Josiah Holland had brought back from Europe and presented to her a few days before. He accepted the gift reluctantly, knowing it probably meant more to her than it would to him. Like the daylilies from earlier, he knew the photograph was Emily's way of saying thank you. "Gratitude is the only secret that cannot reveal itself," she told him. Higginson said he hoped to see her again sometime, and she abruptly interrupted him. "Say in a long time," she corrected, "that will be nearer. Some time is nothing." With a hundred thoughts whirling in his head, Higginson retraced his steps back to the hotel, past the Chinese laundry and the oysters and the livery stables. He needed to go to bed. But before turning in, he compiled notes, trying to recall it all. He pulled out another sheet and wrote a letter to his wife. "I shan't sit up tonight to write you all about E.D. dearest but if you had read Mrs. Stoddard's novels you could understand a house where each member runs his or her own selves.* Yet I only saw her."[50] Miss Dickinson said many things, he told her, some remarks you would have found foolish and some I thought wise, he wrote. Higginson made one final note before retiring, a quick entry in his diary. Meeting Emily Dickinson quite equaled my expectation, he wrote.[51] It had been a momentous day: one he would never forget. As he turned down the lamp, he hoped he would be able to calm his mind and get to sleep. He wanted to wake up early and see the fossils.

---

* Elizabeth Drew Stoddard (1823–1902) is best known for her novel *The Morgesons* (1862), which features a female protagonist struggling between societal norms and her own desire for independence.

Most people in Amherst were unaware of Thomas Wentworth Higginson's visit with Emily Dickinson. They had been preoccupied with the excitement at Mr. and Mrs. Gray's house. Roxalina Gray had a way with plants—and the week before, her rare night-blooming cereus unfolded just as evening fell and then closed forever right before dawn. Mrs. Gray opened her doors the night the flower bloomed and neighbors filed in to witness the phenomenon. The petals were enormous—as big as dinner plates—and smelled like honey.[52] For Emily, Mr. Higginson's visit had been just as miraculous. It felt unreal to her as if a phantom had entered the family parlor and transformed it. "Contained in this short Life / Are magical extents," she wrote.[53] Emily felt elated, emboldened, and slightly off-kilter. Hearing herself talk so much, she said, made her feel as though the words rushing out were not sentences at all, but events.[54] After the call, Emily reached again for the family Shakespeare and turned to *Macbeth*. "Now a wood / Comes toward Dunsinane," she read, reliving how mystical her friend's visit had been.[55] Yet as exhilarated as she felt, it was gratitude that lingered. When she thought about all Higginson had done for her—answering that first letter, writing her from the battlefront when he was wounded, continuing to write even when he felt his life had lost its purpose, urging her to take time to perfect her art—she felt nearly speechless. Higginson's generosity "disables my Lips," she said and magic, "as it electrifies, also makes decrepit."[56] It was not only that he had read her poems—although she was thankful for that. It was that he had been constant. When she sought words to thank him, she reached not for metaphors from nature or images of planets and dreams that she had been working with. She went deeper. She chose anatomy. "The Vein cannot thank the Artery," she told him, "but her solemn indebtedness to him, even the stolidest admit."[57] That's what Emily meant by saying Higginson had saved her life: her connection to him was vital and sustaining. Emily gave poetry to herself, but Higginson had affirmed her choice, and that to her was salvation. Over the next months, the thought of seeing him again played on her mind with eerie repetition. It "opens and shuts," she said "like the eye of the Wax Doll."[58] She hoped he would return to Amherst someday or in "a long time"—perhaps that would be nearer.

Before leaving town, Higginson took in the fossils. The dinosaur footprints looked like the scratches of ancient birds, he thought, or a bit like Emily Dickinson's handwriting. On the train he sat for a while with President Stearns and they talked more about Emily and her family. It was an all-day ride through Vermont and into New Hampshire and Higginson could not stop thinking about Dickinson. He kept recalling her remark about puddings, her light step, and the imposing weight of her ancestral home. Higginson wrote additional notes and placed them in his valise for safekeeping. While he always tried to record his thoughts, he was especially concerned about capturing every particular about meeting the poet—"his" poet. It was as if he had some momentary glimpse into the future and could imagine generations of readers who wanted to know more. He wrote his wife again and told her about running into Edward Dickinson before leaving town. "Thin dry, & speechless," he said, adding, "I saw what her life has been."[59] Jostling along on the tracks, miles from Amherst, he said Emily Dickinson had dazzled him, but had also made him uncomfortable. She was not capable of casual conversation, he told Mary, or of everyday friendship. It took every ounce of his being to meet her level of intellectual intensity. "I never was with any one who drained my nerve power so much," he admitted. "Without touching her, she drew from me. I am glad not to live near her."[60]

When Higginson's train crossed into Vermont, he stared out the window and could barely see the Connecticut River. Rocks and sandbars emerged where there once was rushing current. There had been little rain. Every moment of his life Thomas Wentworth Higginson had studied the natural world. Rivers, hills, and pastures were a source of inspiration, a canvas on which to project his thoughts and search for answers. "Nature' is what We know - / But have no Art to say," Emily once wrote.[61] Passing through Brattleboro, he surveyed the fields. They were as brown as those in Amherst. Grapes had begun to shrivel and farmers were already feeding hay to their cows. In a sign of early autumn, yellow leaves fell to the ground. Yet as dry as everything was, fruit was in abundance.[62] It seemed a wonder. Recently Emily had bitten into a pear that had "hips like hams, and the flesh of bonbons," she said.[63] Years earlier when he'd been a young man, Higginson had spent time at Brook Farm near Boston. That great experiment in communal living had intrigued him, and he had made several trips to examine the dairy and farming operations. Before he became a writer, he had considered becoming a farmer. Growing peaches interested him.[64] He liked the idea of being closely connected to the seasons and imagined planting a tree, watching it grow, picking its fruit, and transforming slices into pies and thick preserves. Down in Amherst, an editor prepared his copy for next week's edition of the newspaper. This season there will be a good crop of apples, he wrote.[65] The New England Seven— as they were called—had names that were poetry themselves: Baldwins, Delicious, Wealthies, Gravensteins, Rhode Island Greenings, Northern Spies, Macintosh.[66] Higginson never got around to asking Emily if she was interested in preparing a book of poetry like Helen Hunt was doing. Perhaps he couldn't find the nerve, feeling that if he pressed too hard, Emily would withdraw, vanishing like those sparkles of light he always associated with her. But the man who never became a peach farmer knew there was a time to sow and a time to reap. For Emily Dickinson, the harvest was yet to come.

Nine

SUCCESS IS COUNTED SWEETEST

Tuesday, October 10, 1876 2 p.m. Temperature 63.4 degrees. Clouds 2 str. Wind SW 3. Barometer 29.431. Humidity 51 Remarks none.
—Sabra Snell, *The Meteorological Journal Kept at Amherst College*

Helen Hunt's first mistake was asking Emily Dickinson for travel advice. Her second was taking it. After Thomas Wentworth Higginson urged the two childhood friends to reconnect, Helen made plans to see Emily again. She stopped by Amherst in August 1873 on her way to New Hampshire, where her sister now lived. After so much travel across the country and in Europe, Helen had taken to viewing her hometown as a backwater. She still had affection for the landscape and memories of her girlhood, but she also was quick to find fault. People didn't dress well. The streets were dusty. Old-timers told the same tiresome stories. And certain preachers bellowed their way through sermons just as they always had. When she checked into the local boardinghouse Emily had recommended, she was not in the best mood. The room was awful: damp and stifling. A recent bout of diphtheria complicated matters and made Helen's persistent problems with her lungs flare up again. She worried things would get worse, and blamed her health—blamed everything—on Amherst. There "was a positive miasm about the house," she complained to her sister. "I was pros-

trated in *twelve* hours! . . . Me! Of all people! If there had not been a
remarkably intelligent & skilled homeopathic Dr. there, I think I
should never have got away alive! . . . [He] checked the dysentery—
& orders me to fly at once."[1] Helen obeyed the doctor's orders and
made her way to Worcester, securing lodgings where she previously
had boarded. Even though she had to share the room with a young
woman who had been in bed for five days with cholera, she found
the conditions an improvement. In retrospect, consulting a woman
as reclusive as Emily Dickinson for travel advice was misguided at
best. And as for her new roommate's cholera, Helen had her suspi-
cions. "Brought from Amherst no doubt," she huffed.[2] Helen's visit
with Emily would have to be postponed, but she would not abandon
plans to see her. Helen never gave up. It was one of her best and—
some would say—worst qualities. For decades, the two old friends
had tried to find the right time to meet and talk about literature.
Helen already had an agenda in mind: she believed Emily should
publish and share her work with the world. While other writers
and editors agreed that the poet's verse should see the light of day,
no one—including Thomas Wentworth Higginson—ever dared to
speak so forcefully to Dickinson. But Helen was not like other people. She was passionate, pragmatic, persuasive, and impossible to
turn away. Dickinson and Helen Hunt would find their moment to
talk soon and—when it came—their conversation would have consequences for generations to come.

From time to time, other girlhood friends wanted to visit Emily,
but she demurred. The letters she once sent friends all but begging
them to visit had tailed off. Nearly all her schoolmates had married,
were raising children, or had moved, and she felt little in common with them. Abby Wood from Emily's Amherst Academy days
had come to visit recently, and was startled to discover Emily had
become the town enigma: darting upstairs when a visitor knocked

or fleeing the garden when a carriage drove up. "Quick as a trout," someone said.[3] Children especially had stories about the secluded Miss Emily. One boy remembered stumbling upon her when he cut through the Dickinson property in search of playmates. There she was, standing on a rug near the barn, potting plants. The boy almost froze. But Emily motioned for him to join her and soon they were talking about favorite flowers. Before he dashed off, Emily snipped blossoms and handed them to the boy for his mother. He raced home, clutching the bouquet as if it were golden treasure.[4] But Abby Wood thought surely that she would not have to rely on cutting through the Dickinson property to see her friend again. After all, she had traveled so far. Since marrying Rev. Daniel Bliss two decades ago, Abby and her husband had settled in Beirut, where they were rearing four children, and where Reverend Bliss had founded the Syrian Protestant College.* Over the years, Abby had sent Emily plant specimens from the Mediterranean and when Austin's First Church building project was near completion, the Blisses had shipped cedarwood from the Holy Land for the new pulpit.[5] Yet even with the kindness Abby had shown her, Emily offered her usual response to a request for a visit: she said no. Abby was astonished, and tried persuading Emily with some good-natured teasing. The second attempt worked, and Emily invited Abby in. Other friends, such as Samuel Bowles, received similar rejection. Once when he'd stopped by, Emily refused to leave her upstairs chamber. He stood at the bottom of the stairs and bellowed for her to come down. He even swore—mildly—calling her a "damned rascal." She relented finally. Later in a note, she thanked Bowles for the visit and signed the letter, "Your Rascal," playfully adding, "I

---

* Daniel Bliss was president of the Syrian Protestant College from 1866 to 1902. The college is now American University in Beirut and enrolls nearly 9,000 students.

washed the Adjective."* The family had a name for Emily's refus-
als and darting out of a room. "Elfing it," they said.[6] There was no
question she delighted in occasional mischief, but Emily was serious about her privacy and required it to accomplish her work. She
had articulated her point of view in a poem years earlier.

> The Soul selects her own Society –
> Then – shuts the Door –
> To her divine Majority –
> Present no more – [7]

Thomas Wentworth Higginson was a person Emily never refused.
On a winter day in 1873, he paid a second call at the Homestead.
His schedule was tight, his visit brief, and he took few notes.
But he wrote his sisters the little he could remember. Emily
only sees a few others, he told them, and never goes outside her
father's ground. This time she had greeted him with a pale pink
flower from her conservatory—a *Daphne odora*—and once more
she dressed in white. Higginson promised his sisters the next
time they came to Newport, he would read some of Dickinson's
verse. He had long ago given up critiquing her poems, and the
letters between the two had taken on a different tone. Now when
they wrote, they shared personal news. We come together as old
and tired friends, Higginson told her. "I hope you will not cease
to trust me and turn to me; and I will try to speak the truth to
you, and with love."[8] Earlier she remembered the season of his
first visit. It was "Mighty Summer," she wrote. "Now the Grass
is Glass and the Meadow Stucco."[9] Perhaps some instinct had put

---

* Some scholars report Bowles called Dickinson "a damned wretch." By "washing
the adjective," she meant she had deleted the "damned." [L515.]

her in a somber mood and she hinted that she thought the second visit could be their last.

The thought of visiting Emily had grown stronger for Helen Hunt. From the many poems Colonel Higginson had been sharing, Helen had created a volume of her friend's verse. She wanted to talk about Dickinson's poems, especially the confounding ones, and she wanted to discuss a writer's responsibility to the world. Once another writer had tried to tell Emily what she owed society and received a stinging reply. A "Miss P" had written, asking for poems to support a worthy cause.* Emily declined the request and burned the letter. It did not seem to bother her that Miss P might be offended. She's probably off "extricating humanity from some hopeless ditch," Emily scoffed.[10] But Helen was undeterred by Emily's resistance, and, she had another reason for wanting to speak with her. When it came to poetry, Helen now spoke from experience. The volume of verses she had worked so hard to write *and* pay for had met with critical acclaim—and rightly so. The book, published under her pen name "H. H." was so popular that publishers issued an expanded edition almost immediately. *Verses,* one critic said, places "H. H." not only above all American poetesses, but all English poetesses as well. Only Elizabeth Barrett Browning shows a greater range of imagination, he added. Other reviewers compared her intellect to Hawthorne, her lyricism to Wordsworth, and her nature poetry to Andrew Marvell and Emerson. With her travel essays, the short stories she was writing and now a book of poetry, Helen Hunt had become a respected and cel-

* Most critics believe "Miss P" was novelist, poet, and essayist Elizabeth Stuart Phelps, although Dickinson biographer Alfred Habegger suggests she might have been Elizabeth Peabody. [Alfred Habegger, *My Wars Are Laid Away in Books: The Life of Emily Dickinson* (New York: Random House, 2001), 545.]

ebrated American writer. Higginson was thrilled and eager to hear what Emily thought of Helen's verse. Dickinson said she liked the poems immensely and pronounced them stronger than any women's poetry since Elizabeth Barrett Browning and Mrs. Lewes.* "Truth like Ancestor's Brocades," she said, "can stand alone."[11] Around the time Helen's verse was published, another girlhood friend produced a volume of poetry. Emily Fowler Ford—Noah Webster's granddaughter, who helped edit the Amherst Academy student publication, *Forest Leaves*—had been publishing for years in newspapers and the *Atlantic*. But the reviews for Mrs. Ford's book did not equal those for Mrs. Hunt's. The *Springfield Republican* observed Emily Ford writes too many poems, and "damages the effect of what she has said by what she keeps on saying."†[12] Regardless of the local opinion of Mrs. Ford, Higginson marveled at the three women writers who were born and raised in Amherst, Massachusetts: Helen Fiske Hunt, Emily Fowler Ford, and Emily Dickinson. What was it, he wondered, about that small college town that had produced so many literary women? "Amherst must be a *nest* of poetesses," he told a friend.[13]

But it was Emily Dickinson who had the most important poems to offer, Helen believed. She did not belittle her own work, but—

* Mary Ann Evans also was known by her married name, Mrs. George Henry Lewes. She wrote under the pseudonym, George Eliot.

† The opening poem of Emily Fowler Ford's book of poetry confirmed the assessment of the *Springfield Republican* reviewer: "I am no poet, and I know it./ But if a wild bloom lingers/ within my loving fingers/ From the woods I joyful bring it;/ In my sweet friend's lap I fling it./ Can you blame me that I show it." Years later after refusing a visit from Mrs. Ford and rejecting her offer to visit Brooklyn, Emily acknowledged receipt of her friend's volume of verse. "The little Book will be subtly cherished," she told her old friend—as noncommittal a statement as Dickinson ever wrote. [L781.]

when it came to poetry—Hunt recognized Dickinson's verse was of a wholly different order. Not only did she want to talk with Emily about literature in general, but she also wanted to talk about publishing. Unlike Higginson, who no longer broached certain subjects, or Abby Wood, who approached her old friend with gentle nudging, or even Samuel Bowles who playfully cursed, Helen simply barreled in. She wanted a serious, face-to-face conversation. But another one of Helen's wanderings delayed the visit even longer. The attack of diphtheria that had shortened Helen's visit to Amherst had also canceled a long-awaited journey to Colorado. She had wanted to see the Rocky Mountains in 1873 with May Alcott, Louisa's sister—but May could not go.[14] She then persuaded a Boston friend, but the two women had to turn back when Helen became ill. That's when she had ended up in the damp Amherst boardinghouse. But now that she was feeling better, Helen wanted to set out again for Colorado. She had heard the mountains offered the perfect climate for people with respiratory disease. Not taking any chances on a second attempt across the plains, she convinced the Amherst homeopathic doctor to accompany her, along with a nurse. Once they'd reached Colorado's eastern slope, Helen's first sight of the mountains was dispiriting. "There stretched before me, to the east, a bleak, bare, unrelieved, desolate plain. There rose behind me, to the west, a dark range of mountains, snow-topped, rocky-walled, stern, cruel, relentless." It was not what she'd hoped for. "One might die of such a place alone," she wrote.[15] Yet as she always did, Helen made the best of it. The doctor and nurse returned to Massachusetts, and Helen found a room in a Colorado Springs boardinghouse on a street known locally as Dead Man's Row. Helen appreciated the dark humor; she was not the only person with lung problems who had moved to Colorado. Besides, she kept herself busy: writing more short stories, getting into a fight with William Dean Howells over grammar, and fuming over a review in the *Nation* that declared her poems lacked womanly grace. In 1872, Roberts Brothers of Boston—a new publisher for her—released Helen's book of essays, *Bits of Talk about Home Matters*, an ironic title, considering Helen had never owned a home. Over time Colorado had become more appealing to her. "Mrs. Helen Hunt's health is greatly improved by the 'marvelous sunshine' of Colorado Springs," the *Springfield Republican* reported. "She says 'it is enough, almost, to raise the dead.' "[16] As much as she was growing to love the west, Helen still thought about a trip back east—and Emily Dickinson. But that was before Samuel Bowles introduced her to William Sharpless Jackson, a Colorado banker and executive with the Denver and Rio Grande Railroad. At first Mr. Jackson did not seem the kind of man Helen would find engaging. He was literal-minded, devoted to his financial books, and not prone to the kind of enthusiasm Helen always displayed. But he was taken with her independence and vitality, and she found his stability a comfort. Helen called him Will and, for some inexplicable reason, he called her Peggy. They spent nearly every Sunday outdoors in the mountains, and once when Helen wanted a perfect view of the sun coming up over Pikes Peak, the two camped on the floor in an empty Manitou Springs tollbooth, waiting for sunrise.[17]

It was just as well that Helen Hunt did not return to Amherst anytime soon. Emily had other concerns, and was especially worried about her father. As early as 1871, Edward had begun having health problems. When an unspecified illness made him take to his bed, Emily feared he would die. "Now in a piercing place," she had written Fanny and Loo Norcross.[18] Her father's strong sense of duty and determination to erase the failures of his own father had exacted a price. College officials hailed Edward as perfectly "perpendicular," but that was the problem.[19] He never played, Emily said, and seldom gave in to an easy moment. One of his rare displays of exuberance was the purple ink he used to write letters home. But the letters themselves were filled with the driest of details and often trailed off with empty phrases, such as "nothing new," "no more to say," or "I can think of nothing particular."[20] Even the "straightest engine has its leaning hour," Emily wrote her cousins.[21] Edward eventually recovered from that illness, and when the Panic of 1873 threw most of the nation's railroads into receivership, he once again ran for political office. Railroads were everything to him. Arguably the proudest moment of his life came when the Amherst, Belchertown Palmer Line named a locomotive after him: the *Edward Dickinson*.[22] Against every vow he'd made about leaving politics forever, he placed his name on the ballot in 1873 for the Massachusetts House of Representatives. He won—and the next year, the seventy-one-year-old legislator trudged between Amherst and Boston as a freshman representative. His absence was hard on the family. Austin and Sue's adolescent son, Ned, recently had an attack of inflammatory rheumatism and worried the family. As much as Edward was concerned about his grandson, he was also committed to using his political clout to complete the Hoosac Tunnel, linking rail service between Boston and Albany. The project had been mired in problems for years: financial debacles, engineering mistakes, and blasting disasters.* During a legislative recess, Edward had made a trip home and—before leaving Boston—he'd stopped at a bookstore to select two volumes he thought Emily might enjoy: a biography of Theodore Parker and new book of poems by Mrs. Lewes.

---

* The nearly five-mile-long Hoosac Tunnel was constructed in the Berkshires of Western Massachusetts near the town of North Adams. Until the twentieth century, it was the longest tunnel in North America. The tunnel opened in 1875, and still is used today for freight rail service.

But even while home, he worked demanding hours in his Amherst law office. A local judge noticed the light burning in Edward's legal chambers long after most residents had retired for the night.[23] On June 16, 1874, Representative Dickinson was back in Boston, and rose to make a speech on the statehouse floor on behalf of the railroad. It had been a miserably hot day with lowering thunderclouds.[24] As he spoke, Edward felt faint and sat down. Alarmed, a colleague asked if he could walk the stricken Mr. Dickinson back to his hotel on Tremont Street. Edward said yes. He knew something was wrong and wanted to return to Amherst immediately.[25] That evening Emily was eating supper with her mother and Vinnie when Austin burst through the Homestead door, a telegram in his hand. She instantly knew by the look on his face that something terrible had happened. Father is ill, her brother said, and he and Vinnie must go to Boston at once. Everyone jumped and rushed to retrieve valises and hats. It was six o'clock. The train had already gone through. Vinnie and Austin would have to take the carriage. From the barn came the clatter of harnesses and straps as a stablehand dressed the horses. Then another dispatch arrived. It was too late. Edward Dickinson was dead.*[26]

It seemed fitting that a locomotive should bring Edward Dickinson's body home. An undertaker met the train at the depot and escorted the coffin up the hill to the Homestead. When he finished his work and left the house, Austin stared down at his father's face as if for the first time. Then he leaned over and kissed him. "There, father, I never dared do that while you were living," he said.[27] Over the next three days, the town of Amherst came to a standstill.

---

* A Boston doctor conjectured Edward's cause of death was apoplexy—what would now be considered a stroke. Later the family discovered the physician had administered morphine to Mr. Dickinson. That drug was poison to Father, Austin said.

First Church canceled its strawberry festival, the college suspended classes, and out of respect for Amherst's leading citizen, the bank, the marble works, and even tonsorial artist James A. Williams closed their doors. The only businesses still busy were the hotel and the livery stables: so many lawmakers, judges, mayors, and college trustees had arrived for the funeral, extra hands were needed. On July 19, 1874, workers carried College Hall settees over to the Homestead for crowds gathering on the lawn. Not everyone could fit into the Dickinsons' parlors or library. Vinnie was everywhere, consoling friends, tending to details of the service, and making sure neighbors had a place to sit. Her strength did not escape Austin's notice; he'd marveled at his sister's composure, and his mother's too. Austin, however, was another matter. His sorrow was so overwhelming it blurred his thinking. He could not remember to whom he had talked or what anyone said. His grief frightened his seven-year-old daughter, Mattie, who tried to do whatever she could to make things better. She scurried around the house setting out vases of lilacs and daisies. Although no one had seen Emily, Mattie knew where she was. Aunt Emily was upstairs alone in her chamber with the door opened a crack. She had caught her niece's attention and whispered a caution in her ear: don't cut all the blossoms from the garden, she told her.[28] Emily never came downstairs. The only friend she spoke to that day was Samuel Bowles. Perhaps she knew he would never leave without seeing her. After a brief service in the family library, a line of eighteen pallbearers carried Edward's coffin through the back fields behind the Homestead to the cemetery. Emily stayed behind in her room as the coffin was lowered into the ground next to the graves of Edward's mother and father. Later someone said Edward Dickinson's death reversed all the laws of nature for his eldest daughter. "I thought I was strongly built," Emily wrote weeks later, "but this stronger has undermined me."[29] She did not visit her father's grave the day he was buried. She did not visit his grave the rest of her life.[30]

In one of the last letters Edward wrote home, he had been worrying about pears. It seemed such a mundane concern: were the pear trees in the family orchard producing the best fruit? But Edward had the future on his mind. He wanted to clear away dead limbs and splice new shoots onto the trees so they would bear fruit for years and years to come.[31] What he needed, he had thought, was a graft to produce descendants—a single worthy scion. Emily kept thinking of the sound of her father's voice. There was the militant way he thundered out morning prayers, in a voice that startled her: "'I say unto you!' "[32] But she also recalled a voice that came in fugitive moments, she said, when he forgot the lawyer and became the man. Then he sounded lonely and adrift: a foreigner, she observed.[33] Edward once told Emily that he felt his entire life had been passed in a wilderness or on an island. She knew what he meant. She could hear the way his voice often sounded faraway and removed—a "sea tone," she called it.[34] The last afternoon they were together, she heard that voice again. It had been during the legislative recess, when Edward was working so late in his law office. "The last Afternoon that my Father lived," she later wrote, "though with no premonition – I preferred to be with him, and invented an absence for Mother, Vinnie being asleep. He seemed peculiarly pleased as I oftenest stayed with myself, and remarked as the Afternoon withdrew, he 'would like it not to end.' His pleasure almost embarrassed me," she continued, "and my Brother coming – I suggested they walk. Next morning I woke him for the train – and saw him no more." Edward's vulnerability in their last moments together was too much for Emily to bear. "His Heart was pure and terrible," she said, "and I think no other like it exists."[35]

After hearing the news, Mr. Higginson wrote Emily gently. Are you working yet? Are you able to read? Yes, she replied. She was able to dip into books, but grief had overpowered her ability to concentrate.[36] Emily wanted Higginson to come again to Amherst. She always did. It would be priceless, she told him, precious.[37] But his schedule would not permit it and so she spent months shuffling around in what she called "Little — wayfaring acts."[38] She visited with her father's old friend Judge Otis Lord, who was in Amherst for a week, gathered up fruit for neighbors, and sent orders to Cutler's stores for family provisions: 10 cents' worth of brown sugar, 1 can of corn, 1 cup prunes, 35 bars of soap, and 2 corsets—one later returned.[39] She also made out her will. Oddly, Edward Dickinson had not prepared a document, leaving Austin to sort out everything. Now more keenly aware of the problems such a situation could produce, Emily wrote her final wishes, bequeathing to Vinnie "all my estate, real and personal, to have and to hold the same to her and her heirs, and assigns forever." Judge Lord's wife, Elizabeth, served as one of the witnesses to her signature. Neighbor Luke Sweetser and Margaret Maher, the Dickinsons' faithful maid, were the others.[40] Grief continued to weigh on her. "Affection . . . helps me up the Stairs at Night," she wrote.[41] The books her father had selected in Boston before his last trip home—the Theodore Parker and Mrs. Lewes—lay unread in the family library. She did not have the strength to open, let alone read, them.[42] Emily wanted Higginson to have the books—a gesture linking the two most important men in her life. He demurred at first, a bit embarrassed, as he had been when Emily offered the postcard of Elizabeth Barrett Browning's grave that Josiah Holland had given her. Why she always was quick to give away personal gifts, he must have wondered.* Before Emily could restore herself emotionally, another family tragedy hit.

---

* Higginson appears to have accepted the book of George Eliot poems, informing Emily he already owned the Parker biography.

Almost a year to the day her husband died, Emily Norcross Dickinson suffered a stroke. Her memory was impaired, she wandered around the house looking for Edward, and paralysis weakened her hand and foot. Her "Will followed my Father," Emily said, "and only an idle Heart is left, listless for his sake."[43] Once again, shades at the Homestead were drawn, and the rooms were saturated with the smell of camphor and roses.[44] Higginson wrote with his concern and inquired again if she had the concentration to write. This time Emily was definitive. "You asked me if I wrote now," she said. "I have no other Playmate."[45]

The losses altered everyone in the family. Austin "set a face of flint to the world," some said.[46] He was worried about Ned's health, made constant visits across the path to check on his mother and sisters, sometimes eating his breakfast there instead of at home. He also took on more work. Amherst College Trustees appointed him treasurer of the college, succeeding his father and grandfather. The new position meant additional income, but it came with headaches. Austin discovered the college books were not in the best order, and he found it exasperating to manage the college's money in the first place. "It is the most almighty queer thing that I should be picked out to spend my life handling dirty money," he said. "I don't care a thing about it!"[47] One day at the Amherst train station, he lost his temper completely. As Austin waited to board, a friend got off. Neighbors greeted the man cheerfully and asked about a recent fishing trip. Austin stood by, envious and fuming. In a voice loud enough for everyone to hear, he berated his friend for having fun, declaring he had little time for recreation. Townspeople stood with their mouths agape at Austin's anger.[48] Nothing, however, pointed more to the aggrieved state of his mind than the way he drove his horse and carriage home every night. Mattie remembered her father would fly down the street at breakneck speed, heedless of who or what might be in his way. The horse's nostrils flared, dust flew, and cats and the family's favorite turkey scattered for cover. As he reached the house, Austin would turn the corner on one wheel and violently yank the horse to a stop at the carriage shed.[49] His actions were reckless, dangerous even. Perhaps he intended them to be.

For Vinnie, the family's sorrow ended a chance for life on her own. Long ago, she had stopped going on walks with suitors. Mr. Howland, who gave her a ring when they were young, had settled into married life and had children. Another suitor, Joseph Lyman, was dead.* Vinnie once told Joseph she had half a mind to give up gentlemen admirers altogether, and by the age of forty-two she had.[50] When her father was alive, she feared her flirtations—or any action—would displease him. She still did. She said she felt she had a right to freedom, but was not strong enough to take it.[51] Lavinia could not be called reclusive like Emily, but she spent more time at home than she used to. Once shopping for bonnets in Northampton—all of seven miles away—she admitted to being homesick.[52] On summer nights, she often sat with Emily on the side terrace overlooking the garden. With Margaret's help, they would drag the big *Daphne odora* from the conservatory and ring the sitting area with jasmine and tall oleanders in green tubs—a fortress of plants. When it came to the flowers and vines, Vinnie loved profusion, nothing pruned, everything in tumult.[53] She looked over the garden with its dense tangle and knew this was her life. She was not unhappy, exactly. With her father gone, she had risen in rank, becoming the

---

* William Howland moved to Lynn, Massachusetts, where he worked as a lawyer for the rest of his life. He died in 1880. After his romance with Lavinia in 1854, Joseph Lyman married, had children, and became a New York journalist. He died in 1872.

family's lieutenant: mindful of everyone's needs, protecting Emily's privacy, and keeping track of commitments, invitations, and grudges. Mattie said she admired her aunt's ability to locate anything from a lost quotation to last year's muffler.[54] But to Emily, Vinnie shouldered an invisible burden. My sister, she said, lives in "the State of Regret."[55]

With her father gone, Emily almost missed the family obligations she once dreaded. For decades during Amherst College commencement as guests spilled out over the lawn and crowded the house, she would position herself by the east window in the dining room, next to the sherry decanter. From six in the evening until eight, she stood with a flower in her hand and dutifully poured wine for guests. She remembered the bread she baked for her father—round loaves so there would be more crust.[56] When she looked at her enfeebled mother, it was difficult to recall a time when Emily Norcross Dickinson supervised the entire house: banging carpets every spring, gathering eggs in her apron, and remembering to send shoe blacking to her daughter at Mount Holyoke. It was even more difficult to imagine her mother as a young woman who had moved away from her family to study chemistry in New Haven. Few people—including Emily—credited her mother with having intellectual interests. Too often all they saw was a quiet woman who stirred custard and mended socks. Now at night Mrs. Dickinson called out and could not understand why Edward wasn't home. "Home is so far from Home, since my Father died," Emily wrote.[57] With both daughters tied to her mother's needs, Emily asked neighbors to mail her letters and packages. Seventy-year-old Luke Sweetser took Emily's postings and sent them off.[58] But for private letters, Emily entrusted only Elizabeth Holland. Mrs. Holland had been sending Emily's letters to Reverend Wadsworth for years, addressing them in her own hand

and mailing them from her residence in New York City. Now back in Philadelphia after years in San Francisco, Charles Wadsworth was leading a new church, and still earning acclaim for his powerful words. "I once more come, with my little Load," Emily wrote to Mrs. Holland, thanking her for "beloved Acts, both revealed and covert."[59]

Sue also felt Edward Dickinson's loss. She tried her best to send one of the children over with "some dainty" each Sunday for her mother-in-law, but she was too busy to do it as often as she'd like.[60] A friend worried Sue looked "used up."[61] During one commencement, both children had the measles and it was all she could do to deal with guests and her children's fevers. Austin did not seem to pay much attention to Sue or his son and daughter. On one of his many visits to New York to frequent art galleries and buy landscape paintings, he neglected to retrieve Mattie from one of his stops, and several hours later found her sitting in front of a seascape and staring at the waves.[62] After Edward's death, Sue took Ned and Mattie and joined her brother at a resort hotel in Swampscott, where she walked the rocky ledges above the Atlantic. Young Mattie wouldn't go near the ocean. The force terrified her. "The tide was enough," she later said, "and too much."[63] Sometimes Sue would stay away from Amherst and Austin for a month at a time, and Emily knew all was not well.[64] After Edward died and before Emily Norcross Dickinson suffered her stroke, Sue learned she was pregnant—again. On August 1, 1875, she gave birth to her third child—a son, Thomas Gilbert. Gib they called him. Sue was forty-four years old with a son who was fourteen, a daughter who was eight, a crying infant—and a husband who had removed himself. Life was so upended, she must have wished for nothing more than Edward's Sunday-morning knock at the door. The coffee at the Homestead had always been too weak for her father-in-law. He would steal over to the Evergreens for a secret cup. Like Edward, Susan sought quiet, order, and a strong brew.[65]

The fall of 1875, when Gib was born, Helen Hunt was again in New England. But she wasn't making her usual gallop around the countryside gathering research for essays. She was getting married. "Peggy" and Will had a small wedding at the home of Helen's sister, who had moved to Wolfboro, New Hampshire, in the White Mountains. Emily sent a congratulatory note and a few lines from a longer poem she had written earlier. "Have I a word but Joy?" she wrote, adding,

> Who fleeing from the Spring
> The Spring avenging fling
> To Dooms of Balm — [66]

Helen was pleased to hear from Emily, but baffled by the verse. What did "dooms" mean and how did the idea of calamity connect to her wedding? In her usual direct way, Helen asked Dickinson for an explication, and sent the poem back, along with a warning. "This is *mine*, remember," she wrote. "You must send it back to me, or else you will be a robber."[67] Emily did not return the verse, at least not right away, and Helen was on her again. "You did not send it back, though you wrote that you would. Was this an accident, or a late withdrawal of your consent? Remember that it is mine — not yours — and be honest."[68] Sensing she might be overstepping her bounds, Helen offered reassurance that she simply wanted to understand what Emily meant.* She also reiterated her long desire to see Emily.

---

* Dickinson scholar Jay Leyda later found the poem among Helen Hunt Jackson's papers, years after her death. [Richard B. Sewall, *The Life of Emily Dickinson* (New York: Farrar, Straus and Giroux, 1974), 580.]

She always was full of questions and had many for her girlhood friend. Mainly she could not understand Emily's ambivalence toward publication. For Helen, every essay or poem needed to find its way into print. Publishing always was the final step—for reasons of both ambition and money. But to Emily, publication was far from her mind. Helen confronted her in a letter. "When you are what men call dead," she said, "you will be sorry you were so stingy."[69] Emily might have shrugged off the remark or even been amused by the force of it, but she could not ignore another sentence. In more personal tones, Helen told Emily she hoped they would get to know each other better, and write from time to time—only when it does not bore you, she added. Then she declared what she most wanted to say. "You are a great poet," she said, "and it is a wrong to the day you live in, that you will not sing aloud."[70] Emily always remembered when someone called her a poet: the word was almost too sacred to be uttered, let alone claimed. She recalled something Judge Lord had once told her: the joy we most revere, we profane in taking.[71] As much as sharing her poems with the world unsettled her, she at least was willing to listen to Mrs. Jackson. Emily and Helen made a plan. Next fall, when Helen Jackson was on her annual trek through New England, she would call at the Dickinson Homestead. Emily could only imagine what Mrs. Jackson would say next.

That autumn as students began the new term at Amherst College, Professor Ebenezer Snell went about his usual tasks: teaching, checking his weather apparatus three times a day, and recording meteorological details. On Friday, September 15, 1876, he walked up the hill to the college and met with all his classes, but he felt odd. He was light-headed, and fainted. He blacked out several more times at home and grew increasingly weak. His family sent for the doctor, who did not have good news. Ebenezer Snell was rapidly declining, he said. He did not expect him to live through the weekend. That Monday, when Emily heard the college bells toll, she knew why. Professor Snell was dead at age seventy-four. "I had a father once," she wrote the family—a single sentence conveying her condolence.[72] College officers said no one could compare to Ebenezer Snell. He was in the first graduating class of the college and taught generations of Amherst students for half a century. Although he had little money, they said he was one of the college's greatest benefactors—giving all he had in service to Amherst.[73] Snell's family knew his tender side. He never got over the idea that although people who loved each other might be apart, they could gaze up at the sky and see the same stars and the same moon.[74] The scientist in him understood the phenomenon, but the poet in him appreciated the wonder. During his brief illness, the meteorological journal Snell kept so meticulously did not miss a day. His daughter Sabra collected the measurements. She had been working by her father's side for some time and shared his devotion to the record. On the day her father died, she pulled down his heavy leather ledger and entered the data just as he had instructed her to do: "61 degrees. Stratus, minimal clouds."* In the remarks column where Ebenezer Snell once noted all the atmospheric phenomena that thrilled him—halos, and parhelia, and the blazing Northern Lights—she made a simple notation: "Professor Snell died Rainy day."[75]

Several weeks later, on October 9, Helen Jackson was in New England as planned. She stood at the base of a mountain and looked up. The Mount Holyoke summit towered above her, but she was undaunted. Before seeing Emily Dickinson the next day, she wanted to spend the night at a hotel on top of the mountain.

---

* For the next twenty-six years, Sabra Snell would continue recording weather data in the journal started by her father.

One time, when Helen was researching a travel article about a cog railroad that transported passengers to the top of New Hampshire's Mount Washington, she had convinced the conductor to let her ride outside the train engine for a better view.[76] If she survived the 2,700-foot ascent of Mount Washington, surely she could tackle Mount Holyoke's 935 feet. To reach the top, she had three options. She could tramp two miles to the summit. She could climb 522 steps up a rustic staircase. Or she could choose the most precarious way: the Old Sleigh. Workers had created a cable funicular by nailing two wooden sleighs together to form a cart. A single rope then hoisted four passengers to the top—two facing forward and two backward. A horse, sometimes a team of oxen, and later a steam engine did the hoisting. The Old Sleigh was not for the timid. As the horse moved the rope around a turntable below, the sleigh would lurch unpredictably, sending passengers perilously close to the edge. When the contraption finally made its way to the summit, the sleigh rolled to an opening near the Prospect House.* That's where Helen would spend the night. From the mountain peak, she could see everything familiar to her: thirty-eight towns, Mount Holyoke Female Seminary, and Amherst College. A telescope positioned at the drop-off allowed her to see even farther. The hotel staff said that if you looked through the glass, you could set your watch by the clock tower at the United States Armory all the way down in Springfield. That night, when Helen stood on the hotel's wide wraparound porch, the view was especially beautiful. The Connecticut River curled like a ribbon through dark-green pastures. Sometimes

---

* Emily Dickinson made the trek to the top of Mount Holyoke along with Vinnie and several friends on October 9, 1849. Her name still appears in the Prospect House registry. [Jay Leyda, *The Years and Hours of Emily Dickinson*, vol. 1 (New Haven: Yale University Press, 1960), 158–59.]

a blanket of fog settled on the valley making pumpkin fields and barns disappear. What made the view so exceptional, people said, was the perspective. There were no foothills to obstruct the scene or long slopes that made the world seem distant. While Helen could see for miles, the view had a human scale. She could trace all the roads that had brought her to this single spot.[77]

The next morning, Emily Dickinson came down from her chamber and waited. On those rare occasions when she did agree to see friends—Bowles, Abby Wood, Higginson—the calls had been social. But Emily knew Helen wanted to talk business. Months earlier she had sent Dickinson a circular from a publisher in Boston, announcing the start of an unusual series of books. "The Messrs. Roberts Brothers, of Boston will begin soon the publication of a series of original American novels and tales," a newspaper reported, "to be published anonymously under the title of 'No Name.'"[78] The idea for the series had come from Thomas Niles Jr., a brilliant editor known for spotting new talent and stirring up excitement. Niles predicted that curious readers would buy the books and enjoy speculating about who had written them. Helen knew Mr. Niles planned a volume of anonymous poetry further down the line, featuring both famous and unpublished poets. Like many publishers, Niles was especially interested in presenting the work of women writers. The series would be perfect for Emily, Helen thought. "Authors like it hugely," Niles wrote a friend. "The idea of being able to write fearlessly, intrenched behind an anonymous, and all the critics at bay, is pleasing. We shall all have a good deal of fun."[79] Niles had made a name for himself at Roberts Brothers by encouraging Louisa May Alcott to write what he called a girls' story. *Little Women* had been a success for both Alcott and Niles. He asked Miss Alcott if she might consider writing for No

Name. Anything she wanted, he said, perhaps a novel full of mystery and suspense.* Knowing authors might risk writing something not in their usual style, he assured Alcott and others that anonymity would be guaranteed. He hired copyists to transcribe manuscripts and made sure even Roberts Brothers employees did not know the identities of No Name writers. The first book already had been released: *Mercy Philbrick's Choice*. Like many of the volumes to come, it focused on New England and the lives of women—and was a sensation. Nearly 4,000 books sold in two months and newspapers across the country were filled with conjecture about the author. It's Louisa May Alcott, one newspaper reported. No, it's Harriet Beecher Stowe, another guessed. Louisa Chandler Moulton, Harriet Prescott Spofford, Susan Coolidge, others proposed.† To make it easy to track the possibilities, Niles included

---

* In 1877 the No Name series issued Louisa May Alcott's *A Modern Mephistopheles*, a dark thriller based on Goethe's *Faust*. In her journal, Alcott wrote that she enjoyed writing the novel, "being tired of providing moral pap for the young." [Louisa May Alcott, *Little Women: An Annotated Edition*, ed. Daniel Shealy (Cambridge: The Belknap Press of Harvard University Press, 2013), 2.]

† Helen Hunt Jackson wrote *Mercy Philbrick's Choice*, and some characters in the novel bear a striking resemblance to Dickinson. "One cannot walk through the streets of a New England village," the book began, "without being impressed by a sense of the futile semblance of barrier, this touching effort of withdrawal and reticence." The main character is a shy woman with poetic sensibilities—a woman who led a secluded life, and whose personality was marked by "the loneliness of intense individuals." Some local readers thought Dickinson may have been the novel's author. [Karen Dandurand, "Dickinson and the Public," in Martin Orzbeck and Robert Weisbuch eds., *Dickinson and Audience* (Ann Arbor: University of Michigan Press, 1996), 272–73; Leyda, vol. 2, 257.] The No Name series ran between 1876 and 1886 and published a total of thirty-seven volumes. Each book was bound in green cloth with symbols of good luck on the cover: a four-leaf clover and a horseshoe.

a blank page in the back of each book entitled "GUESSES AT THE AUTHORSHIP of *MERCY PHILBRICK"S CHOICE*."[80]

As Helen's carriage pulled into Amherst on October 10, 1876, the town was empty. The college had declared Tuesday to be Mountain Day, and students took the day off to enjoy the outdoors. Many Amherst College faculty were not present anyway; they were off visiting the Centennial Exposition in Philadelphia. Helen had already made the trip to celebrate the anniversary of the nation's first one hundred years—an experience she labeled a great chore.[81] She preferred the countryside, not a quarter of a million people crammed into stuffy exhibition halls. From down the road, Mattie Dickinson could see Mrs. Jackson's carriage passing Phoenix Row. Her father was away at the exposition, but with fourteen-month-old Gib teething and Ned's troubles developing into a rheumatic heart—her mother was at home. She had told Mattie all about Mrs. Jackson. The girl was so full of anticipation she called the day one of the "excitingest" moments of her young life.[82] Mattie peered out the window as the team of gray horses came to a stop. Mrs. Jackson stepped out, fluffed her full skirts, and marched right up to the Homestead. Aunt Emily's door opened and then it closed. For the rest of the afternoon, all Mattie would see was the livery driver walking his horses down to a tree, then turning around, and walking back to Homestead's front gate—over and over again.[83]

Emily took pride in her appearance. She always did—the clean white dress, the brown velvet net over her hair.* For special occasions, she would add a white-and-gold cameo pin or wear a small

---

* Emily cared about the way she looked and once apologized to Sue, who had dropped by for a quick visit. "I would have liked to be beautiful and tidy when you came," she wrote her sister-in-law. "You will excuse me, wont you. . . . How it would please me if you would come once more, when I was palatable." [L383.]

watch draped from her belt. When Helen first saw her, she was shocked. Emily looked small, mothlike, and pale.[84] Helen wondered if she had been ill and asked about Emily's health, regretting almost immediately the words that fell out of her mouth. In Dickinson's delicate presence, Helen said she felt like an ox and thought she sounded clumsy and stupid.[85] Emily took no offense. She found Helen kind and noble, and worried more about disturbing her or doing something that might turn her away.[86] But Dickinson knew why Helen was there, and it was not to discuss her appearance. She wanted to talk about the circular. Emily had not tossed it away as she had Miss P's letter soliciting poems. They began talking. Will you give me some poems for Roberts Brothers, Helen asked. She appreciated Emily's desire for privacy and offered to copy the verses in her own hand to ensure double anonymity. Helen abhorred publicity herself, and turned down requests for speaking engagements, even when Higginson encouraged her otherwise. She said public attention was foreign to her instinct and she lacked the courage to address an audience.[87] Helen's work always had appeared under a pseudonym, if not H.H.—then Saxe Holm, Rip Van Winkle, or Jane Silsbee. Friends said Helen once bit off Louisa Moulton's head when Moulton reviewed one of her books and referred to her by name rather than her pseudonym.*[88] Yet as much as Helen understood the use of a pen name, she could not understand why Emily did not publish at all. When Emily said how much she had enjoyed Mrs. Jackson's recent

---

* When the *Springfield Republican* revealed Helen Hunt had written a series of anonymous short stories, she was furious with Samuel Bowles and wrote him directly. "I will not be found out," she later wrote a friend, "not even to sell 10 000 of the book in one week!" [Leyda, Vol. 2, 216.] To another friend she said, "I *intend* to deny it, till I die. *Then* I wish it to be known." [Kate Phillips, *Helen Hunt Jackson: A Literary Life* (Berkeley: University of California Press, 2003), 198.]

book of verses, Helen saw an opening to make her case. Surely your
poems would give others pleasure, she told Dickinson.[89] Emily listened carefully, sitting as she usually did on a straight-backed chair
with her hands neatly folded. But Dickinson thought she owed the
public nothing. Her devotion was to the work itself, not the world. A
poem she had among her loose sheets placed the importance on the
poetry, not the poet. It was the words themselves that lived.

> The Poets light but Lamps —
> Themselves — go out —
> The Wicks they stimulate
> If vital Light
>
> Inhere as do the Suns —
> Each Age a Lens
> Disseminating their
> Circumference — [90]

It was not so much that Emily didn't believe in publishing. She
didn't want to engage in the advertising that went along with it. Perhaps her poems might become public sometime, but now was not
the time. She wanted to hold on to verses, reworking them, mining
them for other poems, "Our own Possessions though our own / 'Tis
well to hoard anew," she wrote.[91] She had written a hundred or more
new poems over the past few years, and many Helen would like: "A
little Madness in the Spring," "The Heart is the Capital of the Mind,"
and "There is no Frigate like a Book." There were scores of fragments, too, jotted down between tending to her mother and helping
Margaret prepare supper: phrases written on a note to the dress-
maker, a few words on the back of the Massachusetts Agricultural
College commencement program, a line or two on Mrs. Kingman's

bill for milk. Once her family had discovered a complete poem
written on the flyleaf of Edward Dickinson's edition of Washington
Irving. "The most pathetic thing I do," the poem began, "Is play I
hear from you."[92] But even with so many poems—both old and new—
to choose from, Emily believed her verses were not yet ready, and
she felt incapable of agreeing to Mrs. Jackson's request. She told
her no, but Helen did not accept the answer. She thought Emily was
perfectly able of writing poems and seeing them through to print.
She even carried some Dickinson verses in her own valise and
knew many by heart. She offered to help Emily choose which poems
to include in the Roberts Brothers book. But then Helen started
talking too forcefully and fell right back into pushing too hard: she
accused Emily of wanting to live in darkness. Sensing Dickinson's
unease, Helen changed course, telling Emily she need not make a
decision immediately. Jackson was patient, but she would not give
up. As they said goodbye, the two women clasped hands. The day
was beautiful. Fall colors were at their peak: sugar maples already
orange and oaks turning brown. The hemlocks outside Emily's
front door stood tall like sentinels. The livery driver who had been
waiting with the horses assisted Mrs. Jackson into the coach. As the
team headed north out of town, Helen could almost still feel Emily's hand in hers. It felt to her like a wisp.[93]

√

AFTER HELEN'S VISIT, Emily had second thoughts. She worried she
had said the wrong thing, and fretted she had handled the conversation poorly. She looked at the No Name circular, folded it, and put
it in a letter to Mr. Higginson, asking for advice and an alibi. "I am
sorry to flee so often to my safest friend," she wrote. She hoped he
would be willing to write Helen, saying he disapproved of Dickinson publishing her verse. Helen will believe you, she said.[94] But

Higginson misunderstood the request and thought Mrs. Jackson
had asked Emily to submit short stories or a novel for the series.
Fiction is not in your line, he told Emily, unaware that Roberts
Brothers had also planned a volume of verse.[95] Higginson left the
decision up to Emily. Meanwhile, Helen spent a few days in Ashfield, a hilltown near Amherst. The weather had turned sharply
colder and snow had fallen. "Cold as Greenland," she wrote in her
diary.[96] Austin had returned from the expedition and come down
with chills and fever. Perhaps Helen had been right: the Philadelphia Centennial *was* unhealthy. Sue consulted a physician in
Springfield, who diagnosed Austin with malaria. Remember he is
not of common clay, Sam Bowles wrote Sue.[97] Sue handed her husband glasses of quinine and brandy.[98]

Faithful to her word, Helen did not give up. She wrote Emily
from Ashfield and apologized for being pushy, but then she pushed
again. She had spent the morning looking over Emily's poems—the
last batch Dickinson had sent her. She continued to find a few verses
inscrutable, but when she read them again and more deeply, she
had determined that "the dimness must have been in me."[99] Still,
she liked the most direct poems best, the ones whose words did not
baffle the way that "dooms" had in the wedding verse Dickinson
had sent. Later back home in Colorado, Helen resumed the cam-
paign, telling Emily she herself would contribute to the volume. It
would be fun, she added, having the two of them participate in the
national guessing game. Could you do it for me as a personal favor?
she pleaded.[100] Emily wavered. It "almost seems sordid to refuse
from myself again," she wrote Higginson.[101] Thomas Niles was busy
assembling copy for the book, and had been in touch with Mrs. Jackson. Already he had secured poems from Louisa May Alcott, Bronson Alcott, William Ellery Channing, Annie Fields, Sidney Lanier,
Rose Hawthorne Lathrop, James Russell Lowell, Christina Rossetti,

and Celia Thaxter.[102] In her continued appeals to Dickinson, Helen reduced the number of poems she asked her to contribute. First she had requested "some," then one or two, and then finally only a single verse—a poem she had always loved and had memorized. Emily had written the poem almost two decades before and had published it during the Civil War in the *Brooklyn Daily Union*. Helen may not have realized the verse represented an idea that had absorbed Dickinson all her life. It was a poem about the reach, the miss, and the poignancy of the almost. No one knew the space between effort and accomplishment better than Dickinson:

> Success is counted sweetest
> By those who ne're succeed.
> To comprehend a Nectar
> Requires the sorest need.
> Not one of all the Purple Host
> Who took the flag to-day,
> Can tell the definition,
> So plain, of Victory,
> As he defeated, dying,
> On whose forbidden ear
> The distant strains of triumph
> Break, agonizing clear.[103]

Emily gave Helen permission to submit the poem. She had been worn down by repeated requests, and finally relented to turn the poem over to Thomas Niles. In truth, it would be the third time Emily had directly submitted her own work for publication. The first was *Forest Leaves* back when she was a schoolgirl at Amherst Academy. The second was more recently, when Mattie had asked her to contribute to a short-lived neighborhood newspaper, *The*

Fortnightly Bumble Bee—the name for the publication suggested by Aunt Emily herself.[104] But with "Success is counted sweetest" in the new volume from Roberts Brothers, Emily achieved something she had never accomplished in her life: her first poem published in a book she could hold in her hands.

The years Helen Jackson spent urging Emily to publish her poems had made Dickinson respect Helen all the more. No one else felt such a mission in trying to convince Emily to share her work with the world. Thomas Niles was ecstatic to include Dickinson's poem in the 1878 publication of *A Masque of Poets*, and he gave the verse a prominent place at the end of a section. Helen was pleased, too, and grateful. "I hope you have not regretted giving me that choice bit of verse for it," she wrote.[105] No one guessed Emily Dickinson was the author of "Success is counted sweetest." The poem had been altered slightly and had a title attached to it, "Success"— but she voiced no concerns. Thomas Niles wrote Emily directly and sent a complimentary copy of the book. The guessing game over "Success" elicited much speculation, he told her. Most people thought Ralph Waldo Emerson had written the poem. In Concord, Mr. Emerson set the record straight. He did not write the poem, Emerson said. He had not submitted a verse to the volume at all. Readers do not like my poetry much, he said.[106]

Ten

CALLED BACK

Saturday, May 15, 1886 9 p.m. Thermometer 55.2. Rain/Snow 0.
Clouds 0. Winds 0. Thermometer Attached to Barometer 72.1. Dry
Bulb 55.3. Wet Bulb 54.5. Force of Vapor .411. Humidity 93.
—Sabra Snell, *The Meteorological Journal Kept at Amherst College*

Alone at her desk at night, Emily looked up and stared into the darkness. Even as she approached fifty, Emily continued to write at night. Sometimes the sound of the wind woke her, or her invalid mother called out from another room or a thought intruded on her sleep and wouldn't let go. Once roused, Emily would walk ten steps to her desk, light a lamp, and get to work. The only sound interrupting her solitude was the scratch of mice going after candy Vinnie kept on the top kitchen shelf.[1] "Time, why Time was all I wanted!" Emily was fond of saying, even if the hours she snatched were in the middle of the night.* After her father's death, Emily told Higginson that nothing had changed—at least externally.[2] She still had her mother and Vinnie. Austin, Sue, and their three children remained next door at the Evergreens. But there were

---

* The remark was a paraphrase from Robert Browning's poem "Any Wife to Any Husband." [Jane Donahue Eberwein, *Dickinson: Strategies of Limitation* (Amherst: University of Massachusetts Press, 1986), 92.]

internal changes—profound ones. Everything now seemed more tenuous, as if the world Emily had once known could disappear in a flash or at least not be the same as it was. In the days following Edward Dickinson's death, Emily said she did not—at first—feel "danger." She didn't feel much of anything, wandering around in a daze and all but unconscious. But the sense of threat came later in what she called the after, slower days.[3] Emily fixed her gaze out the western window and tried to discern what was before her. In the dark, the pupils in her brown eyes grew large, trying to absorb light. She could barely see the ghostly line of hemlocks, the tall oak tree, and the edge of the veranda where Sue liked to be alone with her thoughts.[4] At night the glass in Emily's window turned into a mirror, reflecting her face as much as it did the shadows before her. She did not turn away as others might have, those who claimed there was nothing to see. For Emily, there was always something to see, even in the dark—especially in the dark. Years earlier she had imagined groping her way across a pitch-black landscape without the benefit of light or moon or good eyes. "We grow accustomed to the Dark – " the poem began.

> Either the Darkness alters –
> Or something in the sight
> Adjusts itself to Midnight – .[5]

As much as Emily refused to turn away, she could not see what was coming, including her own death. Before that spring day in 1886, there would be unimaginable loss, a surprising kindling of romantic love, and—up until the end—more poems.

On too many nights as Emily stared out the window, lamps suddenly blazed inside the Evergreens, and her reflection would vanish. When the space between the two houses flooded with light, Emily knew it was happening again. Ned, her older nephew, was ill. Austin would awaken to a violent shaking, as if heavy wagons were passing on the road and sending reverberations throughout the house. He'd run into Ned's room to find his fifteen-year-old son moaning and gasping for breath. Nothing could make the seizures stop as Austin tried to hold his son and keep Ned from biting his tongue. The boy cried out, foamed at the mouth, and his whole body contorted with spasms.[6] After the first seizure in 1877, Austin and Sue stood watch over their son the entire night, and sent for the doctor first thing in the morning. The physician examined the young man and believed the convulsions were related to a heart condition, possibly triggered by Ned's earlier bout with rheumatism. He did not expect the seizures to reoccur and Austin and Sue eased, thinking the previous night's scare was the end of it. But then the convulsions returned. In his diary, Austin kept track of each episode, and noted the way his son's eyes darkened hours before an attack. Epilepsy, the doctor said. Austin was devastated, saying Ned is "sick with rheumatism and most everything else."[7] Neighbors found Sue distracted, nervous, and exhausted—"unstrung," a friend said.[8] One night, when Emily once again saw the Evergreens' lamps burning in the middle of the night, she darted over to the house. Her niece, Mattie, caught a glimpse of her out a window by the rosebushes. "'Is he better?'" Emily whispered. Startled to see her aunt alone at that hour, Mattie could only nod. But before Mattie could get to the door to let her in, Emily had disappeared.[9] Later she made pies, wrote poems to Ned, and sent over the season's first batch of maple sugar.[10] She may have thought that the sense of danger she had been living with was a premonition of Ned's epilepsy. But the fright over her nephew was only the beginning.

Tragedy struck Samuel Bowles next. "Dear Mr Bowles found out too late," Emily wrote, "that Vitality costs itself."[11] Years of hard work, travel, and late hours editing the *Springfield Republican* had sapped his energy and taxed his body. Everyone—even Bowles himself—suspected it. Once, after visiting Emily, Bowles sent her a note: "I hope I may oftener come face to face with you. I have little spare strength or time for writing."[12] He died January 16, 1878, of apoplexy at age fifty-one. When she thought of him, Emily could still see the sparkle of his eyes—"those isolated comets"—and thought his countenance the "most triumphant Face out of Paradise."[13] Bowles loved purple hues, and in the afternoon, when Emily looked east to the Pelham Hills, she thought—there's Sam's color.[14] After Bowles, death took his friend and coeditor, Josiah Holland. Holland and Bowles had been Emily's earliest literary champions, publishing her valentine and asking for more work from the promising young writer. A heart attack ended Holland's life on October 12, 1881, and his family notified Emily by telegram. During one of her restive nights, Emily pulled open a drawer, where she kept a memorial edition Scribner's had published as a tribute to Dr. Holland. "It shall always remain there – nearest us," she wrote his wife. She recalled one brilliantly clear morning when, after a visit, Holland placed one hand on Vinnie's head and another on Emily's, and said he would always remember the sunshine around them.[15] "The Things that never can come back, are several," Emily wrote Elizabeth Holland

Childhood – some forms of Hope – the Dead –
Though Joys – like Men – may sometimes make a Journey –
And still abide – [16]

In April 1882, it was Charles Wadsworth, Emily's mysterious minister from Philadelphia. A few years earlier, he had appeared unannounced on the Homestead steps and rang the bell, asking

Margaret if he could see Miss Dickinson. Vinnie had heard him
enter the front hall and rushed to alert her sister, who was in her
garden conservatory. "The Gentleman with the deep voice wants to
see you, Emily," she said.[17] Dickinson was surprised, even startled,
to find him in Amherst, let alone in her own home. She asked why he
had not told her he was coming, and he replied that he hardly knew
himself. "I stepped from my Pulpit . . . to the Train," he said.[18] Earlier, Wadsworth had remarked that he was liable to die at any time,
but Emily had not taken him literally: he had always been opaque.
But now that he was dead of pneumonia at age sixty-seven, she
wanted to know more about his life and sought out others who knew
him. She located a mutual acquaintance in Brooklyn and asked him
questions: Did Wadsworth have brothers and sisters, what did he
say on his deathbed, do either of his sons have his remarkable face,
does his daughter regret her "flight from her loved Father"?[19] For a
man she considered "my closest earthly friend," Emily knew strikingly little about him.[20] She shared her skepticism about heaven
with his New York friend. "Are you certain there is another life?"
she asked. "When overwhelmed to know, I fear that few are sure."[21]

Seven months later, Emily's mother died. Emily Norcross Dickinson's death on November 14, 1882, was not a surprise. A larger
mother had died before, Emily said, thinking of the neuralgia, the
depression, the stroke, and the broken hip that had plagued the
seventy-eight-year-old woman and limited her life.[22] In many ways
her passing was a blessing—both for the suffering Mrs. Dickinson
and the steadfast daughters who cared for her. Emily admitted she
and her mother had not always been close. "But Mines in the same
Ground meet by tunneling," she wrote, "and when she became our
Child, the Affection came."[23] The day before Mrs. Dickinson died,
she had seemed better, and Emily fed her mother beef tea, custard,
and lemonade.[24] The next morning, after being lifted from bed to

chair, Mrs. Dickinson admired a cluster of grapes a friend had sent, called out for Vinnie not to leave her, then gasped and died. Her funeral was a simple one. Amherst shops did not close as they had for her husband. There were no Boston dignitaries present. To the few who saw Emily the day of her mother's service, the poet looked pale and worn.[25] "There was no earthly parting," Emily wrote her Norcross cousins. "She slipped from our fingers like a flake gathered by the wind, and is now part of the drift called 'the infinite.' We don't know where she is, though so many tell us. I believe we shall in some manner be cherished by our Maker – that the One who gave us this remarkable earth has the power still farther to surprise that which He has caused. Beyond that all is silence."[26] When she looked back over the many years her mother had been ill, Emily had one regret: She wished her mother had been better friends with the sky. Nature had always been Emily's preferred companion. "That is 'sociability,'" she wrote, "that is fine and deathless."[27] Even while expected, her mother's death left Emily chilled. It was always that way with her: when grief or terror struck, Emily turned to ice. "Her dying feels to me like many kinds of Cold," she wrote, "at times electric, at times benumbing – then a trackless waste."[28] The poet was right, though, in suspecting that life might still surprise. In the months after her mother's death, Emily Dickinson fell in love.

Otis Phillips Lord was a justice on the Massachusetts Supreme Judicial Court. An Amherst College graduate, former politician, and staunch old-school Whig, he was recognized for being forceful, high-minded, and at times stiff. He had known Emily since she was a girl and—as one of Edward Dickinson's closest friends—he had often visited the family. Once at the Dickinsons' dinner table, he had spontaneously launched into the somber hymn "My Thoughts on Awful Subjects Rolls." Sue and Vinnie could barely contain their amusement, and Vinnie defused the awkward moment with her own ren-

Fig. 26: Frazar Stearns (right), lieutenant Massachusetts 21st Volunteer Infantry. "His big heart shot away by a 'minie ball.'"

Fig. 27: Johnson Chapel at Amherst College, site of the cannon dedication ceremony for Frazar Stearns and the Massachusetts 21st.

Fig. 28: The *Atlantic Monthly* and *Springfield Republican* in the Dickinson family library. Both publications played significant roles in the publication of Emily's poetry.

Fig. 29: Thomas Wentworth Higginson, Dickinson's literary mentor. "You were not aware that you saved my Life."

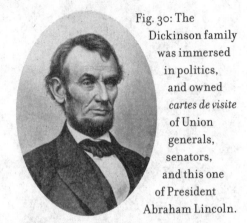

Fig. 30: The Dickinson family was immersed in politics, and owned *cartes de visite* of Union generals, senators, and this one of President Abraham Lincoln.

Fig. 31: The Dickinsons often walked "up-street" to the center of town for books, gloves, French chocolate, or oysters at Frank P. Wood's Dining Rooms.

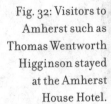

Fig. 32: Visitors to Amherst such as Thomas Wentworth Higginson stayed at the Amherst House Hotel.

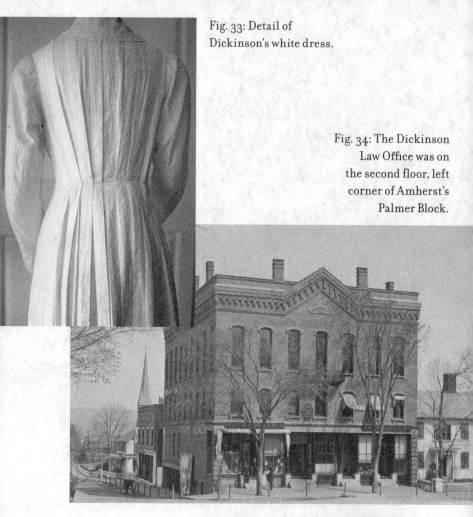

Fig. 33: Detail of Dickinson's white dress.

Fig. 34: The Dickinson Law Office was on the second floor, left corner of Amherst's Palmer Block.

Fig. 35: Ralph Waldo Emerson. Emily said he seemed to "come from where dreams were born."

Fig. 36: Upon returning home from treatment in Boston for an eye disorder, Dickinson climbed the stairs to the family attic where, alone, she recited Shakespeare.

Fig. 37: Nephew Edward "Ned" Dickinson wanted a house where his mother could live in peace. "No fame, no brains, no family, no scholarship. *No Anything.*"

Fig. 38: Niece Martha "Mattie" Dickinson. "Don't cut all the blossoms," Emily told her.

Fig. 39: Nephew Gilbert "Gib" Dickinson at around six years old. He died two years later. "I see him in the Star, and meet his sweet velocity in everything that flies."

Fig. 40: Mabel Loomis Todd. An alternate signature to her name underscores her affair with Dickinson's brother, Austin.

Fig. 41: Before animosities over Austin's affair, Mabel Loomis Todd and Susan Dickinson enjoyed outings with friends. They jokingly called their group the Shutesbury School of Philosophy. Mabel Loomis Todd (standing in white dress), Susan Dickinson (holding son Gib), Martha Dickinson (in straw hat), Ned Dickinson (with tennis racket), and David Peck Todd (behind Ned in dark suit).

Fig. 42: Judge Otis P. Lord. "My Church," Dickinson called him.

Fig. 43: Helen Hunt Jackson with unidentified woman at her home in Colorado Springs. Jackson was relentless in urging Dickinson to publish.

Fig, 44: After young Gib's death, Austin and Susan left their son's bedroom untouched.

Fig. 45: Marsh Undertaking in Amherst took Dickinson's final measure: "Death: May 15. Funeral to take place: May 19. Place of Funeral: House. Length to Heel: 5 feet 6 inches."

Fig. 46: Homestead's back door through which workmen carried Dickinson's coffin. "Dying is a wild Night and a new Road."

Fig. 47: Emily Dickinson's grave, and two of the last words she ever wrote. West Cemetery, Amherst, Massachusetts.

Fig. 48: Dickinson never lost her fascination for plants. Her conservatory, adjacent to the family library, was both a laboratory and refuge for her.

Fig. 49: "I see – New Englandly." The cupola atop the Homestead offered Dickinson a panoramic view.

Fig. 50: The "Pony Express" path between the Dickinson Homestead and the Evergreens.

dition of a more uplifting psalm. Judge Lord might not have minded their giggles. In private moments he exhibited a warm sense of humor, and he and Emily had fun swapping droll newspaper stories.

NOTICE!

My wife Sophia Pickles having left my bed and board without just cause or provocation, I shall not be responsible for bills of her contracting.

SOLOMON PICKLES

NOTICE!

I take this means of saying that Solomon Pickles has had no bed or board for me to leave for the last two months.

SOPHIA PICKLES[29]

When their relationship began around 1882, Judge Lord was seventy years old, a widower with no children, a resident of Salem, and eighteen years Emily's senior. She called him "my Church," and letters to him were filled with affection.[30] Judge Lord's legal work brought him to nearby Northampton twice a year, and he often stayed in Amherst accompanied by nieces who kept house for him. Perhaps Emily felt a newfound sense of freedom after so many years focused on her mother's care. Perhaps she finally was ready to open herself to the vulnerabilities of love. While Emily and Otis did not see each other often, they exchanged weekly letters—missives that Emily took care in drafting and kept copies of in her room. Whether she mailed all the letters she drafted was unclear. What was certain, however, was her passion. "My lovely Salem smiles at me," she wrote. "I seek his Face so often . . . I confess that I love him – I rejoice that I love him – I thank the maker of Heaven and Earth that gave him me to love – the exultation floods me – I cannot find my channel – The Creek turns to Sea — at thought of thee."[31] When the time was right, she said she would lift the bars and lay him in the moss.[32] Yet as much as Emily poured out her love, she also held back. "Dont you know you are happiest while I withhold and not confer," she wrote. "Dont you know that 'No' is the wildest word we consign to Language?"[33] Soon after Emily pledged her love, Judge Lord asked her to marry him—or seemed to.* "You said with loved timidity in asking me to your dear Home, you would 'try not to make it unpleasant.' So delicate a diffidence," she wrote.[34] She played with writing her name as if they were married, first joking about his reference to her slight frame. "Emily 'Jumbo'! Sweetest name, but I know a sweeter — Emily Jumbo Lord."[35]

But Judge Lord's health was precarious. Shortly after his relationship with Emily began, Vinnie and Austin read in the newspaper that he had collapsed. Vinnie asked Emily if she had seen the paper and when she said no, her sister broke the news. Again Emily felt the cold grip of panic take hold and her sight blurred. When Tom Kelley, a family workman, appeared at the door, Emily ran to his blue jacket.[36] Miraculously, Otis Lord recovered and he and Emily returned to their correspondence. "The love I feel for you, I mean, your own for me [is] a treasure I still keep," she wrote in rare stumbling formality.[37] There never would be a marriage or anything as official as an engagement. The thought of uprooting Emily Dickinson to Salem was unrealistic. Amherst ran too deep in her veins. She may also have thought that marriage came at too high a price, as if it would distract from her poetry or impede words. "Sleeplessness makes my Pencil stumble," she wrote Judge Lord one night. "Affection clogs it — too."[38] She preferred to live in a familiar place—as fearsome and

---

* All but one of the letters from Otis Lord were burned after Dickinson's death. Lord's words to the poet are inferred from the drafts of letters she left behind that ended up in Austin's possession, and eventually with Mabel Loomis Todd.

eruptive as it was. In a poem she shared with no one, she described living on a precipice.

Volcanoes be in Sicily
And South America
I judge from my Geography
Volcanoes nearer here
A Lava step at any time
Am I inclined to climb
A Crater I may contemplate
Vesuvius at Home[39]

Around 1882, Austin also fell in love. But unlike Emily's relationship with Judge Lord, Austin's love affair was clandestine and eventually tore the family apart. Mabel Loomis Todd had moved with her husband, David, to Amherst in the autumn of 1881. David Todd was the new professor of astronomy at Amherst College and his twenty-five-year-old wife became the toast of the town—or so Mabel would be the first to tell anyone. She was a beautiful young woman, lively and talented. Upon her arrival in Amherst, she became a close friend of Susan's. Mrs. Austin Dickinson is the "real society person here," Mabel gushed, and said Sue's presence filled every room with grace and elegance.[40] Mabel started spending time in Austin and Sue's drawing room, playing the piano and singing. Ned, only five years younger than Mabel, was smitten. Austin's fascination went deeper. Austin and Mabel took walks alone and she found him dignified, if also a little odd.[41] Vinnie and Emily were impressed with the newcomer, although the poet declined to see her as she did most everyone else. When Mabel played the piano for the Dickinson sisters at the Homestead, Emily would listen from the top of the stairs and send down a glass of wine or a poem. Mabel found Austin's mysterious sister captivating. "I must tell you about the *character* of Amherst," she wrote her parents. "It is a lady whom the people call the *Myth*." According to town gossip, she said, Emily had not been out of the house in fifteen years and never saw anyone. She allowed children to visit once in a while or would lower treats to them from her window. She dressed totally in white, had a brilliant mind, and wrote beautifully. "Isn't that like a book?" she said.[42] Sue shared some of Emily's poems with Mabel, and Mrs. Todd wrote them down to study at home. She was seriously interested and called the poems "full of power."[43] David Todd often was away from Amherst on astronomical expeditions, and was rumored to have romantic affairs of his own.[44] On a picnic to nearby Sunderland one day, Austin told Mabel he wanted to be buried where crickets would forever chirp around him. She was transported. He is "a true, if silent, poet," she confided in her diary, and declared fifty-three-year-old Austin Dickinson was "almost in every particular my ideal man."[45] By 1883, after Mabel returned from an out-of-town trip, Sue's cordiality turned to hostility. She'd learned that Austin and Mabel had become lovers, with at least the tacit acknowledgment of his sisters, and perhaps others in town. Vinnie sided with Austin and barely spoke to Sue. She urged Mabel to rise above her sister-in-law's icy behavior.[46] Ned was furious with his father, started smoking, and told Mattie that all he wanted was one day to have a house of his own where his mother could live in peace. "No fame, no brains, no family, no scholarship, *No Anything*."[47] Sue let her unhappiness spill over and told her daughter that the time might come when she would not be there for her children. Hope "lies far behind me," she said.[48] Emily tried to stay above the rancor and not choose sides. She continued to send notes to Sue and stirred berries over a kettle to send over to the Evergreens.[49] But she rarely saw Sue: the berries would be delivered to the house by someone else, and a family stableman let Emily know if Mrs. Dickinson seemed weary. Emily did not check on Susan herself, and—too worn by the ruin around her—Sue apparently did the same.

"Whom not seeing I still love," Sue wrote in a book inscribed to Emily, and sent across the path between the houses.[50]

Constancy for Emily was her poems. She continued to work, and started corresponding with the new champion of her verses, Thomas Niles. Mr. Niles was the Roberts Brothers publisher and Helen Hunt Jackson's great friend. After the publication of *A Masque of Poets*, Niles had expressed admiration for Dickinson's work. Emily knew Helen had been praising her poems and had urged the publisher to consider publishing a Dickinson volume. "The kind but incredible opinion of 'H. H.' and yourself I would like to deserve," Emily wrote the Boston publisher.[51] But she then played her usual trick with people who sought to bring her work to the public: she didn't say yes and she didn't say no. She did, however, send Niles more poems, a clear indication that she wanted to keep the door open. Just as she had twenty years before with her first letter to Mr. Higginson, Emily sorted through the many poems in her room—forty fascicles and hundreds of loose poems now, some old verses that she loved and some new ones she had been working on. She selected a few. While the quantity of her poems had been reduced over the years, she still produced around thirty or so new poems a year—and the quality of the work had not diminished. Her methods never altered; there were always drafts, alternate phrasings, and endless revisions. And even as she aged, her subject matter remained the same: poems about love, immortality, death and—always—nature. There were some wonderful new poems she wanted to share with Mr. Niles— verses as good as any she had ever written. She chose one to send, and off it went to Boston—a poem about a hummingbird.

A Route of Evanescence,
With a revolving Wheel –
A Resonance of Emerald
A Rush of Cochineal –

And every Blossom on the Bush
Adjusts it's tumbled Head —
The Mail from Tunis — probably,
An easy Morning's Ride — [52]

When Emily received Niles's reply, she was pleased with his reaction—happy that the poem with its burst of color and whirl of motion had captured the essence of the bird. Earlier he had admired a poem she had sent about a blue jay, remarking that the verse seemed true to him.[53] Commending one of her poems for being *true* was the highest praise anyone could offer Emily. Encouraged, she sent him another. It was one of her older poems, a verse she had shared with Higginson seventeen years earlier. She had reworked the stanzas many times and looked over the elegy again.

Further in Summer than the Birds —
Pathetic from the Grass
A minor Nation celebrates
It's unobtrusive Mass —
No Ordinance be seen —
So gradual the Grace
A gentle Custom it becomes —
Enlarging Loneliness —

Antiquest felt at Noon
When August burning low
Arise this Spectral Canticle
Repose to typify —
Remit as yet no Grace —
No furrow on the Glow —
But a Druidic Difference
Enhances Nature now — [54]

For the woman who more than once had called herself a pagan, the poem celebrated the natural world—beginning low in the grass with chirping crickets and ending in the ancient realm of the Druids. It captured the haunting sounds of autumn and moved with the same majestic sweep she had achieved in "Safe in their Alabaster Chambers." She knew the cricket's lonely August chant made one sense a difference that could be felt, but not named. Conjuring up the ineffable was, after all, her territory. "My Cricket," Emily announced in presenting the poem to Mr. Niles.[55] Niles wrote back enthusiastically, saying he had read and reread the poems she was sending. Could Roberts Brothers publish a collection of her verse, he boldly asked. "That is, if you want to give them to the world through the medium of a publisher."[56] Mrs. Jackson had already acquainted Mr. Niles with Dickinson's reluctance.

After their many conversations over *A Masque of Poets*, Emily and Helen had forged a close relationship. Dickinson had also sent her friend the hummingbird poem and a bluebird one, which Helen had committed to memory. "That is more than I do of any of my own verses," Jackson said.[57] They also enjoyed sparring over poems, and when Helen all but dared Emily to write a poem about an oriole, Emily fired one back in her next letter. "One of the ones that Midas touched," it began.[58] While still spending her days writing, Helen had all but left poetry behind. Another occupation had overtaken her. On a recent trip out west, she had been appalled by the living conditions of Ponca Indians and was attending political meetings to protest their poor treatment by the US government. The work consumed her, and she wrote to a friend that someday she would be found dead with "Indians" engraved on her brain.[59] She vowed to write a serious political treatise pointing out the government's injustice. The title for the book came to her suddenly, she said, "as if someone spoke them aloud in the room."[60] In 1881 she published *A Century of Dishonor*, and gave copies at her own expense to every senator and congressman in Washington.[61] Two years later President Chester Arthur appointed her a special agent of the department in charge of surveying the needs of Mission Indians in Southern California. Not only was Helen absorbed with her government report, she also had a flickering idea for a novel. She already had a name for the book—*Ramona*—and told her old friend Colonel Higginson, "If I could write a story that would do for the Indian a thousandth part of what Uncle Tom's Cabin did for the Negro, I would be thankful the rest of my life." [62] Helen was so focused on her work that she let her correspondence with Emily slip, and Dickinson nudged her with a note and a photograph of her young nephew Gib. The young boy had captured Emily's heart and that of everyone else around him. He had the unusual ability to bring out the best in people, even his warring parents. Once, on his birthday, he marched around the Dickinson grounds with a band of friends, beating drums and waving party hats. His aunt leaned out the window and applauded.[63] Emily hoped Helen would love the little boy as much as she did and told her to keep the photograph.

The last half of 1883 proved to be ruthless. Austin and Sue argued to the point of oblivion and Austin promised Mabel he would straighten things out or "smash the machine."[64] In late September Gib had been outdoors, riding his velocipede around town and splashing in puddles with friends. Within two days he became mysteriously ill—seriously so. Sue and Austin hovered over their eight-year-old child as the little boy's fever soared. Mabel waited for Austin to come round with news. She wrote in her diary that doctors suspected typhoid or malarial fever.[65] In the early morning hours of October 5, Emily crept over to the Evergreens to see what she could do. She had not been in the house in years. By the time she saw him, Gib was hallucinating, sweating, and thrashing in bed. The stringent smell of disinfectant sitting in buckets around the house made Emily's stomach churn. While she wanted to stay, her physical distress would not allow it. Her head throbbed and she vomited. Emily had to get out of the house, and she rushed back home across the dark path. As the night wore on, Gib's condition worsened. "Open the Door, open the Door," he cried in delirium. "They are waiting for me."[66] By five o'clock the next evening, he was dead. A neighbor observed that the Dickinson family—once the symbol of Amherst's vitality and strength—seemed to collapse overnight.[67] Sue shut the door and saw no one. A doctor treated Vinnie for exhaustion. Austin was nearly dead, Mabel wrote in her diary. "Gilbert was his idol, and the only thing in his house which truly loved him."[68] Emily lay in her bed unable to move. "*Who* were waiting for him," she asked herself, "all we possess we would give to know."[69]

Somehow Emily managed to write. Her letter of condolence to Sue was astonishing, drawing on the full power of her genius. She had never written a more beautiful epistle and she had never more keenly felt the triumph of life over death. That she was able to find words at all was remarkable.

Dear Sue —

The Vision of Immortal Life has been fulfilled —

How simply at the last the Fathom comes! The Passenger and not the Sea, we find surprises us —

Gilbert rejoiced in Secrets —

His Life was panting with them — With what menace of Light he cried "Dont tell, Aunt Emily"! Now my ascended Playmate must instruct me. Show us, prattling Preceptor, but the way to thee!

He knew no niggard moment — His Life was full of Boon — The Playthings of the Dervish were not so wild as his —

No crescent was this Creature — He traveled from the Full —
Such soar, but never set —
I see him in the Star, and meet his sweet velocity in everything
that flies — His Life was like the Bugle, which winds itself away,
his Elegy an echo — his Requiem ecstasy —
Dawn and Meridian in one.

Wherefore would we wait, wronged only of Night, which he left
for us —

Without a speculation, our little Ajax spans the whole —

> Pass to thy Rendezvous of Light,
> Pangless except for us —
> Who slowly ford the Mystery
> Which thou hast leaped across!

Emily[70]

Later, Sue asked Emily if she would always be beside her. "The first section of Darkness is the densest, Dear," Emily replied. "After that, Light trembles in — You asked would I remain? Irrevocably, Susan — I know no other way."[71]

The next year, Judge Lord died. A stroke killed the seventy-five-year-old jurist in 1884 while he was reading the newspaper, searching perhaps for articles to send Emily. "Dear Mr Lord has left us," Emily wrote a friend. "After a brief unconsciousness, a Sleep that ended with a smile, so his Nieces tell us."[72] On her way to bed, Emily would stop before a portrait of Otis. She looked at his curly white hair, his stern expression much like her father's—a face not so much dignified as wanting to appear so. If she had not loved his expression, Emily said, she would have feared it. His face "had such ascension."[73] She once asked Judge Lord what she should do

for him after he died. "'Remember Me,'" he had said.[74] She took out
her pencil as if in reply.

> Go thy great way!
> The Stars thou meetst
> Are even as Thyself —
> For what are Stars but Asterisks
> To point a human Life?[75]

On June 14, 1884, three months after Judge Lord died, Emily
was in the kitchen at noon making a cake, when suddenly a great
darkness came over her. She fainted and did not recover consciousness until evening. When she came to, Austin, Vinnie, and a
physician were standing over her. Emily thought she was dying or
already was dead—"all was so kind and hallowed," she said.[76] The
poet had never fainted in her life, and for weeks she was bedridden
until strong enough to sit a few hours in a chair. The doctor's diagnosis was "revenge of the nerves," and he prescribed sedatives,
tinctures for headaches, and a syrup of French lettuce.[77] Emily had
her own diagnosis. "The Dyings have been too deep for me," she
said.[78] Two months later, while back home in Colorado, Helen Hunt
Jackson fell down a flight of stairs and broke her leg. Emily saw the
notice in the *Republican* and wrote her friend immediately. "It was
not quite a 'massacre,'" Helen replied with her usual pluck. "But
it was a very bad break — two inches of the big bone smashed in
— & the little one snapped: as compound a fracture as is often com-
pounded!"[79] She assured Emily she was all right, managing well
on crutches, and confident she would be walking soon with a cane.
It was merely an involuntary rest cure she told her.[80] Helen did
need the rest. She had finished her Indian novel in three months,
faster than anything she had ever written.[81] *Ramona* caused a sen-

sation and sold 15,000 copies in a matter of months. Thomas Niles was ecstatic. "My life-blood went into it," Helen wrote her publisher, "all that I had thought, felt, and suffered for five years on the Indian Question."[82] Perhaps thinking the California climate would help her recover, Helen hired a nurse and took rooms in a Los Angeles boardinghouse. She described for Emily the view from her bed. "I am looking straight off towards Japan – over a silver sea – my foreground is a strip of high grass, and mallows, with a row of Eucalyptus trees sixty or seventy feet high."[83] But Helen did not improve. Sick as she was, she still thought about Dickinson's verse—was still praising it, and still admonishing Emily for not sharing it with the world. "I wish I knew what your portfolios, by this time, hold," she wrote.[84] While a doctor treated her for malaria, he suspected stomach cancer was the underlying cause. He wired William Jackson in Colorado and told him to come at once. By the time Helen's husband arrived, it was nearly too late. When he saw her, William broke into pieces.[85] For all her ceaseless wanderings, Helen had proved to be the perfect match for William Sharpless Jackson. He adored her passion for life, her independence, her love of adventure, and what he called her "too muchness."[86] When Emily received word that Helen had died on August 12, 1885, she wrote Mr. Jackson. "Helen of Troy will die, but Helen of Colorado, never," she said. "Dear friend, can you walk, were the last words that I wrote her. Dear friend, I can fly—her immortal (soaring) reply."[87]

Dickinson never fully recovered. Fainting in the kitchen was the beginning of the end. Three months after Helen's death, she was again confined to her bed. She read, wrote letters, and on occasion drafted a poem. She worked on one about Helen, returning again to the image of stars and asterisks. "Did you not give her to me?" she wrote Higginson.[88] By the beginning of the year in 1886,

Emily's family kept close watch over her. Austin canceled travel plans to Boston in order to be near, and he and Vinnie had a serious talk about their sister's health. A neighbor looked up at the big yellow house sitting behind the hemlock hedge and said everything was dark.[89] Inside Emily was thinking of flowers, Reverend Wadsworth, Thomas Wentworth Higginson, Helen Hunt Jackson, and nurturing what she called a "pink and russet hope."[90] Years earlier she had dashed off a note to her Norcross cousins, telling them they had left something behind after a visit at the Homestead. Loo had forgotten a tumbler of sweet peas on top of a bureau, and Emily had an idea about what to do with them. She proposed leaving the flowers in the bureau drawer until they had withered and made pods. They'll sow themselves in the dark, she wrote, and be ready to blossom later on.[91] It was like that now in her room. That spring as she looked around her chamber, everything Emily had sown was blossoming. All the fascicles stitched with thread, all poems hiding in dark drawers. Nearly 2,000 verses in all.* There was a long-ago note from the college boy who printed her first valentine, inviting her to a candy pull—with a poem on the back. "Corn," "Wheat," "Ice Cream" scrawled on pieces of paper—and poems on the reverse. A fragment of an old Amherst Academy penmanship lesson with a verse scribbled across it. An envelope with the flap opened to resemble a peaked roof—"The way Hope builds his House" written inside.[92] Nearly everything

---

* Dickinson did not retain all of the poems she wrote. Some were sent to correspondents without an original kept in the poet's possession. In the late twentieth century after all of the known poems were collected, most scholars believe Dickinson wrote just under 1,800 poems. That number fluctuates depending on how scholars define a poem. Some phrases embedded in letters are counted as poems by some scholars, and not by others.

she touched became a surface on which to write or a poem itself. Blossoming sweet peas. And there were letters—hundreds and thousands of letters written to Emily over a lifetime, and drafts of her own. The mysterious Master Letters were there too. If Reverend Wadsworth were the intended recipient of those agonizing missives, the poet did not say. From her bed, Emily could see the sun dipping radiant and alive beyond farmhouses to the west. She would remember the singsong of phoebes and the smell of mud when farmers turned over the soil in the spring. She would recall Gilbert's uncomplicated joy and the way he tipped his cap. She could see her brother at his happiest, planting azaleas and little oaks from the Pelham Hills, and feel Vinnie's ferocious loyalty. She could hear her father's triumphant "Amen" after morning prayers, smell her mother's warm doughnuts. And Carlo, always big, beloved Carlo looking out the window, padding near her. The round, fragrant orange on the dining-room sideboard. The soft folds of the *Springfield Republican* lying unopened on a chair in the library. The pink roses of her chamber wallpaper, the smell of hyacinths on the windowsill, the afternoon light that fell across on her desk, shining like the lustrous tail of a comet streaming just out of sight. "Should you ask what happened here," she had written, "I should say nothing perceptible. Sweet latent events — too shy to confide."[93]

It had been raining and cloudy in Amherst the second week of May 1886. When the showers finally let up and the sun started shining, strawberries all over the Connecticut River Valley turned red. Frank Wood would have the first of the season for his customers. He always did, unloading big crates of berries at his dining room in the center of town.[94] Across the Notch in South Hadley, Mount Holyoke Female Seminary principal Miss Blanchard was counting heads; fifteen students from Mount Holyoke would be spending an afternoon at Amherst College's art museum. If the weather continued to hold, clerks from Phoenix Row would play a game of baseball with the nine from the local hat shops.[95] Everything in Amherst that May was about baseball. In his diary, Austin kept track of Emily's declining health. "Emily feeling poorly—and so I have kept within her call," he wrote on May 13.[96] Sometime earlier Dickinson had written a note to Fanny and Loo Norcross. "Little Cousins, Called back. Emily." Five words. Three lines. Nine beats. 4-2-3. Her final poem.[97] On Saturday evening May 15, 1886 as choir practice was beginning across the street at First Church, Emily took her last breath. Austin's diary told the story. "It was settled before morning broke that Emily would not wake again this side. The day was awful. She ceased to breathe that terrible breathing just before the whistles sounded for six. Mrs Montague and Mrs Jameson were sitting with Vin. I was near by."[98] That night the last vestiges of the week's clouds disappeared, and the sky over Amherst was clear. Ned, Mattie, and Gib loved studying the heavens and even had a favorite star, Algol. The night Emily died the stars were especially brilliant. The moon was almost full and in the south, Jupiter and Mars were shining brightly. Barely visible and just above the horizon, Algol started to rise, like an asterisk.[99]

⸓

"DYING IS A wild Night and a new Road," Emily had written.[100] She knew well the chill aftermath of death: the stillness, the numbness, the nerves sitting "ceremonious, like Tombs."[101] Austin and Lavinia went over instructions Emily had left. Mr. Higginson should be contacted in Cambridge. Ask him to read Emily Brontë's poem at the funeral. All papers should be burned. A simple coffin. A brief service at home. No hearse. The family's Irish workmen as pallbearers. Austin summoned undertaker Edwin Marsh, who took Dickinson's final measure. "Death: May 15. Funeral to take place: May 19. Place of Funeral: House. Length to Heel: 5 feet 6 inches." Dr. Bigelow completed the physician's certificate: Bright's disease. Length of illness—2 1/2 years.* The town clerk added the remaining facts. Twenty-second death of the year in Amherst. Female, single. Fifty-five years. Five months and five days. Occupation: At Home.[102]

In the end, Susan was there. "The tie between us is very fine," Emily had written her most treasured friend, "but a Hair never dissolves."[103] "Thank you, dear Sue — for every solace," she had written before her death, and another: "Dear Sue, Thank y ," the last two letters never finished.[104] Sue took care of the most intimate of duties. She arranged for the local seamstress to sew a white flannel robe in which to wrap Emily's body. "When we come into the world we are wrapped in soft, white flannel," Sue said. "I think it fitting that we should leave it that way."[105] She then went to work on the obituary for the newspaper. She wanted to make sure people understood Emily's seclusion was not a rejection of the world or them. She wanted to stress that Emily's faith was not repudiation of God, but of dogma. And she wanted to declare that Emily's words were unparalleled—gleaming, startling, and rapturous.

> The death of Miss Emily Dickinson, daughter of the late Edward Dickinson, at Amherst on Saturday, makes another sad inroad on the small circle so long occupying the old family mansion. It was for a long generation overlooked by death, and one passing in and out there thought of old-fashioned times, when parents and

---

* Bright's disease was a general term for kidney ailments. Given Dickinson's headaches, fainting spell, and family history, it would appear she also suffered from hypertension.

children grew up and passed maturity together, in lives of singular uneventfulness ... Very few in the village, except among the older inhabitants, knew Miss Emily personally, although the facts of her seclusion and her intellectual brilliancy were familiar Amherst traditions. ... As she passed on in life, her sensitive nature shrank from much personal contact with the world, and more and more turned to her own large wealth of individual resources for companionship, sitting thenceforth, as some one said of her, "in the light of her own fire." Not disappointed with the world, not an invalid until within the past two years, not from any lack of sympathy, not because she was insufficient for any mental work or social career—her endowments being so exceptional—but the "mesh of her soul," as Browning calls the body, was too rare, and the sacred quiet of her own home proved the fit atmosphere for her worth and work. All that must be inviolate.[106]

That Wednesday afternoon, May 19, the funeral service took place in the Dickinsons' family library. "To Amherst to the funeral of that rare & strange creature Emily Dickinson," Thomas Wentworth Higginson wrote in his diary. When he looked down at Emily's face in the coffin, he was astonished. She looked like a young woman. There was not a gray hair or a wrinkle. Vinnie bent over beside him and placed two heliotropes by Emily's hand. To "take to Judge Lord," she whispered.[107] The funeral was as simple and plain as Emily had wanted. As instructed, Mr. Higginson read lines from Emily Brontë's poem. But before he did, he added a few words of his own: "Our friend who has just now put on Immortality, and who seemed scarce ever to have taken it off," he said.[108] Then he began, "No coward soul is mine / No trembler in the world's storm-troubled sphere." Higginson looked around at Edward Dickinson's

old books that still lined the library shelves and smelled spring-
time blossoms drifting from Emily's conservatory. The first time
he had been in the house was a quarter of a century earlier, when
he'd listened as Emily spoke with barely a pause about puddings
and clocks and how a poem made her feel. So cold no fire ever can
warm me, he remembered her saying.[109] He thought about one
question she had asked him that memorable afternoon—a question
that at the time was so odd and perplexing he wrote it down: "Could
you tell me what home is," she had inquired.[110] The answer seemed
simple to him. Home was this very house that she loved with all
her heart. Home was Amherst. Better than heaven, she said. But
Higginson now knew that's not what Dickinson meant. Home to
her was much more. It was the wild terrain of her mind. A world
of hummingbirds and crickets and alabaster and dots on a disc of
snow. To Emily Dickinson, home was consciousness itself—a continent of language where metaphor was her native tongue.

I dwell in Possibility –
A fairer House than Prose –
More numerous of Windows –
Superior – for Doors –

Of Chambers as the Cedars –
Impregnable of eye –
And for an everlasting Roof
The Gambrels of the Sky –

Of Visitors – the fairest –
For Occupation – This –
The spreading wide my narrow Hands
To gather Paradise – [111]

No one who attended her funeral that day knew Emily Dickinson would become someone else after death. Or that Vinnie would find her cache of poems and not have the heart to burn them.[112] No one knew that several years later Thomas Wentworth Higginson and Mabel Loomis Todd would approach Thomas Niles at Roberts Brothers in Boston with hundreds of her verses—surely enough for a volume, they thought. No one knew that the book Mr. Niles would publish in 1890 would sell faster and wider than anyone ever could have imagined. No one knew in the centuries that followed that Dickinson would be proclaimed one of the greatest poets in the English language. All the small group of people who gathered in the family library knew was that Emily Dickinson would be laid to rest next to her parents in the village cemetery. Undertaker Marsh was waiting for them. Sue had made sure the new grave was lined with pine boughs. Across town that afternoon Sabra Snell collected details to enter in her father's weather journal: *Temperature 66. A few clouds. Light breeze.*[113] It was a beautiful day. Buttercups and violets dotted the grass. At the backdoor of the Homestead, Austin, Sue, Vinnie, and Thomas Wentworth Higginson watched as half a dozen Irish workmen lifted Emily's coffin. Then the quiet procession headed out past the barn, across the fields, and into the light.

ACKNOWLEDGMENTS

"My friends are my 'estate'," Emily Dickinson wrote, and I have many to thank.

I am grateful to Dickinson biographers and critics who have come before me, especially Ralph Franklin, Lyndall Gordon, Alfred Habegger, Thomas Johnson, Jay Leyda, David Porter, Adrienne Rich, and Richard Sewall. Current scholars have generously shared their time and expertise, among them Christopher Benfey, the late Jed Deppman, Julie Dobrow, Jane Eberwein, Suzanne Juhasz, Cynthia MacKenzie, Cristanne Miller, Aife Murray, Emily Seelbinder, and Susan Snively. The entire Emily Dickinson International Society community has shaped my thinking, and I am indebted to them for their insights and fellowship. I would also like to thank Kate Phillips, whose work on Helen Hunt Jackson has been particularly helpful.

Countless archivists have made my work more precise, and a lot more fun. For answering questions with patience and good humor, I would like to thank Margaret Dakin and Mike Kelly at Amherst College, Cynthia Harbeson at the Jones Library, Leslie Fields and Deborah Richards at Mount Holyoke College Archives, Jessy Randall at Colorado College, and Dan Lombardo.

Over many decades, I have relied on the kindness and hard work of the Emily Dickinson Museum staff. Every time I walk through the

Museum door, I find laughter, imagination, and good will. I would like to express my appreciation to Lucy Abbott, Brooke Steinhauser, and Michael Medeiros. Cynthia Dickinson and Jane Wald deserve a special thank you. Not only have they helped me each time I called but also they have enriched my life with their long friendship.

The conceit of this book began in an upstairs room at the Dickinson Museum, where for nearly two decades I taught an Emily Dickinson seminar. My Mount Holyoke College students brought me joy every Tuesday afternoon, and they challenged me in ways that happily complicated my understanding. I am grateful for those moments when Dickinson's words grabbed my students on a personal level. At times they were stunned into silence or deeply unsettled when the world suddenly seemed to shift under their feet. Watching them grapple with Dickinson's genius reminded me of what is at the heart of literature, and teaching.

Many friends have read these chapters. First and foremost, I would like to thank Joanne Dobson for her dedicated and meticulous read. When it comes to All-Things-Dickinson, I trust no one more. I met Joanne and Karen Dandurand years ago when we were graduate students at the University of Massachusetts. Our boundless conversations during those years and the years that followed provided the bedrock for my study of Dickinson. In Karen and Joanne, I found my tribe—and this book is dedicated to them.

I also would like to thank friends who read these pages or who put up with me talking endlessly about them. They are: Christina and Sara Barber-Just, Jane Crosthwaite, James Fitzgerald, Julia Hendrix, and Mary Young. Kathy Dempsey Zimmerman read with enthusiasm and curiosity, and helped me anticipate readers' questions. James Gehrt deserves special thanks. James is my neighbor and former colleague at Mount Holyoke College. He brought his artistic eye to the project, providing many photographs for the book. I always have fun when I'm on a photography adventure with James, and I always learn from what he sees.

I have been a lucky duck to land at W. W. Norton. I'd like to thank my editor, Jill Bialosky, for believing in this project and for her astute ear for poetry. Jill's comments pushed me in ways that deepened this work and opened new doors in my thinking. Drew Elizabeth Weitman provided a steady hand with everything from deadlines to sizing photos. I appreciate her know-how and attention to detail. Sarahmay Wilkinson designed the cover, a strikingly beautiful concept based on the poet's bedroom wallpaper. Rachelle Mandik's careful copyediting made this book tighter, clearer, and saved me from more than one goof. Rose Sheehan and Rachel Salzman steered promotion with vigor and enthusiasm. And what good fortune to have Lauren Abbate guiding this book through production. Lauren is a former Mount Holyoke College student of mine who years ago took my Dickinson seminar. I was in good hands with Lauren as production manager, and it brings me a particular pleasure to see her doing the job so well.

Ellen Geiger has been my literary agent for over twenty years, and always knew this Dickinson book was in me. Thank you, Ellen, for being the best champion *These Fevered Days* could have. It was a stroke of luck that brought me into your orbit years ago. I'm grateful for your good advice, and all the good times we have shared.

Finally, my deepest thanks go to my wife, Ann Romberger. Ann has always said she doesn't "really understand poetry"—and that makes convincing her to give Emily Dickinson a whirl all the more challenging—delightfully so. Ann has read every one of these words three, four, five times or more—through all the multiple drafts, even the really rotten ones. By now, she's earned her poetry stripes. But you know what? I think she always knew more than she let on. All along she realized I had to find Dickinson for myself. Thank you, Ann, for knowing what matters most.

ILLUSTRATION CREDITS

Fig. 1: Amherst College Archives and Special Collections
Fig. 2: [Dickinson Room]. Houghton Library, Harvard University.
Fig. 3: [MS Am 1118.99b 18]. Houghton Library, Harvard University.
Fig. 4: Amherst College Archives and Special Collections
Fig. 5: Jones Library Special Collections, Amherst, Massachusetts
Fig. 6: Emily Dickinson Museum, Amherst, Massachusetts
Fig. 7: Todd-Bingham picture collection [MS 496E]. Manuscripts & Archives, Yale University.
Fig. 8: Jones Library Special Collections, Amherst, Massachusetts
Fig. 9: Mount Holyoke College Archives and Special Collections
Fig. 10: Mount Holyoke College Archives and Special Collections
Fig. 11: Amherst College Archives and Special Collections
Fig. 12: James Gehrt
Fig. 13: Jones Library Special Collections, Amherst, Massachusetts
Fig. 14: Amherst College Archives and Special Collections
Fig. 15: Private Collection
Fig. 16: Amherst College Archives and Special Collections
Fig. 17: Amherst College Archives and Special Collections
Fig. 18: [MS Am 1118.99b 49]. Houghton Library, Harvard University.
Fig. 19: Presbyterian Historical Society
Fig. 20: Jones Library, Special Collections, Amherst, Massachusetts
Fig. 21: James Gehrt
Fig. 22: James Gehrt
Fig. 23: James Gehrt
Fig. 24: Jones Library Special Collections, Amherst, Massachusetts
Fig. 25: Amherst College Archives and Special Collections
Fig. 26: Amherst College Archives and Special Collections
Fig. 27: Amherst College Archives and Special Collections

Fig. 28: James Gehrt

Fig. 29: [MS Am 1118.9b 45]. Houghton Library, Harvard University.

Fig. 30: [MS AM 1118.99b 54]. Houghton Library, Harvard University.

Fig. 31: Jones Library Special Collections, Amherst, Massachusetts

Fig. 32: Jones Library Special Collections, Amherst, Massachusetts

Fig. 33: James Gehrt, from the collection of the Amherst Historical Society, Amherst, Massachusetts

Fig. 34: Jones Library Special Collections, Amherst, Massachusetts

Fig. 35: From the collection of the Amherst Historical Society, Amherst, Massachusetts

Fig. 36: James Gehrt

Fig. 37: [MS Am 1118.99b 19]. Houghton Library, Harvard University.

Fig. 38: [MS Am 1118.99b 2]. Houghton Library, Harvard University.

Fig. 39: [MS 496E Series 1 Box 16 Folder 172]. Todd-Bingham picture collection. Manuscripts & Archives, Yale University Library.

Fig. 40: Mabel Loomis Todd papers [MS 496C]. Manuscripts & Archives, Yale University Library.

Fig. 41: Todd-Bingham picture collection [MS 496E]. Manuscripts & Archives, Yale University Library.

Fig. 42: [MS Am 1118.99b 55]. Houghton Library, Harvard University.

Fig. 43: Helen Hunt Jackson Papers [Part 1, Ms 0020, Box 6, Folder 3], Colorado College Special Collections

Fig. 44: James Gehrt

Fig. 45: Jones Library Special Collections, Amherst, Massachusetts

Fig. 46: James Gehrt

Fig. 47: James Gehrt

Fig. 48: James Gehrt

Fig. 49: James Gehrt

Fig. 50: James Gehrt

PERMISSIONS CREDITS

NOTES

Emily Dickinson's poems are identified by their Franklin number (F), the number assigned by R. W. Franklin in his *The Poems of Emily Dickinson*. Variorum edition. (Cambridge: The Belknap Press of Harvard University Press, 1998). The numbers reflect Franklin's estimate of the poems' chronological order in Dickinson's oeuvre. Dickinson's letters are identified by the number assigned by editor Thomas H. Johnson in his *The Letters of Emily Dickinson* (Cambridge: The Belknap Press of Harvard University Press, 1958). The Johnson number (L) reflects his estimate of the letters' chronological order.

AUTHOR'S NOTE

1   L268.
2   F446.
3   L972.
4   L939.
5   Suzanne Juhasz. " 'The Landscape of the Spirit' " in *Emily Dickinson: A Collection of Critical Essays*, ed. Judith Farr (Upper Saddle River, NJ: Prentice Hall, 1996), 137.
6   F690.
7   George S. Merriam, *The Life and Times of Samuel Bowles*, Vol. 1 (New York: The Century Co., 1885), 236.
8   L281.
9   Richard Wilbur, "Altitudes," in *Collected Poems, 1943–2004* (New York: Harcourt, Inc., 2004), 305.
10 L342a.
11 L268.

ONE: ALL THINGS ARE READY

1   Ebenezer Snell and Sabra Snell, *The Meteorological Journal Kept at Amherst College*, Ebenezer Snell Papers, Amherst College Archives and Special Collections.

2   *The Letters of Emily Dickinson*, ed. Thomas H. Johnson. (Cambridge: The Belknap Press of Harvard University Press, 1958), L80.

3   L6.

4   L7; L184.

5   Jay Leyda. *The Years and Hours of Emily Dickinson*, vol. 1, (New Haven: Yale University Press, 1960), 27.

6   Ibid., 53.

7   L7.

8   Ibid.

9   Ibid.

10 Ibid.

11 Ibid.

12 L9.

13 L5.

14 Alfred Habegger, *My Wars Are Laid Away in Books: The Life of Emily Dickinson* (New York: Random House, 2001), 8.

15 Leyda, vol. 1, 50.

16 Ibid., 24.

17 L2.

18 L1.

19 Leyda, vol. 1, 8, 56.

20 Ibid., 81.

21 Ibid., 31.

22 L159.

23 Leyda, vol. 1, 82.

24 L116.

25 L176.

26 L133.

27 *Franklin and Hampshire Express*, Friday, August 1, 1845.

28 L827.

29 L11.

30 Leyda, vol. 1, 24; L6, L5.

31 L6.

32 Frederick Tuckerman, *Amherst Academy: A New England School of the Past, 1814–1861*, (Amherst: Printed for the Trustees, 1929), 103.

33 Habegger, 143.

34 Leyda, vol. 1, 29.

35 L6.

36 L8.

37 L7.

38 Leyda, vol. 1, 21.

39 Leyda, vol. 1, 87.

40 L7.

41 Carolyn Lindley Cooley, *The Music of Emily Dickinson's Poems and Letters* (Jefferson, NC: McFarland Publishing, 2003), 18.

42 L184.

43 Leyda, vol. 1, 59.

44 L6.

45 L3.

46 L91.

47 Ibid.

48 Leyda, vol. 1, 81.

49 L5.

50 Tuckerman, 113.

51 Leyda, vol. 1, 19

52 Ibid., 36.

53 Kate Phillips, *Helen Hunt Jackson: A Literary Life* (Berkeley: University of California Press, 2003), 51.

54 Ibid., 17.

55 L6.

56 Habegger, 171.

57 Ibid.

58 L11.

59 Leyda, vol. 1, 86.

60 Ibid.

61 Ibid.

62 Ibid., 86, 87.

63 L13.

64 L7.

65 Ibid.

66 L8.

67   L7.
68   Ibid.

TWO: IT IS HARD FOR ME TO GIVE UP THE WORLD

1   L16, L304, L320, L645, L927, L471, L809, L32, L39, L907, L179.

2   L12.

3   *Eleventh Annual Catalogue of the Mount Holyoke Female Seminary in South Had-
     ley, Mass., 1847–8*. Mount Holyoke College Archives and Special Collections;
     Fidelia Fiske, *Mary Lyon, Recollections of a Noble Woman* (London: Morgan,
     Chase and Scott, n.d.), 42.

4   L12.

5   Recorded Items, Mount Holyoke Female Seminary, 1840s, Mount Holyoke
     College Archives and Special Collections; http://clio.fivecolleges.edu/mhc/
     rg02/4statutes/box02_ff01/behavioral/01.htm

6   L13.

7   L14.

8   L18; *Catalogue of the Officers and Students at Amherst College for the Academi-
     cal Year 1846–47*. Amherst College Archives and Special Collections; Fiske,
     23; *Mount Holyoke College Journal Letter September 1847–June 2, 1848*, 2; *Eleventh
     Annual Catalogue of the Mount Holyoke Female Seminary*; L11, 18; L8; L13.

9   Mary Dickinson to Edward Dickinson, December 22, 1822, Edward Dickin-
     son Papers, Houghton Library, Harvard University.

10   *Eleventh Annual Catalogue of the Mount Holyoke Female Seminary*; Martha Ack-
     mann, *The Matrilineage of Emily Dickinson*, PhD Dissertation, University of
     Massachusetts, 1988, 35.

11   Edward Hammond Clarke, *Sex in Education, Or, a Fair Chance for the Girls*
     (Boston: James R. Osgood and Company, 1874), 51.

12   E. A. Andrews, "The Religious Magazine and Family Miscellany," 1 (1837).

13   James E. Hartley, ed., *Mary Lyon: Documents and Writings* (South Hadley, MA:
     Doorlight Publications, 2008), 317.

14   Jay Leyda, *The Years and Hours of Emily Dickinson*, vol. 1 (New Haven: Yale Univer-
     sity Press, 1960), 115; William H. Gibbs, *Address Delivered Before the Literary Asso-
     ciation of Blandford, Mass* (G. W. Wilson, printer. Springfield, MA, 1850), 34; Celia
     S. Wright Strong files, Mount Holyoke College Archives and Special Collections.

15   L17.

16   Edward Hitchcock, *The Power of Christian Benevolence Illustrated in the Life
     and Labors of Mary Lyon* (New York: Published by the American Tract Society,
     1858), 4.

17   Susan Danley, "Mount Holyoke: The Grandest Cultivated View in the World." in *Changing Prospects: The View from Mount Holyoke*, ed. Marianne Dozema (Ithaca: Cornell University Press, 2002), 13–19.

18   Edward Hitchcock, *Reminiscences of Amherst College: Historical, Scientific, Biographical, and Autobiographical with Other and Wider Life Experiences* (Northampton, Mass: Bridgman & Childs, 1863), 159.

19   Leyda, vol. 1, 150; Alfred Habegger, *My Wars Are Laid Away in Books: The Life of Emily Dickinson* (New York: Random House, 2001), 15; Lucretia Dickinson to Edward Dickinson, March 26, 1823, Edward Dickinson Papers, Houghton Library, Harvard University.

20   Ackmann, 56; *Mount Holyoke College Journal Letter September 1847–June 2, 1848*, 5; Leslie Fields, email to the author, December 3, 2015, referencing Sarah Packard's 1846 journal; Elizabeth Alden Green, *Mary Lyon and Mount Holyoke: Opening the Gates* (Hanover: University Press of New England, 1979), 86.

21   L15.

22   L5.

23   Kate Phillips, *Helen Hunt Jackson: A Literary Life* (Berkeley: University of California Press, 2003), 54.

24   L22.

25   Mary Lyon Collection, Mount Holyoke College Archives and Special Collections; *Eleventh Annual Catalogue of the Mount Holyoke Female Seminary*.

26   Vivian Pollak, ed., *A Historical Guide to Emily Dickinson* (New York: Oxford University Press, 2004), 33.

27   L18.

28   Malvia Stanton Lang to Louisa Cowles, January 5, 1904, Mount Holyoke College Archives and Special Collections; Louisa Dickinson to John Morton Graves, May 1, 1857, Amherst College Archives and Special Collections.

29   Fiske, 32, 42.

30   L16.

31   Elizabeth Hall to her friends, September 20, 1848, Mount Holyoke College Archives and Special Collections.

32   Elizabeth Haven to her brother, October 28, 1839, Mount Holyoke College Archives and Special Collections.

33   L10; L5.

34   Ibid.

35   Fidelia Fiske Papers, Mount Holyoke College Archives and Special Collections; Fidelia Fiske to Abigail Moore, August 19, 1843, Mount Holyoke College Archives and Special Collections.

250 NOTES TO PAGES 41–51

36 L22.

37 L23.

38 Prayer Meeting Notes, Mary Lyon Collection, Mount Holyoke College Archives and Special Collections; Writing of Mary Lyon Respecting Property, Mount Holyoke College Archives and Special Collections; Amanda Porterfield, *Mary Lyon and Mount Holyoke Missionaries* (New York: Oxford University Press, 1997), 14; Sarah D. Stowe, *History of Mount Holyoke Female Seminary During Its First Half Century, 1837–1887* (Springfield, Mass: Springfield Publishing Company, 1887), 78.

39 Habegger, 14.

40 L9.

41 *Mount Holyoke College Journal Letter September 1847–June 2, 1848*, 18–20.

42 Leyda, vol. 1, 135–36.

43 Ibid., 135.

44 Prayer Meeting Notes, Mary Lyon Collection, Mount Holyoke College Archives and Special Collections.

45 L20.

46 L10.

47 Ibid.

48 *Mount Holyoke College Journal Letter, September 1847–June 2, 1848*; Mary Lyon Collection, Mount Holyoke College Archives and Special Collections.

49 Mary Lyon Collection. Mount Holyoke College Archives and Special Collections.

50 Ibid.

51 L10.

52 L23.

53 L35, L750.

54 *Mount Holyoke College Journal Letter, September 1847–June 2, 1848*, Mount Holyoke College Archives and Special Collections.

55 Ibid.

THREE: I'VE BEEN IN THE HABIT *MYSELF* OF WRITING SOME FEW THINGS

1 L76; Jay Leyda, *The Years and Hours of Emily Dickinson*, vol. 1 (New Haven: Yale University Press, 1960), 252.

2 L23.

3 L86.

4 L82.

5   Leyda, vol. 1, 211–12.

6   Ibid., 245.

7   *Andover Theological Seminary Necrology, 1898–99* (Boston: Beacon Press, 1899), 354–55.

8   L95.

9   L71.

10   Leyda, vol. 1, 193.

11   Ibid., 183.

12   Ibid., 222.

13   Ibid., 225.

14   Ibid., 193.

15   L53.

16   Leyda, vol. 1, 216.

17   Cynthia Harbeson, email to the author, Jones Library, Amherst, Massachusetts, June 23, 2016.

18   Esther Howland files, Mount Holyoke College Archives and Special Collections.

19   L27.

20   L34.

21   Leyda, vol. 1, 167–68; *The Indicator,* February 1850, Amherst College Archives and Special Collections.

22   L280.

23   L63.

24   L31.

25   L30; Alfred Habegger, *My Wars Are Laid Away in Books: The Life of Emily Dickinson* (New York: Random House, 2001), 223.

26   L31.

27   L29.

28   L31.

29   Leyda, vol. 1, 243; Kate Phillips. *Helen Hunt Jackson: A Literary Life.* Berkeley: University of California Press, 2003, 74; L60.

30   L62.

31   L29.

32   L86.

33   Leyda, vol. 1, 203.

34   Ibid., 203.

35   L53.

36   L45.

37   Edward Hitchcock, *The Power of Christian Benevolence Illustrated in the Life and Labors of Mary Lyon* (New York: American Tract Society), 4.

38   Elizabeth Alden Green, *Mary Lyon and Mount Holyoke: Opening the Gates.*
      Hanover, NH, University Press of New England, 1979), 313.
39   *Recollections of Mary Lyon with Selections from Her Instructions to the Pupils of
      Mt. Holyoke Female Seminary.* (Boston, American Tract Society, 1866), v.
40   Ibid., 24.
41   L59.
42   L30.
43   L36.
44   L79.
45   L54.
46   L30.
47   Ibid.
48   L43.
49   L85; L36; Habegger, 243; L66.
50   Richard B. Sewall, *The Life of Emily Dickinson* (New York: Farrar, Straus and
      Giroux, 1974), 405.
51   Phillips, 69.
52   L31.
53   L36; L85.
54   L57.
55   Phillips, 65.
56   Ibid., 72–73.
57   Ibid., 75.
58   Ebenezer Snell, *The Metereological Journal Kept at Amherst College*, February
      1852.
59   L936.
60   Leyda, vol. 1, 248.
61   Ibid., 249.
62   L45, L58.
63   L73.
64   *The Poems of Emily Dickinson, Variorum Edition*, 53–55.
65   Acts 2:19.
66   L35.
67   L36.
68   Cynthia Harbeson, email to the author, Jones Library, Amherst, Massachu-
      setts, June 10, 2016.
69   *Springfield Daily Republican*, February 20, 1852.
70   Ibid.

71 L77.
72 Millicent Todd Bingham, *Emily Dickinson's Home: The Early Years as Revealed in Family Correspondence and Reminiscences* (New York: Dover Publications, 1967), 268.
73 L79.
74 L46.
75 Leyda, vol. 1, 246.
76 Ibid., 251.
77 L110.

FOUR: DECIDED TO BE DISTINGUISHED

1   L199.
2   *The New York Times*, January 5, 1859.
3   *Hampshire and Franklin Express*, January 7, 1859.
4   *Hampshire and Franklin Express*, December 31, 1858.
5   L176.
6   L212.
7   Ibid.
8   L77.
9   L85.
10 L182.
11 Ibid.
12 Ibid.
13 Ibid.
14 Jay Leyda, *The Years and Hours of Emily Dickinson*, vol. 1 (New Haven: Yale University Press, 1960), 294.
15 Ibid., 266.
16 Ibid., 291.
17 L131.
18 L108.
19 Leyda, vol. 1, 332.
20 L102.
21 L96.
22 L94.
23 L118.
24 Leyda, vol. 1, 302.
25 L88.

26 L159.

27 L144.

28 L88.

29 Martha Dickinson Bianchi, *Recollections of a Country Girl 18—to 1900.* Unpublished manuscript (1935), Brown University Library, Special Collections Department, Manuscript Division, 145–46.

30 L199.

31 Ibid.

32 Ibid.

33 L731.

34 Alfred Habegger, *My Wars Are Laid Away in Books: The Life of Emily Dickinson* (New York: Random House, 2001), 309.

35 L185.

36 L133.

37 Ibid.

38 *Biographical Encyclopedia of Massachusetts* (Boston: Metropolitan Publishing and Engraving Company, 1883), 185.

39 L159.

40 Leyda, vol. 1, 302.

41 L78.

42 L176.

43 L85.

44 L166; L79.

45 L93.

46 L154.

47 L176.

48 Judith Farr "Emily Dickinson and Marriage: The 'Etruscan Experiment,'" in *Reading Emily Dickinson's Letters: Critical Essays,* eds. Jane Donahue Eberwein and Cindy MacKenzie (Amherst: University of Massachusetts Press, 2011), 186.

49 L199.

50 Leyda, vol. 1, 253.

51 Kate Phillips, *Helen Hunt Jackson: A Literary Life* (Berkeley: University of California Press, 2003), 85.

52 L178.

53 Helen Hunt Jackson Papers, Part 6, MS 0353, Colorado College, Tutt Library, Special Collections & Archives.

54 Richard B. Sewall, *The Life of Emily Dickinson* (New York: Farrar, Straus and Giroux, 1974), 451–52, 460.

55 Habegger, 298.
56 Coleman Hutchison, "Eastern Exiles: Dickinson, Whiggery, and War," *Emily Dickinson Journal* 13, no. 2, 2.
57 L97.
58 Habegger, 328.
59 L94.
60 L182.
61 L155.
62 F6.
63 F33.
64 L195.
65 L114.
66 *The Manuscript Books of Emily Dickinson*, R. W. Franklin, ed. (Cambridge: The Belknap Press of Harvard University, 1981), 28.
67 F23.
68 L146.
69 L187.
70 F21; F24; F26.
71 L199.

FIVE: TALLER FEET

1 *Hampshire Franklin Express*, November 22, 186; William A. Stearns, *Adjutant Stearns* (Boston: Massachusetts Sabbath School Society, 1862), not paginated; Jay Leyda, *The Years and Hours of Emily Dickinson*, vol. 2 (New Haven: Yale University Press, 1960), 26, 31.
2 L245.
3 L234.
4 L217.
5 *Hampshire Franklin Express*, November 9, 1860; Leyda, vol. 2, 26.
6 L298.
7 Wayne E. Phaneuf and Joseph Carvalho III, *Not So Civil War: Western Massachusetts at Home and in Battle*, vol. 1 (Springfield, MA: The Republican Heritage Series, 2015), 13, 11, 45; *Hampshire and Franklin Express*, March 7, 1862.
8 *Hampshire and Franklin Express*, September 27, 1861.
9 L269.
10 Susan Dickinson to Dwight Gilbert, January 10, 1853, Houghton Library, Dickinson Collection.

11   Henry Root to Helen Hunt, Wednesday p.m., Helen Hunt Jackson Papers, Colorado College, Tutt Library, Special Collections and Archives.

12   Helen Hunt to Henry Root, February 26, 1855, Colorado College, Tutt Library, Special Collections and Archives.

13   Leyda, vol. 1, 268.

14   Alfred Habegger, *My Wars Are Laid Away in Books: The Life of Emily Dickinson* (New York: Random House, 2001), 304.

15   L93.

16   L167; Leyda, vol. 1, 309, 311, 314; Habegger, 304—5.

17   L173.

18   F4.

19   Leyda, vol. 2, 38.

20   F24, F38, F44, F32, F48, F115, F110, F112, F181, F135.

21   L238a.

22   F945.

23   L233.

24   L248.

25   Ralph Waldo Emerson, "The Poet," in *Selected Writings of Emerson* (New York: Random House, 1950), 319—41.

26   Jack Capps, *Emily Dickinson's Reading: 1836—1886* (Cambridge: Harvard University Press, 1966), 116.

27   Leyda, vol. 1, 350—51.

28   Susan H. Dickinson, "Magnetic Visitors," in *Amherst* (Alumni Quarterly) 33:4 (Spring 1981), 8—15, 27. ("Magnetic Visitors" is a slightly condensed reprint of Susan's essay "Annual of the Evergreens" archived in the Houghton Library, Harvard University.)

29   F45.

30   F1263.

31   For the intricacies regarding the multiple drafts of this poem, I have used Ralph W. Franklin, ed., *The Poems of Emily Dickinson: Variorum Edition* (Cambridge: Harvard University Press, 1998). All subsequent reference to this poem derive from this transcription of "Safe in their Alabaster Chambers," F124.

32   L277.

33   George Merriam, *The Life and Times of Samuel Bowles*, vol. 1 (New York: The Century Co., 1883), 34.

34   Dickinson, "Magnetic Visitors," 13.

35   Habegger, 451. Bowles's tendency to turn a thoughtful moment into humor also may have stemmed from insecurity about his education. While a man of wide-ranging intelligence, Bowles knew he had a poor education. He often

found himself the only man in the room who had never gone to college, and the realization undermined him. Stephen G. Weisner, "Embattled Editor: The Life of Samuel Bowles," PhD Dissertation, University of Massachusetts at Amherst, 1986, 9.

36 Leyda, vol. 2, 28, 47; L241.

37 Leyda, vol. 2, 41.

38 Leyda, vol. 1, 368.

39 Weisner, "Embattled Editor," 66.

40 Richard B. Sewall, *The Life of Emily Dickinson* (New York: Farrar, Straus and Giroux, 1974), 489–90.

41 F11; Karen Dandurand, "Another Dickinson Poem Published in her Lifetime," *American Literature*, 54 (October 1982) 434–37.

42 *The Poems of Emily Dickinson: Variorum Edition*, 1.

43 Ibid., F124, 161.

44 Ibid.

45 Ibid.

46 Ibid., F124, 162.

47 *Hampshire Franklin Express*, March 7, 1862.

48 *Hampshire Franklin Express*. February 21, 1862.

49 Ibid.

50 Leyda, vol. 2, 48.

51 *The Poems of Emily Dickinson: Variorum Edition*, F124, 161.

52 The Amherst regiment named itself "The Amherst Boys." *Hampshire Franklin Express*, September 9, 1861; William A. Stearns, *Adjutant Stearns* (Boston: Massachusetts Sabbath School Society, 1862), not paginated.

53 Stearns. *Adjutant Stearns*.

54 Ibid.

55 Ibid.

56 L298. Habegger notes that Thomas Johnson misdated this letter as "1864?" Jay Leyda correctly moved it to December 1862. Habegger, 400.

SIX: ARE YOU TOO DEEPLY OCCUPIED TO SAY IF MY VERSE IS ALIVE?

1 Edward W. Chapin, "On College Hill," *Amherst Graduates Quarterly*; *Student Life at Amherst College*, 102–3; *Hampshire and Franklin Express*, July 11, 1862.

2 William A. Stearns, *Adjutant Stearns* (Boston: Massachusetts Sabbath School Society, 1862), not paginated; Charles Folsom Walcott, *History of the Twenty-First Regiment Massachusetts Volunteers* (Boston: Houghton Mifflin and Co, 1882), 64–68.

3   Polly Longsworth, "Brave Among the Bravest: Amherst in the Civil War," *Amherst* (Summer 1999), 25–31; Walcott, *History of the Twenty-First*, 64–68; William Eleazar Barton, *The Life of Clara Barton, Founder of the Red Cross*, vol. 1. (Boston: Houghton Mifflin and Co., 1922), 190.

4   Stearns, *Adjutant Stearns*.

5   L246.

6   F384.

7   Edward Crowell, *Record of the Services of Graduates and Non-Graduates of Amherst College in the Union Army or Navy During the War of the Rebellion* (Amherst College 1905); Margaret Dakin, " 'Your Classmate and Friend,' " *The Consecrated Eminence*, March 4, 2013, https://consecratedeminence.wordpress.comAASC; Longsworth, "Brave Among the Bravest," 25–31.

8   L252.

9   L256.

10 George S. Merriam, *The Life and Times of Samuel Bowles*, vol. 1 (New York: The Century Co., 1885), 404.

11 Bowles was known for occasionally working forty-two continuous hours. Stephen G. Weisner, "Embattled Editor: The Life of Samuel Bowles," PhD Dissertation, University of Massachusetts, Amherst, 1986, 54.

12 Merriam, vol. 1, 315.

13 Ibid., 305, 303.

14 Jay Leyda, *The Years and Hours of Emily Dickinson*, vol. 2 (New Haven: Yale University Press, 1960), 49, 71.

15 Merriam, vol. 1, 308.

16 Andrew Elmer Ford, *The Story of the Fifteenth Regiment Massachusetts Volunteer Infantry in the Civil War, 1861–1864* (Clinton Press of W. J. Coulter Courant Office, 1898), 382; *Hampshire Franklin Express*, September 27, 1861.

17 L261.

18 F242.

19 F260.

20 F225.

21 L269.

22 L261.

23 L342b.

24 Leyda, vol. 2, 7–8. While Jay Leyda places the date of Wadsworth's visit in early 1860, other scholars suggest it may have occurred later in the poet's life.

25 L248a.

26 F347.

27 Leyda, vol. 2, 50.

28 Thomas Wentworth Higginson, "Letter to a Young Contributor," *Atlantic Monthly*, April 1862.

29 Newton Manross to William Clark, April 20, 1862, Amherst College Archives and Special Collections.

30 *Hampshire Franklin Express*, April 18, 1862.

31 Newton Manross to William S. Clark April 20, 1862, Amherst College Archives and Special Collections; Patrick Browne, "Two Friends at Antietam," June 8, 2011, historicaldigressions.com; *Springfield Republican*, April 15, 1862; *Hampshire Franklin Express*, April 18, 1862.

32 Higginson, "Letter to a Young Contributor."

33 F207.

34 F269.

35 F312.

36 F314.

37 F320.

38 F372.

39 F409.

40 F479.

41 F236.

42 F282, F204, F304.

43 Thomas Wentworth Higginson, "Emily Dickinson's Letters," *Atlantic Monthly*, October 1891; Higginson, "Letter to a Young Contributor."

44 L238.

45 L260.

46 Higginson, "Emily Dickinson's Letters."

47 Wendy Martin, *An American Triptych: Anne Bradstreet, Emily Dickinson, and Adrienne Rich* (Chapel Hill: University of North Carolina Press, 1984), 108.

48 *The History of the Town of Amherst, Massachusetts*, Compiled and Published by Carpenter and Morehouse (Amherst: Press of Carpenter & Morehouse, 1896) 492; Dan Lombardo, email to the author, November 22, 2016.

49 L262.

SEVEN: BULLETINS ALL DAY FROM IMMORTALITY

1 All quotations from this paragraph are L261.

2 L265, L261.

3 L261.

4 Ibid.

5 Ibid.

6   L290.

7   L261.

8   Thomas Wentworth Higginson, "Emily Dickinson's Letters," in the *Atlantic Monthly*, October 1891, www.theatlantic.com/magazine/archive/1891/10/emily -dickinsons-letters/306524/.

9   L352.

10   L788.

11   L268.

12   L265.

13   L271.

14   L268.

15   L265; L271.

16   L271.

17   L274.

18   Thomas Wentworth Higginson, *The Complete Civil War Journals and Selected Letters*, ed. Christopher Looby (Chicago: University of Chicago Press, 2000), 229.

19   L280.

20   Ibid.

21   Higginson, *Complete Civil War Journals*, 310.

22   L274.

23   James R. Guthrie's study of Dickinson's vision is indispensible for understanding the problems with her eyes and how reduced sight affected her poetry. James R. Guthrie, *Emily Dickinson's Vision: Illness and Identity in Her Poetry* (Gainesville: University of Florida Press, 1998), 9, 10, 13, 18, 20, 21, 30, 178, 180; L439

24   L285.

25   Ibid.

26   Ibid.

27   L286.

28   Karen Dandurand, "Dickinson and the Public," in *Dickinson and Audience*, Martin Orzeck and Robert Weisbuch, eds. (Ann Arbor: University of Michigan Press), 269.

29   Mike Kelly, "Emily Dickinson and the New York Press," Consecrated Eminence, July 15, 2013. Amherst College Archives and Special Collections. Consecratedeminence.wordpress.com.

30   Dandurand, "Dickinson and the Public," 255–77; Karen Dandurand, "New Dickinson Civil War Publications," *American Literature* 56, no. 1 (March 1984), 17–27; *American Newspaper Directory*, ed. George Presbury Rowell

(New York: Printers' Ink Pub. Co., 1870), 669; In addition, I am indebted to Karen Dandurand for countless conversations about Dickinson's publication history.

31 James R. Guthrie and I share the belief that Dickinson was worried her poor eyesight would bring an end to her poems. Guthrie, *Emily Dickinson's Vision*, 22, 24, 30.

32 L268.

33 Wayne E. Phaneuf and Joseph Carvalho III, *A Not So Civil War: Western Massachusetts at Home and in Battle*, vol. 1 (Springfield, MA: The Republican, 2015), 134–135; Patrick Browne, "Billy Yank and Johnny Reb and Christmas on the Rappahonnock, 1862, *Historical Digression*, December 22, 2015. historical digression.com; Higginson, *Complete Civil War Journals*, 216; Walter L. Powell, "'So Clear of Victory': Emily Dickinson's Gettysburg Address, Lecture at the Amherst History Museum, November 9, 2013, sponsored by the Emily Dickinson Museum; Walter L. Powell, email with the author, March 14, 2019.

34 Higginson, *Complete Civil War Journals*, 350.

35 Ibid., 305.

36 Leyda, vol. 2, 90.

37 L290.

38 F824.

39 L290.

40 Boston Public Library, https://www.digitalcommonwealth.org/search /commonwealth:kho4mv993.

41 L290.

42 Ibid.

43 Guthrie, *Emily Dickinson's Vision*, 9.

44 L292.

45 n.a., "Iritis" in *Hospital, a Weekly Journal of Science, Medicine, Nursing and Philanthropy* (London: London Hospital, vol. 11, Dec. 12, 1891), 131–32.

46 n.a., "The Treatment of Iritis" in *Hospital, a Weekly Journal of Science, Medicine, Nursing and Philanthropy* (London: London Hospital, vol. 42, July 15, 1899), 260; L293.

47 Richard B. Sewall, *The Lyman Letters: New Light on Emily Dickinson and Her Family* (Amherst: University of Massachusetts Press, 1965), 76.

48 L289.

49 L289, L294.

50 L291.

51 F484.

52   Guthrie shares this view of one possible benefit of Dickinson's illness.
     Guthrie, *Emily Dickinson's Vision*, 13.

53   L583.

54   F681.

55   L293.

56   L289, L295.

57   L289.

58   L293, L294.

59   L295.

60   L294, L306.

61   L296.

62   Ibid.

63   L302.

64   L296.

65   Higginson, *Complete Civil War Journals*, 220.

66   Ibid., 7.

67   Critic Helen Vendler in describing Dickinson's "supposed person" wrote,
     "Although she sometimes did write the sort of first-order poem that reads
     like a transcription of a life-event, such as a vigil around a deathbed, more
     often she found a second order 'algebraic' equivalent for emotional occa-
     sions, whether rapturous or troubling." Vendler cites "Before I got my eye
     put out – " (F336) as an example of a "symbolic equivalent" that arose from
     "emotional torture." Helen Vendler, *Dickinson: Selected Poems and Commen-
     taries* (Cambridge: The Belknap Press of Harvard University Press, 2010), 9.

68   F336. Guthrie contends Dickinson's "description of scenes she would look
     upon, were she to regain full use of her eyes, is so rapturous that we may
     infer her transgression had been to admire the visible world excessively."
     Guthrie, *Emily Dickinson's Vision*, 15.

69   *Cambridge Chronicle*, November 12, 1864.

70   L297.

71   L290.

72   Sewall, *The Lyman Letters*, 69.

73   Dickinson's poems that reference illness, darkness, and blindness are
     many. A few notable ones from this period are: "The Soul has Bandaged
     moments – ," F360; "Renunciation – is a piercing Virtue – ," F782; "They
     say that 'Time assuages' – ," F861; "Some say good night – at night – ," F586;
     "My first well Day – since many ill – ," F288; and "What I see not, I better
     see – ," F869.

74   L280.

EIGHT: YOU WERE NOT AWARE THAT YOU SAVED MY LIFE

1   Richard B. Sewall, *The Lyman Letters: New Light on Emily Dickinson and Her Family* (Amherst: University of Massachusetts Press, 1965) 76.

2   L304; Paraic Finnerty, *Emily Dickinson's Shakespeare* (Amherst: University of Massachusetts Press, 2006), 43.

3   L308.

4   Frank Prentice Rand, *The Village of Amherst: A Landmark of Light* (Amherst: The Historical Society, 1958), 123.

5   *Cambridge Chronicle*, April 8, 22, and 29, 1865.

6   L306.

7   L311.

8   L316.

9   Jay Leyda, *The Years and Hours of Emily Dickinson*, vol. 2 (New Haven: Yale University Press, 1960), 120.

10 L319.

11 Brenda Wineapple, *White Heat: The Friendship of Emily Dickinson and Thomas Wentworth Higginson* (New York: Alfred A. Knopf, 2008), 162.

12 Ibid., 197.

13 Ibid., 97.

14 L316.

15 L316; Leyda, vol. 2, 110, 112.

16 Leyda, vol. 2, 110, 111.

17 Ibid., 132.

18 L330a.

19 L330.

20 Wineapple, 163.

21 Leyda, vol. 2, 110.

22 Kate Phillips, *Helen Hunt Jackson: A Literary Life* (Berkeley: University of California Press, 2003), 93.

23 Ibid., 139.

24 Ibid., 95.

25 Leyda, vol. 2, 130.

26 Phillips, 125.

27 Ibid., 101.

28 Richard B. Sewall, *The Life of Emily Dickinson* (New York: Farrar, Straus and Giroux, 1974), 566.

29 Leyda, vol. 2, 102.

30 Aife Murray makes a compelling case for Margaret Maher providing more

time for Dickinson to write. *Maid as Muse: How Servants Changed Emily Dickinson's Life and Language* (Lebanon: University of New Hampshire Press, 2010).

31   Millicent Todd Bingham, *Emily Dickinson's Home: The Early Years as Revealed in Family Correspondence and Reminiscences* (New York: Dover Publications, Inc., 1967), 414.

32   Alfred Habegger, *My Wars Are Laid Away in Books: The Life of Emily Dickinson* (New York: Random House, 2001), 321.

33   L318.

34   Wineapple, 21.

35   L330a.

36   Ibid.

37   L342.

38   Wineapple, 170.

39   Ibid., 176.

40   Rand, 172.

41   *Amherst Record*, August 24, 1870.

42   *Amherst Record*, August 10, 1870.

43   *Amherst Record*, August 17, 1870.

44   L342a.

45   Leyda, vol. 2, 112.

46   L342a.

47   L477.

48   L342a. All subsequent quotations of Higginson's visit with Dickinson are found in L342a and L342b.

49   Leyda, vol. 2, 154.

50   L342a.

51   Leyda, Volume. 2, p. 151.

52   *Amherst Record*, August 8, 1870.

53   F1175.

54   L352.

55   Finnerty, 130.

56   L622.

57   L352.

58   L553.

59   L342b.

60   Ibid.

61   F721.

62   Growing seasons with wet springs and dry summers produce especially

sweet apples. Conversation with Tom Clark, Clarkdale Orchards, September 4, 2017.

63 L343.

64 Wineapple, 21.

65 *Amherst Record*, August 24, 1870.

66 Rand, 114.

NINE: SUCCESS IS COUNTED SWEETEST

1   Helen Hunt to Mrs. E. C. Banfield, August 16, 1873, Helen Hunt Jackson Collection, Tutt Library Special Collections and Archives, Colorado College; Jay Leyda, *The Years and Hours of Emily Dickinson*, vol. 2 (New Haven: Yale University Press, 1960), 204.

2   Helen Hunt to Mrs. E. C. Banfield, August 16, 1873.

3   Martha Dickinson Bianchi, *Emily Dickinson: Face to Face* (Boston: Houghton Mifflin Company, 1932), 17.

4   MacGregor Jenkins, "A Child's Recollections of Emily Dickinson," *Christian Union*, October 24, 1891, B215–217; Leyda, vol. 2, 240.

5   Mary Alden Allen, *Around a Village Green: Sketches of Life in Amherst* (Northampton: Kraushar Press, 1939), 31.

6   Bianchi, 63.

7   F409.

8   L405a.

9   L381.

10 L380.

11 L368.

12 Leyda, vol. 2, 193.

13 Ibid.

14 Kate Phillips, *Helen Hunt Jackson: A Literary Life* (Berkeley: University of California Press, 2003), 168.

15 Ibid., 169.

16 Leyda, vol. 2, 218.

17 Phillips, 172.

18 L360.

19 Millicent Todd Bingham, *Emily Dickinson's Home: The Early Years as Revealed in Family Correspondence and Reminiscences* (New York: Dover Publications, 1967), 444.

20 Ibid., 460–64.

21 L360.

22   Leyda, vol. 2, 71.

23   Ibid., 223.

24   *Daily Bulletin of Weather Reports, Signal Service, US Army*, June 16, 1874, 4:34
     p.m. (War Department. Washington, DC, 1877), 92–94.

25   Leyda, vol. 2, 224.

26   Ibid.; L414; Mary Todd Kaercher, email to the author, October 13, 2017.

27   Leyda, vol. 2, 224.

28   Leyda, vol. 2, 225.

29   L414.

30   Leyda, vol. 2, 225–226; *Amherst Record*, June 24, 1874; Bingham, 473; Alfred
     Habegger, *My Wars Are Laid Away in Books: The Life of Emily Dickinson* (New
     York: Random House, 2001), 562; L432, note 538.

31   Bingham, 411.

32   L432.

33   Richard B. Sewall, *The Lyman Letters: New Light on Emily Dickinson and Her
     Family* (Amherst: University of Massachusetts Press, 1965), 70–71.

34   Ibid.

35   L418.

36   L413.

37   L418; L470.

38   L450.

39   Leyda, vol. 2, 244–45.

40   Ibid., 237.

41   L432.

42   L449.

43   L460.

44   Bianchi, 14.

45   L513.

46   Martha Dickinson Bianchi, *Recollections of a Country Girl*, unpublished man-
     uscript (1935), Brown University Library Special Collections Department,
     Manuscript Division, 120.

47   Habegger, 559–60; Bianchi, *Emily Dickinson*, 124.

48   Leyda, vol. 2, 229.

49   Bianchi, *Emily Dickinson*, 129–30.

50   Sewall, *Lyman Letters*, 34.

51   Leyda, vol. 2, 231.

52   Bianchi, *Emily Dickinson*, 104.

53   Ibid., 39.

54 Martha Dickinson Bianchi, *The Life and Letters of Emily Dickinson* (Boston: Houghton Mifflin Company, 1924), 13.

55 Sewall, *Lyman Letters*, 70.

56 Bianchi, *Emily Dickinson*, 15; Betsy Johnson, email to the author, October 25, 2017.

57 L441.

58 Letters, 549.

59 Leyda, vol. 2, 184; L475; L491.

60 Bianchi, *Emily Dickinson*, 14.

61 Leyda, vol. 2, 177.

62 Bianchi, *Emily Dickinson*, 125.

63 Bryant E. Tolles Jr., *Summer by the Seaside: The Architecture of New England Coastal Resort Hotels, 1820–1950* (Hanover, NH: University Press of New England, 2008), 91; Bianchi. *Recollections of a Country Girl*, 48.

64 L428.

65 Bianchi, *Life and Letters*, 13.

66 L444.

67 L444 notes.

68 L444a.

69 Ibid.

70 Ibid.

71 L477.

72 L474.

73 *Amherst Record*, September 20, 1876.

74 Catherine E. Kelly, *In the New England Fashion: Reshaping Women's Lives in the Nineteenth Century* (Ithaca: Cornell University Press, 1999), 130.

75 Ebenezer Snell and Sabra Snell, *The Meteorological Journal kept at Amherst College*, Amherst College and Special Collections; Marta Werner, email to the author, October 23, 2017.

76 Phillips, 155.

77 Prospect House file, Jones Library Special Collections, Amherst, Massachusetts; *Daily Hampshire Gazette*, November 19, 1975; *Burt's Illustrated Guide of the Connecticut Valley*, 1866.

78 *Quincy* (Illinois) *Daily Whig*, September 11, 1876.

79 Madeleine B. Stern and Daniel Shealy, "No Name Series," *Studies in the American Renaissance* (1991), 376.

80 Ibid., 385, 386.

81 L476a.

82   Bianchi, *Emily Dickinson*, 35.

83   *Amherst Record*, October 11, 1876; Bianchi, *Emily Dickinson*, 36.

84   L476c.

85   Ibid.

86   L476.

87   Phillips, 140–41.

88   Leyda, vol. 2, 236.

89   L476c.

90   F930.

91   F1267.

92   F1345.

93   L476c.

94   L476; L486.

95   L476b.

96   Helen Hunt Jackson Diary, October 13, 1876, Helen Hunt Jackson Collection, Tutt Library Special Collections and Archives, Colorado College.

97   Leyda, vol. 2, 260.

98   Ibid., 261.

99   L476c

100 L573b.

101 L477.

102 Stern and Shealy, 389.

103 F112; The version of the poem included here is the way it appeared in *A Masque of Poets*. In seeking to standardize the poem, Niles eliminated dashes, altered a line break, and switched capital letters to lowercase, among other edits. *A Masque of Poets, including Guy Vernon, a Novelette in Verse* (Boston: Roberts Brothers, 1878), 174.

104 Leyda, vol. 2, 260.

105 L573c.

106 Stern and Shealy, 390.

TEN: CALLED BACK

1   L665.

2   L735.

3   L522.

4   Jay Leyda, *The Years and Hours of Emily Dickinson*, vol. 2 (New Haven: Yale University Press, 1960), 448.

5   F428.

6   Lyndall Gordon, *Lives Like Loaded Guns: Emily Dickinson and Her Family's Feuds* (New York: Viking, 2010), 135.
7   Habegger, 608.
8   Leyda, vol. 2, 320.
9   Martha Dickinson Bianchi, *Emily Dickinson: Face to Face* (Boston: Houghton Mifflin Company, 1932), 66–67.
10 L549, L493.
11 L542.
12 Habegger, 572.
13 L830, L489.
14 L536.
15 L738.
16 L733.
17 L1040.
18 Ibid.
19 L773; L1039.
20 L765.
21 L827.
22 L785.
23 L792.
24 L779.
25 Leyda, vol. 2, 384.
26 L785.
27 L521.
28 L788.
29 Martha Dickinson Bianchi, *The Life and Letters of Emily Dickinson* (Boston: Houghton Mifflin Company, 1924), 70.
30 L790.
31 L559.
32 L562.
33 Ibid.
34 L790.
35 L780.
36 L752.
37 L790.
38 L750.
39 F1691.
40 Leyda, vol. 2, 353.
41 Ibid., 354.

42   Ibid., 357.

43   Ibid., 361.

44   Brenda Wineapple, *White Heat: The Friendship of Emily Dickinson and Thomas Wentworth Higginson* (New York: Alfred A. Knopf, 2008), 245.

45   Leyda, vol. 2, 377.

46   Ibid., 405.

47   Ibid., 433, 445.

48   Ibid., 438.

49   L858.

50   Leyda, vol. 2, 336.

51   L749.

52   F1489.

53   L814.

54   F895.

55   L813.

56   L813b.

57   L601a.

58   F1488.

59   Kate Phillips, *Helen Hunt Jackson: A Literary Life* (Berkeley: University of California Press, 2003), 228.

60   Ibid., 229.

61   Ibid., 234.

62   Ibid., 252.

63   Habegger, 618.

64   Ibid., 612.

65   Leyda, vol. 2, 406.

66   L873.

67   Leyda, vol. 2, 411.

68   Ibid.

69   L873.

70   L868.

71   L874.

72   L890.

73   L967.

74   L968.

75   L967.

76   L907.

77   Leyda, vol.2, 425.

78 L939.
79 L937a.
80 Ibid.
81 Phillips, 253.
82 Valerie Sherer Mathes, *The Indian Reform Letters of Helen Hunt Jackson, 1879–1885* (Norman: University of Oklahoma Press, 2015), 216.
83 L976a.
84 Ibid.
85 Phillips, 272.
86 Ibid., 233.
87 L1015.
88 L1043.
89 Leyda, vol. 2, 466.
90 L1034.
91 L267.
92 F1389; F1453; F1440; F1152; F1512.
93 L619.
94 *Amherst Record*, May 12, 1886.
95 *Amherst Record*, May 19, 1886.
96 Leyda, vol. 2, 470.
97 L1046.
98 Leyda, vol. 2, 471.
99 Bianchi, *Emily Dickinson*, 158–59; Conversation with Alfred Venne, Planetarium Educator, Bassett Planetarium, Amherst College, September 15, 2017, and Alfred Venne, email to the author, September 18, 2017.
100 L332.
101 F372.
102 Emily Dickinson's Death and Funeral File, Jones Library Special Collections, Amherst, Massachusetts.
103 L1024.
104 L1030; Letters, 896.
105 Bianchi, *Emily Dickinson*, 61.
106 Leyda, vol. 2, 472–73.
107 Leyda, vol. 2, 474–75.
108 Paul Crumbley, "Emily Dickinson's Funeral and the Paradox of Literary Fame," *The Emily Dickinson Journal* 26, no. 2 (2017), 55.
109 L342a.
110 L342b.

111 F466.

112 A week after Dickinson's death, Vinnie discovered her sister's poems. While she was well aware that Emily wrote poetry, she had no idea how much. Vinnie first approached Sue with editing the work, but Sue took more time to consider the project than Vinnie wanted. She next asked Mabel Loomis Todd if she would do the work. Mabel transcribed hundreds of poems, while the Dickinson family contacted Higginson. Roberts Brothers published *Poems* by Emily Dickinson, coedited by Todd and Higginson, in 1890 in time for Christmas sales. The book sold out and immediately went into multiple printings. For further information on the disposition of the poems, see R. W. Franklin, "Introduction," in *The Poems of Emily Dickinson*, Variorum Edition (Cambridge: The Belknap Press of Harvard University Press, 1998), 1–43.

113 May 19, 1886, Snell Family Meteorological Journal, Amherst College Archives and Special Collections.

INDEX

THESE FEVERED DAYS

Martha Ackmann

THESE FEVERED DAYS

Martha Ackmann

DISCUSSION QUESTIONS

1. In her introduction, Martha Ackmann acknowledges that "Too often, readers see Emily Dickinson as an artifact in amber: an eccentric spinster who locked herself away from the world" (p. xiv). How does Ackmann's *These Fevered Days* change our received notion of who Dickinson was?

2. The decision to frame Dickinson's very rich biography in just ten moments from her life is an unusual one. How does this distillation heighten each moment and deepen what we know of her larger experience?

3. Every chapter is preceded by the weather of that day, brought to us by Ebenezer Snell and the meteorological journal he kept at Amherst College. We know from her poetry that Dickinson was a watcher of weather; how does knowing the weather for each key moment the book explores give us a more complete picture of Dickinson at that time in her life?

4. In chapter 2, "It Is Hard for Me to Give Up the World," young Dickinson finds herself in seminary, thinking of Miss Mary Lyon's advice: "Don't be a hypocrite" and "be honest" (p. 46). How does what follows relate to those words? Why do you think she doesn't leave a note? How does Miss Lyon's advice carry through to other key moments in the poet's life?

5. Common wisdom about Dickinson tells us that she was a quiet and eccentric recluse, but Ackmann often paints her as anything but, with many cherished friendships and an interest in gossip. What do you think Ackmann gets right about her subject that oth-

ers have often missed? Why do you think these aspects of Dickinson's character were missed by others?

6. In chapter 4, "Decided to Be Distinguished," Ackmann writes, "By the time Emily told Loo she wanted to be distinguished, she already had written nearly fifty poems" (p. 86). Emily is clear that she wants fame, but she doesn't want life in the public sphere. How do you think these are reconciled within her?

7. Dickinson is surrounded by so much death—including the looming death toll from the Civil War. Her life is also deeply affected by her own ailments and frailty. Ackmann writes that, in her poems, Dickinson wanted to contrast the stasis of the dead with the vitality of living. Do you think this was a means of escape—or survival?

8. Famous as a spinster, in *These Fevered Day* it is suggested that Dickinson had at least one romantic love relationship, with Otis Phillips Lord, and several very close attachments to both men and women. Did this surprise you? Did it change your idea of the poet and her poems?

9. In the final chapter, "Called Back," after Dickinson's death and burial, Ackmann writes, "No one who attended her funeral that day knew Emily Dickinson would become someone else after death" (p. 235). What do you think Ackmann means here? Do you think the author has allowed Dickinson to be another someone else with this book?

10. How did *These Fevered Days* defy your expectation for what a literary biography can do? How did its novel-like quality change your understanding of, and feeling toward, the subject?